WEST VANCOUVER MEMORIAL LIBRARY

Withdrawn from Collection

DATE			

Books by Amos Elon

JOURNEY THROUGH A HAUNTED LAND
THE ISRAELIS: *Founders and Sons*
BETWEEN ENEMIES
HERZL: *A Biography*
TIMETABLE
FLIGHT INTO EGYPT
THE ISRAELIS: *Pictures of a Day in May* (editor)
JERUSALEM: *City of Mirrors*

JERUSALEM

AMOS ELON

JERUSALEM

LITTLE, BROWN AND COMPANY

City of Mirrors

BOSTON   TORONTO   LONDON

FIRST EDITION

Maps by d'Art Studio

Library of Congress Cataloging-in-Publication Data

Elon, Amos.
    Jerusalem, city of mirrors / Amos Elon.
        p.   cm.
    Bibliography: p.
    Includes index.
    ISBN 0-316-23388-9
    1. Jerusalem.   I. Title.
DS109.15.E46   1989
956.94'42—dc20   89-34155
                                                        CIP

        10 9 8 7 6 5 4 3 2 1

RRD VA

Designed by Robert G. Lowe

*Published simultaneously in Canada
by Little, Brown & Company (Canada) Limited*

PRINTED IN THE UNITED STATES OF AMERICA

For Beth and Danae

Contents

Acknowledgments

I owe an immense debt of gratitude to many. First and foremost, to my wife, Beth, for her advice, her patience, and her learning; to my agent and dear friend Morton Janklow; and to my editor, Fredrica Friedman, who helped make this a more readable and, I hope, better book. I am also indebted to copyeditor Michael Brandon, to my friends Edna Margalith, Saul Friedlander, Magen Broshi, and Herbert Pundik, as well as to the many authors listed in the Notes — and to none more than Yehuda Amichai, the great modern poet of Jerusalem; wherever I went in the city, I discovered he had been there before.

Chronology

(with special reference to the *main* sieges, captures,
sacks, and destructions suffered by Jerusalem)

Beginnings of Monotheism; early versions of Pentateuch and books of Joshua, Samuel, and Kings circulate in Jerusalem; the great prophets postulate utopia	c. 1900 BC	Jerusalem referred to in Egyptian execration texts; Abraham greeted at Salem in the name of the "most high God"
	c. 1000	David captures Jerusalem
	952	Consecration of the first temple under Solomon
	930	Capture and plunder by Sheshonk I of Egypt
	740–690	Isaiah
	701	Siege of Sennacherib
	625–586	Jeremiah
	587–586	Siege and devastation by Nebuchadnezzar
Under Persian rule, Jewish sectarianism hardens	537–515	Second temple built
	445	Nehemiah rebuilds walls
	c. 350	Probable sack of Jerusalem by Persians
Hellenistic period	320	Destruction by Ptolemy Soter
	168	Destruction by Antiochus Epiphanes; practice of Judaism forbidden
	165	Temple restored by Maccabees
Under direct or indirect Roman rule, Jewish Jerusalem reaches the height of its splendor; the revolts and destructions of the city inaugurate the Jewish dispersion; Jerusalem becomes "Capital of Memory"	63	Siege, capture, and much destruction by Pompey
	40	Capture by the Parthians
	37	Siege and partial destruction by Herod
	20 BC–AD 63	Herod rebuilds second temple
	c. AD 26–30	Ministry and crucifixion of Jesus
	66	Jewish revolt
	70	Devastation by Titus
	132	Capture and devastation by Hadrian; new city renamed Aelia Capitolina; Jews banned

Byzantine rule;	300	Christianity becomes state religion
the height of	335	Holy Sepulchre completed
Christian splen-	614	Capture and sack of Jerusalem by Persians
dor in the city	628	Recapture by Byzantines under Heraclius
A third religion,	638	Arab conquest under Omar
Islam, adopts	692	Dome of the Rock completed
Jerusalem as a	c. 1010	"Mad caliph" al-Hakim destroys Holy Sepulchre
holy city		
Christianity re-	1099	Siege, capture, and massacre of Moslems and Jews by Crusaders
established		
Jerusalem thrives	1187	Recapture by Moslems under Saladin
under the Mam-	1219	Walls razed by Malik al-Muazzam Isa
luk "slave kings"	1244	Capture and sack by Mongols
of Egypt		
The city declines	1516	Ottoman conquest
under Turkish	1537–1541	Walls rebuilt under Suleiman the Magnificent
rule	1808	Fire in the Holy Sepulchre
	1831	Egyptian occupation
	1840	Reoccupation by Turks
Zionists inaugu-	1917	British conquest
rate Jewish	1921	
"Return"; under	1929	Arab riots and uprisings
British rule,	1936	
Jerusalem thrives	1948	War and siege of Jewish Jerusalem by Jordanians
but is frequently		
racked by riots		
and other		
disturbances		
Divided	1948–1967	West Jerusalem becomes capital of Israel; Jordan annexes East Jerusalem
Jerusalem		
Immense growth	1967	War and occupation of Jordanian Jerusalem by Israel; Israel annexes East Jerusalem and its immediate environs
of the city under		
Mayor Teddy		
Kollek, but polit-	1969	Burning of al-Aqsa
ical problems re-	1977	Sadat's visit leads to first Arab-Israeli peace treaty
main unresolved;		
Wars of Religion		
continue in	1985	Plans to blow up Temple Mount foiled
Jerusalem under	1987–	Palestinian uprising
another name		

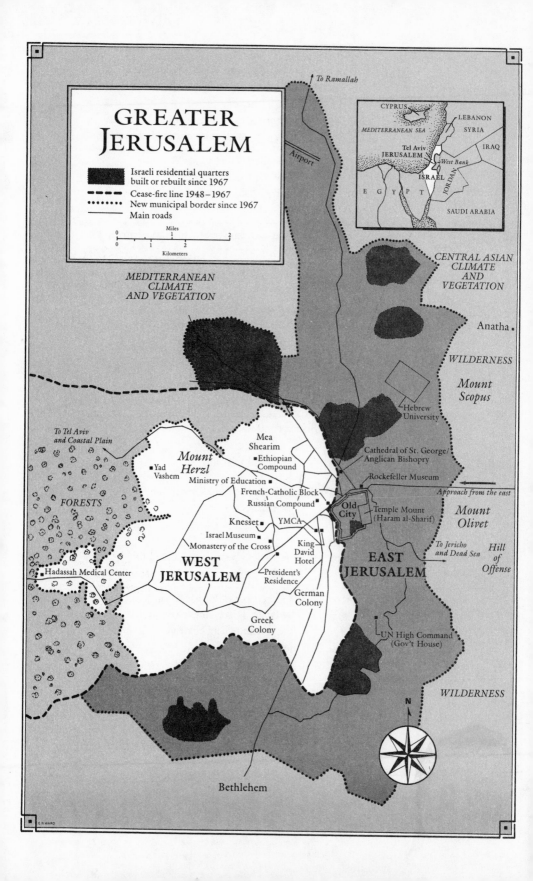

GREATER JERUSALEM

■ Israeli residential quarters built or rebuilt since 1967
- - - Cease-fire line 1948–1967
••••••• New municipal border since 1967
—— Main roads

Miles
0   1   2
0   1   2
Kilometers

CYPRUS
MEDITERRANEAN SEA
LEBANON
SYRIA
IRAQ
Tel Aviv
JERUSALEM
West Bank
ISRAEL
E G Y P T
JORDAN
SAUDI ARABIA

To Ramallah

Airport

MEDITERRANEAN
CLIMATE
AND VEGETATION

CENTRAL ASIAN
CLIMATE
AND
VEGETATION

Anatha ■

WILDERNESS

Mount
Scopus

Hebrew
University

To Tel Aviv
and Coastal Plain

Mount
Herzl

Mea
Shearim

■ Ethiopian
Compound

Cathedral of St. George/
Anglican Bishopry

Rockefeller Museum

Approach from the east

■ Yad
Vashem

Ministry of Education ■

French-Catholic Block

FORESTS

Russian Compound ■

Old
City

Temple Mount
(Haram al-Sharif)

Mount
Olivet

Knesset ■

YMCA ■

To Jericho
and Dead Sea

Hill
of
Offense

Israel Museum ■

Monastery of the Cross ■

King
David
Hotel

EAST
JERUSALEM

Hadassah Medical Center ■

WEST
JERUSALEM

President's
Residence

German
Colony

Greek
Colony

UN High Command
(Gov't House)

WILDERNESS

N

Bethlehem

G. W. WARD

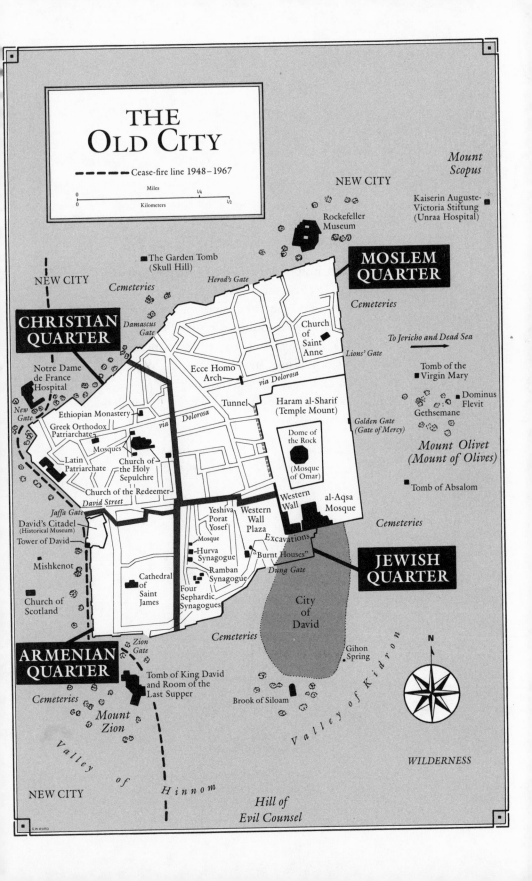

THE OLD CITY

– – – – – Cease-fire line 1948–1967

Miles
0 ——————— ¼
0 ——————— ½
Kilometers

Mount Scopus

NEW CITY

Kaiserin Auguste-Victoria Stiftung (Unraa Hospital)

Rockefeller Museum

MOSLEM QUARTER

Cemeteries

NEW CITY

Cemeteries

The Garden Tomb (Skull Hill)

Herod's Gate

CHRISTIAN QUARTER

Damascus Gate

Church of Saint Anne

To Jericho and Dead Sea

Lions' Gate

Notre Dame de France Hospital

Ecce Homo Arch

via Dolorosa

Tomb of the Virgin Mary

New Gate

Tunnel

Haram al-Sharif (Temple Mount)

Dominus Flevit

Gethsemane

Ethiopian Monastery

via Dolorosa

Greek Orthodox Patriarchate

Dome of the Rock

Golden Gate (Gate of Mercy)

Mosques

Mount Olivet (Mount of Olives)

Latin Patriarchate

Church of the Holy Sepulchre

(Mosque of Omar)

Church of the Redeemer

David Street

Western Wall

al-Aqsa Mosque

Tomb of Absalom

Jaffa Gate

Yeshiva Porat Yosef

Western Wall Plaza

Cemeteries

David's Citadel (Historical Museum)

Mosque

Excavations

Tower of David

Hurva Synagogue

"Burnt Houses"

JEWISH QUARTER

Mishkenot

Ramban Synagogue

Dung Gate

Cathedral of Saint James

Four Sephardic Synagogues

City of David

Church of Scotland

Cemeteries

Gihon Spring

N

Zion Gate

ARMENIAN QUARTER

Tomb of King David and Room of the Last Supper

Cemeteries

Mount Zion

Brook of Siloam

Valley of Kidron

Valley of Hinnom

NEW CITY

WILDERNESS

Hill of Evil Counsel

G.W. WARD

Memory and history are far from being synonymous. They are, in fact, opposites. Memory is life, it is always carried by living people and therefore it is in permanent evolution. It is subject to the dialectics of remembrance and amnesia, unaware of successive deformations and liable to all kinds of uses and manipulation. Memory remains latent for a long time and then suddenly revives. . . . It always belongs to our own time, a living link with the eternal present.

PIERRE NORA
Les Lieux de Mémoire

JERUSALEM

Introduction

THIS is a book about memory and the way it affects an embattled city. Few historic cities have been so bitterly embattled for so long. None has evoked such awe and wonder or at the same time given her name to Peace and to all that is tender in the human soul.

Jerusalem is a middle-sized city, provincial, in many ways modest, yet at the same time a city of invincible attraction. Two universal religions have been founded in Jerusalem; a third, Islam, has incorporated her various traditions into its doctrinal body. No other historic city evokes such inflammatory argument to this day.

In this century alone, Jerusalem has seen intermittent violence for at least seven decades. Jews and Arabs have fought two major wars over her and many bloody skirmishes in between. Even as this book was being written, there was recurrent violence in Jerusalem. Israelis and Palestinians were claiming mutually exclusive jurisdiction over the city in the name of immutable historic and religious rights. In the alleys of the Old City, Jews on their way to prayer were knifed by Islamic fanatics. Hardly a day passed without bloody clashes between flag-waving Palestinian demonstrators and Israeli troops in debris-strewn streets. Firebombs were thrown on passing Israeli cars and buses.

Like acts in a never-ending tragedy — a tragic drama in which there was no catharsis — the violence continued. From the same walls that the Romans scaled in the year 70 and the Crusaders in 1099, Palestinian youths armed (like David) with slingshots pelted passing armored police cars with stones. Helicopters hovered above, dropping tear-gas canisters. Nearby, in the narrow lanes, the sounds of the three faiths that hold the city sacred rose ceaselessly, as they always do, above the noise and clamor, lifting all things unto a sphere of memory and feeling where much of the current trouble started in the first place, a very long time ago: the voice of the muezzin, calling the Moslem faithful to prayer; the toll of church bells; the chant of Jews praying at the Western Wall, the one remaining fragment of their ancient Jewish temple.

The Wars of Religion continue in Jerusalem under another name. It has been said about Jerusalem that she is a necrocracy, the only city where the vote is given to the dead. Everywhere in Jerusalem, you notice the heavy weight of the past on the present. For Jews, she has always been the Capital of Memory. For Moslems, she has been al-Quds, the Holy One, since the rise of Islam in the seventh and eighth centuries. Memory is never static. Memory is always overshadowed, and sometimes manipulated, by power. National and other conflicts feed on it. Jerusalem epitomizes the power of memory over the minds of men and women. There are many ways of writing about such a city. Some are wearisome and some are vain. This book tries to look at the changing images of the past and help the reader see through them the running of history in the present. It examines symbols. Symbols are prisms through which people or peoples look — or are taught to look — at reality. It attempts to reconstitute the emotional life of the past seen through a contemporary temperament.

Jerusalem is a city where history is relentlessly and superstitiously evoked every day by the contesting sides. Nevertheless, this is not a historical narrative, although it includes some history. Nor is this a guidebook or a geography of Jerusalem, even though it refers to sights and sounds and to some of the major monuments. The monuments have a vernacular of their own. They evoke conflicting memories and make up her image as a city dear to more than one people, sacred to more than one faith. The description is not chronological but impressionistic, as it might occur to someone walking from one landmark to the next, as leisurely as is possible under the circumstances.

From the time of Plato, cities have been defined politically — that is, rationally. For Jerusalem, this is not enough. In Jerusalem, as in Belfast, religion bedevils politics. Wars of religion do not lend themselves to rational description. Nor are there at this moment easy or clear-cut answers to the question of how or when the present troubles of Jerusalem might be resolved. The current unrest in the city may die down by the time this book is out, but I doubt that the lull will be more than temporary. Jerusalem lives too deeply in the spell of powerful religious beliefs and secular religions. The pieties and fanaticisms of the warring creeds and nationalities interact. Never has there been a single religious truth in Jerusalem. There have always been many truths. There have always been simultaneously held conflicting images of the city. The images reflect — or distort — one another, and the past is reflected in the present. This book could have been subtitled "Biography of an Image." It might equally well have been designated "Chronicle of an Obsession." I have instead called Jerusalem a "City of Mirrors." The mirrors are sometimes parallel — arranged so the images run to infinity — and sometimes they are oriented like mirrors inside a kaleidoscope. The reflections you see in a kaleidoscope are forever changing with each turn.

In our own time, men have stepped on the moon seeking new Jerusalems in foreign galaxies, but so far the old Jerusalem has not been replaced. She retains an extraordinary hold over the imagination, generating for three hostile faiths, in perfectly interchangeable phrases, the fear as well as the hope of Apocalypse. Religious territorialism is an ancient form of worship here. Nationalism and religion have always been intertwined in Jerusalem, where the idea of a promised land and a chosen people was first patented in the Jewish name almost three thousand years ago. Holy nationalism has since been emulated elsewhere too; in this century alone, at least two great territorial states have widely been thought of as God-lands. In Jerusalem today, religion and territorial politics coincide. On each side of the great divide between Palestinians and Israelis, nationalism and religion overlap. On each side they fuse into a whole that is potentially very explosive.

The ongoing struggle over Jerusalem and, in particular, over the famous holy mountain in her midst — the Jews call it Temple Mount or Moriah, the Moslems Haram al-Sharif — is sometimes described as a likely trigger for the next world war. In this dramatic form, the description is probably overly alarmist. The exaggeration may reflect the traditional religious associations of this spot with the End of Days; and perhaps it is just another instance of Jerusalem hubris, a new version of the ancient belief (rampant since the early Middle Ages) that Jerusalem was the "navel" of the universe. And yet, there is no doubt that the unresolved conflict over Jerusalem is potentially very dangerous. To defuse this potential, if for no better reason, the need for a political Israeli-Palestinian settlement, based on mutual compromise, appears more and more cogent. The religious component of the century-old Arab-Israeli conflict is becoming weightier all the time. In Jerusalem, it may well lead to yet another terrible local war, with untold suffering for all involved.

When Jerusalem was triumphantly reunited by Israel in the Six-Day War of 1967, after nineteen years of division by minefields and barbed wire, it seemed to many that her days of agony in this century might be over. In the aftermath of that war, a comprehensive Arab-Israeli settlement seemed reasonable and therefore — falsely, as it turned out — likely. It was hoped that in the context of such a settlement the two sectors of the city, the Israeli and the Palestinian, would be able henceforth to live in peace. But there was no Arab-Israeli settlement. The intransigence on the Arab side was too great. The Israelis insisted on major territorial changes — including the annexation of the former Jordanian-held parts of Jerusalem — which even the relatively moderate Jordanian government would not concede. Moreover, the two superpowers now engaged themselves in the ongoing Arab-Israeli struggle, which in a sense became a war by proxy between the Soviet Union and the United States.

With the rise, after 1967, of the Palestinian national movement, a new highly explosive element was added to the equation. The Palestinians, more than ever before, now reaffirmed their national identity — a mirror image of Zionism. "Arab Jerusalem" became its shining symbol. Like the Zionism of the Jews, the "Zionism" of the Palestinians was driven by memory, by the myth of the lost city and the bitterness of dispersion and defeat. "If I forget thee, O Jerusalem, let my right hand forget her cunning" became the Palestinians' battle cry, as it had been the Jews' prayer for nineteen hundred years. Simultaneously, "Jewish Jerusalem" was declared Israel's capital city "for ever and ever."

It was after the 1967 war that the idea of writing a book about this tragic city first occurred to me; for personal and professional reasons, I did not start researching and writing until some years later. I should add that I myself grew up in Tel Aviv but have lived in Jerusalem for much of my adult life. Each of us has a general history and a private history; we sort out our personal recollections by anchoring them in public time. I vividly recall the first time I visited Jerusalem as a boy — not because of the exotic sights you could still see in her streets in 1939, but because my father abruptly cut short our visit: World War II had broken out on that day.

The first time I spent any length of time in Jerusalem was as a soldier during the war of 1948. In a way I find hard to explain, I have felt myself to be a Jerusalemite ever since. I cannot pretend that my love for the city is religious or patriotic. Nor is her allure only aesthetic. The passions she arouses derive from geography and history. They go beyond politics or religion.

"For who shall have pity on thee, O Jerusalem? . . . who shall bemoan thee? . . . who shall go aside to ask how thou doest?"

Jerusalem, May 1989

CHAPTER ONE

Eastern Approaches

A TRAVELER making his or her way up the old Roman road to Jerusalem through the stone hills of the Judean desert views a strange land — barren, yellowish and gray. All around in the great dust bowl, the ground is monotonous, gutted and austere. The leaden soil is shallow and washed out. Wild ravines run down from the near mountaintops and rip it apart. Above the vast expanse of desiccated soil, the sky is ablaze in a blinding glare.

The silence is eerie. Away in the wastes stand a few grizzled trees, ashen from the dust. Huge boulders lie about in the gravel, dull and inert. Birds of prey circle above. As you leave your car, you step out onto dry thorns and blistered rocks.

Behind you, in the deeps, the barren coasts and bitter waters of the Dead Sea are visible through the haze. The Dead Sea is only twenty miles distant, but deep down — four thousand feet below, in the Syrian-African rift valley, the lowest spot on earth. The heat soars out from there and sears the skin. As the road climbs through the wilds, it passes below a new Israeli settlement surrounded, like most Israeli outposts in this area (under military occupation since 1967), by grim watchtowers and barbed-wire fences. The harsh, foreboding sight of rust and bare reinforced concrete seems part of the mute, melancholy landscape. It suggests a battlefield. The view is still mostly wild, diaphanous, like a vision on the surface of the moon. Then there is a turnoff from the main desert road and you enter a parched plateau. Instantly, the perspective changes. Ahead, on the high mountain wall, you see the outskirts of a city. A church tower protrudes from clusters of stone houses and green cypress trees. The road is steep. It cuts through the haggard rock in a great, sweeping curve. The air is dry. The stone is still brittle. The wind is less hot now. Lizards flicker on the stones. A faint smell of burning is in the air and here and there smoke rises from unseen brush fires. The face of the mountain nears. There is the muffled roar of car traffic, and, occasionally, the sound of ringing bells.

Presently, the scene quickens. Gaunt little stone houses lie about, lapped in dust and gravel. Still higher, the soil darkens. There are little orchards and vegetable plots. The air is cooler. Up north on the far horizon, a little village is set into the bare hill like teeth into a jaw: Anathot, where Jeremiah was born of a family of priests — today an Arab village, called Anatha by its inhabitants. Though Anatha has been changing in recent years and has become a suburb of Jerusalem, barely four miles away, it still nestles within the distinctive rural setting the prophet so often reflected in his oracles: the same hard-to-till stony fields, the same great triad of olive, barley, and figs, the same dusty vines, the same small flocks of sheep, the same barren heights and depths. Abrupt drops into endless space lurk in the rough terrain. The wilderness is immediately behind. The scale of this wilderness is grand and awesome; it must have suggested to the ancients their vulnerability, their insignificance, their dependence on the whim of a cruel God.

The steep road narrows. Crossing the borderline between the desert and the area that is sown, it climbs in twists and turns the backside of Scopus and Olivet, the two adjoining mountains that overlook Jerusalem from the east. The massive new campus of the Hebrew University comes into view, looking rather like a fortress on the flattened summit of the mountain. Despite more traffic and noise, the scene is still largely rural. There are children on the road now, and women with shopping bags. Men glance up disinterestedly from their work. Dogs bark behind rusty gates. The church tower, nearer now, reaches high above the green. Next to it rises the great hulk of a monastery. The road is even steeper than before. It climbs the last hump and crosses into a hollow between the two mountains, Scopus and Olivet. Then it drops sharply: the hills part to a sudden view of swelling domes and towering minarets.

A walled city heaves below in the dazzling light. The atmosphere is
at once thrilling and unique. Jerusalem is set amid higher mountains on the bank of a deep ravine. Her full strength bursts on you
as soon as you cross the hollow between the two mountains: long
walls and parapets, dark towers, vaulted stone roofs, churches,
synagogues, and mosques. Dominating all is the vast stone platform, half as old as time, of the ancient Jewish Temple Mount —
now a Moslem sanctuary — worn out with the worship of too
many warring gods.

The main business of this platform, for at least three millennia,
has been the traffic in beliefs. Too much holy zeal has been poured
out here, for too long, into too narrow a space. Under the gilded
dome at the center of the stone platform, a flat rock protrudes from
the ground, where successive religions have claimed that the creation of the world began. Here, the first capital crime is said to have
been committed when Cain killed Abel. Here, Abraham bound
Isaac to offer him up as a burnt sacrifice to God. (According to
Moslem lore, the intended victim was Ishmael, not Isaac, and the
place was not Jerusalem but Mecca. It is not the only point of
disagreement among the creeds.)

Today, the great Mosque of Omar, or Dome of the Rock —
lustrous with gold, pale greens, and blues, like a peacock against the
translucent sky — covers this flat rock. The great stone platform
glistens in the light. Touching it in the west — only a stone's throw
away — is the Western Wall, also known as Wailing Wall, where
Jews have come for centuries to pray and lament the destruction of
their temple. Close by, the rounded cupola of the Church of the
Holy Sepulchre rises over the stone rooftops; here, Christians since
the fourth century have worshiped the site of the crucifixion, burial,
and resurrection of Jesus. Within this narrow triangle formed by
Dome, Wall, and Sepulchre, extremes of creed and race and habit
intersect but rarely meet. Sanctities overlap, while all around them
the city is austere and gray, grave, even grim, and yet of a perfect
distinction within her crenellated walls. The walls survey the
ravines. They follow the sunken lines of other walls — walls two
thousand, perhaps three thousand years old — that the Romans
stormed in AD 70 and that the Jebusites, over a thousand years
earlier, vainly defended against the invading Hebrews. Below the

walls, a vast city of the dead encircles the city of the living. Clusters of rickety tombstones crowd the silted banks, tombs of all ages and faiths. No matter where you tread, there are graves. It is that kind of place. The earth falls off below to a ravine that is planted with more tombs and olive trees. The olive tree, Pliny observed, never dies.

Viewed from the summits of Scopus and Olivet, the skyline is elaborate with medieval ramparts and towers and gilded domes and crenellations and tottering Roman and Arab ruins. Pigeons turn above in clouds of silver and amethyst. It is an impression that no amount of familiarity can blunt. Whether you pray or curse, it is a gripping view. If Jerusalem had no peculiar historic association, she would still evoke strong emotions by her extraordinary physical aspect. Under a brilliant morning sky the city gleams in a steady light of almost crystalline clarity. Until quite recently, the two over-riding features of the landscape were harsh light and stone — stone fields, stone mountains, and stone valleys; stone roofs; stone towers; stone walls of immense thickness; lines of stones across the terraced fields (stones less likely put there to mark crude boundaries than simply to get them out of the way). The stone is limestone and chalk — the gray, rough-grained kind that local masons call *mizi yahudi*, the red-spotted *mizi ahmar*, or the bright *mizi hilou*. The blind Jorge Luis Borges, groping his way along a Jerusalem street in 1969, claimed he could tell the stones were pink by their peculiar "touch." Since time immemorial, visitors and residents of Jerusalem have been fascinated — or frightened — by her stones. In the nine-teenth century, with its romantic passion for rocks, some visitors were perfectly obsessed by them. Herman Melville spent eight days in Jerusalem in 1857 and was so overwhelmed by the stony landscape he came back to it in his diary time and again. "Stones to right and stones to left . . . stony tombs; stony hills & stony hearts." Melville thought it was no wonder that stones figured so importantly in the Bible. The Old Testament was filled with stones, both figurative and real. Men were stoned to death. The proverbial seed fell in stony places. Job laid out on "stones of darkness." Jacob took a stone and put it up "for his pillows." Joshua set one up as a witness "by the sanctuary of the Lord." Lot's wife became a stonelike "pil-lar of salt."

In the later Jewish legends, stones rained from the sky. God threw a stone into the waters of the abyss and from this stone the whole world grew, with Jerusalem at its center. There was a magic link between water and stone; the contrast between the two inspired Jerusalem's religions. Water was thrown on the stone altar to abjure drought. God himself came from stone: "the Rock that begat thee."

In Melville's time, the mountains around Jerusalem were especially grim and bare — as though chosen with an unerring eye, many observers thought, to house the temple of the cruel deity of an eye for an eye and a tooth for a tooth. "The city looks at you like a cold grey eye in a cold grey man," Melville wrote. He was the quintessential traveler in that landscape-conscious century. The Jews of Jerusalem, he observed, were "like flies who have taken up their abode inside a skull." There was too little to see and altogether too much dust. "No grace of decay . . . no ivy [in] the unleavened nakedness of desolation."

A century later, the city had more than quadrupled in size, but the immediate environs of the old historic core, within the medieval walls, were still more or less unchanged. Yehuda Amichai, the modern Hebrew poet and a lifelong resident of the city, moaned over "All these stones, all this sadness, all this light." In Jerusalem, he wrote, people lived "inside prophecies" that had come true "as inside a thick cloud after an explosion." Edmund Wilson saw Jerusalem in the early 1950s, some years before the well-watered parks with their great expanses of green lawns were planted in the valleys and on the slopes — new gardens that have thoroughly changed the colors of the landscape and even the quality of light. In Wilson's time, the harsh light of summer still drained the landscape of all color. The stony folds below his window in the King David Hotel — today they are a lovely green park — were still a mined no-man's-land between the Arab and the Jewish parts of the city. Wilson thought it strange that from such harsh contours had come the legends that inspired the chiaroscuro of the Renaissance and the blazing colors of the baroque period — that teeming of pink flesh and gorgeous silks and velvet, beautiful blond Madonnas and blue-eyed shepherds in lush green surroundings of near-Arcadian bliss.

The religious imagination always invented — still invents — its own particular geography, and climate to match.

A traveler with a historical bent might be forgiven if he or she insisted on approaching Jerusalem from the desert in the east. The early Hebrews came in this way — from the desert to the sown — after their crossing of the Jordan; and the Romans and Arabs after them. It is the most spectacular route. The stage is set. The color is switched on. The hills suddenly part like curtains. The drama of the scene, like a trumpet blast in *Fidelio,* is enhanced by its suddenness. Historically, the city's cultural and political orientation was toward that desert in the east; she refused to look west, to the prosperous Greek colonies on the nearby Mediterranean coast, with their thriving literary and material — but pagan — culture. Her fugitives usually ran off toward the east. Visually, too, the single gap in the hills surrounding her historic core was to the east. The city faced the desert, not the sea. All other directions were blocked by higher mountains. Historians have read much into this fact. Josephus Flavius, the first-century historian, wanted Jerusalem to be more oriented toward the lush, Mediterranean, Hellenic west. He observed ruefully that the single full prospect from Jerusalem's highest tower was "toward Arabia." George Adam Smith, the nineteenth-century geographer and historian, speculated that her facing toward the east might explain why the Greeks never struck roots in Jerusalem, and why Hellenism, though firmly entrenched on the Mediterranean coast not forty miles away, never made her its own; why even Christianity failed to hold Jerusalem, and the Moslems, as they look down "her one long vista toward Mecca," feel themselves "securely planted on her site."

Mount Scopus was so named, Josephus wrote, because as you come up from the desert in the east, it permitted a first "sight of the city and the grand pile of the temple gleaming afar." It still does. Here the generals, from Nebuchadnezzar to Dayan, habitually paused for a covetous first look, or a last, before the final assault. Here, over the centuries, countless pilgrims knelt to give thanks in prayer on reaching the famous city of their quest; the Jews among them rent their garments in mourning for her ruins. Here, at nearly 2,700 feet above sea level, the air is fresh and cool. Directly behind, over the other side of the saddle, the desert mountaintops swelter in the heat.

Few capital cities stand so high or are so splendid and at the same time so terrifying as Jerusalem viewed from the dry, lunar backdrop of the eastern desert. The name Zion — which comes from the Hebrew *ziya,* meaning "parched desert" — denotes her dryness. The surrounding valleys have suffered the intrusion of modern housing and even some industry in recent years. They are still marked by a brooding, bleak, not easily definable beauty.

The beauty seems to derive from a rare combination of luminosity and bareness. There is a merciless clarity in the sunlit air. Everything is open to the sky. On a fine day, the Old City is sharply carved out within the hills as in an etching. In the early morning, light and shade sweep over the rooftops and hills — stony and steep — bringing successively into strong relief every point of interest. At noon, the sky burns like a heated opal. With the sun directly above, there are — as in the mind of a fanatic — only blacks and whites below, no muted colors in between. This is Jerusalem's most distinctive moment.

The afternoon softens the harsher edges. The setting sun lights the stone walls with an exquisite glow, as of pure fire. The low sun shortens the perspective. If the atmospheric conditions happen to be right, they will conjure up in the dry mountain air a wonderful optical illusion. The far mountains of Moab, pink and rosy, will loom in the east above the frozen undulations of the desert, across the deep hollow of the Dead Sea. They are more than fifty miles away in Jordan, but in the evening light they will appear as though on the outskirts of the city. There is something uncanny in this. The city never seems more part of the desert world than on evenings such as these. Then, the sky darkens, rather abruptly. The pinks dissolve into grays and blacks.

Nights, especially during the long summer months, are splendid. Enormous stars hang in the dry darkness like great chandeliers. Winter nights are bleak. But under a foot of snow the surrounding hills gleam in the dark with their own hidden light, like a transfiguration by El Greco. When it snows, it usually snows day and night until the city is sealed up like a village in Norway and the authorities declare a state of siege. Nineteenth-century travelers were often overwhelmed by the Jerusalem nights. They preferred Jerusalem by night to Jerusalem by day. Darkness hid the decay and reawakened the ancient spell. In the harsh daylight, the spell vanished. "I had stood alone within the awful circle of the Coliseum, when faintly touched by the light of the rising moon," W. H. Bartlett, the famous English engraver wrote in 1843, "but this nocturnal approach to the ancient capital of Judea, across her bleak and desolate hills, awoke a more sublime and thrilling emotion."

A person standing on Scopus or Olivet four thousand years ago and looking west across the ravine would have seen a small, fortified city climbing up to a rocky peak. Where the great temple platform is today, with its mosques and minarets, there was in ancient times a small plateau, an acropolis. The large, flat rock, still visible today under the great golden Dome, served as an altar to Baal, or some other pagan god. By the curious economy governing sacred sites, the same rock would play a major role in a succession of mutually hostile creeds.

Jews called it Stone of Foundation, the spot where they claimed the creation of the universe began and Adam was born of dust. The legend of Abraham making ready to sacrifice his son on this rock was later interpreted as a parable intended to dramatize a higher form of religion — one in which faith was enough and the deity no longer needed to be placated by gifts. But this was a relatively late interpretation of the legend. What its deeper origins might have been in the Oedipal psyche of primitive fathers and sons is still the subject of extensive conjecture. The same rock is said to have been the Jebusite Araunah's threshing floor, which David bought for fifty shekels but found barely large enough for his little shrine, "the ground around it being precipitous and steep." David's son, Solomon, walled up the eastern side toward the ravine to make more ground available for the first Hebrew temple. The rock may have served as the temple's altar. The perforations and holes in it suggest lines of drainage for water or blood. Or it may have been the temple's "Holy of Holies." The Holy of Holies was the innermost part of the sanctuary, a dark chamber that only the high priest entered, once a year, on the highest holiday. In the days of Solomon, the tablets of the law, which Moses was said to have brought down from Mount Sinai, were kept there. A thousand years after Solomon, the second temple, that of Herod the Great, rose up over the same rock high above the ravine, "the grandest ever heard of by man," wrote Josephus. Perhaps Josephus exaggerated. Judging from what is left of the Herodian walls and in the vast stone platform that has remained almost intact on its artificially raised base, the exaggeration cannot have been very great.

Here nurtured the religions of half of today's world. Their nerves still quiver in the dry and stony soil. Here, even the nonbeliever must confront and come to terms with the phenomenon of faith and its concomitant, sacredness. It has to do with power and the imagination — God, in Paul Tillich's words, being the name for that which concerns man ultimately. Here, time and again, the curious observer is struck by the uniqueness of the religious experience, for in the eyes of the true believer, God is not necessarily an abstraction or a moral allegory but a terrible power, manifested by His wrath. The nonbeliever sees this, perhaps, with a keener eye than the believer, since the nonbeliever is more likely to assume from the very outset that the religious experience has little to do with rationality.

Here was born the rumor of a single invisible God, a father figure, authoritarian — at once petulant and magnanimous, vindictive and merciful; and the sadomasochism of "in my wrath I smote thee, but in my favour I had mercy" was first articulated in religious terms.

But why here? Why of all places in Jerusalem? There is a temptation to read much, perhaps too much, into the majestic landscape. The grandiose view over the bare mountaintops out into the open desert is conducive to meditation and thought and wonder at the meaning of life. But so are many other landscapes. Ernest Renan recommended "reading" this landscape as the "fifth gospel," a key to the understanding of the canonical four. The desert was *monothéiste*, Renan argued. The monotonous landscape, under the dazzling sky, cleansed the mind of earthly distractions, and allowed it to concentrate on the heavenly and the divine. And yet no one is more conscious of earthly things than the desert dweller, more aware than the Beduin of every line in the sand, changing with the wind, every speck of dust, every lizard and every fly.

Was it the climate, then? The ancient Hebrews were a peasant people. Meteorology plays an important part in the Old Testament. The sky over Jerusalem is clear at night for eight months of the year and invites the worship of heavenly objects. "The heavens declare the glory of God," sang the psalmist. The simple rhythms of nature, of night and day, winter and summer, cold and heat, are more dramatic here than in northern climes. The elements may have lent wings to the cosmology of a divinely ordered world. (Voltaire surmised that Mohammed, who forbade wine in Arabia, would have been stoned to death had he done so on the banks of the Dwina or "in Switzerland, especially before going to battle.")

Similar ideas of a divinely ordered universe circulated elsewhere in the ancient world. Elsewhere, however, religion was not necessarily linked to ethics. In Jerusalem, it was. Greek philosophers toyed with the idea among speculations of an entirely different character; they deduced their morals from man, rather than from God. Indeed, most ancient religions had no ethical content at all. The closest parallel, the monotheism of Amenhotep IV, or Akhenaton — perhaps a contemporary of Moses — who worshiped the sun-disk, was equally devoid of it. Akhenaton's religion was contemplative rather than practical. In Jerusalem, apparently for the first time, religion became both.

Here was waged the first battle in the long war between the invisible God of the austere desert mountains and the graven sensual gods of the green plains. Other ancient religions postulated a sky-god or a single deity. Here, perhaps for the first time, God was conceived as righteous and transcendent, completely outside nature, unbounded by any form of physical existence, the sole creator of the universe. Religion, until then best defined as a form of extreme fear, was made moral. The idea of a righteous god was first broached sometime between 900 and 800 BC when the Jewish prophets, for some reason, took to exalting the savage tribal god of their ancestors as one who loved justice and hated iniquity. Their message was vivid, deeply emotional, and intolerant. Not the democratic "Let us see," as in Plato, but the authoritarian "Thus saith the Lord," as in Isaiah.

Here, the Jews began to live morally — as the Japanese have done literally — in a house of paper: the Bible. Here, they first became, however reluctantly, people of the Book. Here, probably long before the Greeks, they achieved the intellectual feat of composing a connected narrative of history — their own and that of the world — enmeshed in the five books of Moses. Here, a national identity was defined, perhaps for the first time, by articulating a philosophy of history. And here, the idea of progress was first broached. In its time, it was an absolutely sensational idea. Thucydides still thought it was worth writing the history of the Peloponnesian war because its events inevitably would be repeated. The scribes and prophets of Jerusalem challenged the prevailing notion that history necessarily moved in circles, repeating itself again and again. They invented utopia, the possibility of a better world. They enunciated hope on a grand scale. They postulated the possibility of a linear progression toward a better, more worthwhile life.

Versions of the Pentateuch and the books of Joshua, Samuel, and Kings circulated in Jerusalem, as oral traditions, early in the eighth or ninth century BC. In Greece, Homer was at work on his great epic. As in the Homeric epics and other great books from before the age of literary record, the poetic form ensured the relatively correct transmission of these fragments from generation to generation. The poetic form served another purpose that the ancient Greeks had ignored: it endowed ideas, especially ethical ideas, with such emotional force they became laws.

Some of the factual details in these biblical fragments were remarkably accurate. Archaeological and epigraphical evidence has repeatedly shown this to be so. There is still no archaeological evidence of Joshua or David or Isaiah and perhaps there never will be. But there is ample evidence of Sennacherib's and Nebuchadnezzar's military exploits in the neighborhood of Jerusalem. Proper names mentioned in the Book of Kings turn up in epigraphic finds. Judging from the average quality of composition in the Bible, literary works must have been extremely good in ancient Jerusalem; better, perhaps, than anywhere we know in the ancient world outside of Greece. Even more extraordinary is the fact that the Bible, as it was written in Jerusalem, unlike the books of other ancient peoples, was not the literature of a major or regional power nor even of a ruling elite, but the literature of a minor, remote people — and not the literature of its rulers, but of its critics. The scribes and the prophets of Jerusalem refused to accept the world as it was. They invented the literature of political dissent and, with it, the literature of hope.

Here, according to the biblical account of David — itself a small literary masterpiece, always human, dramatic, and under the stress of great passions — the king "danced before the Lord with all his might" and carried into the city, behind a curtain, the ark of the God nobody had ever seen and most outsiders mocked, and placed it on Araunah's rock. The pagans were at a loss to understand what anyone could possibly worship in a temple destitute of pictures and effigies. When, in the autumn of 63 BC, Pompey arrived in Jerusalem to inspect Rome's latest conquest, he entered the inner sanctum forbidden to all except the high priest, Tacitus reports, and found there to his stupefaction "nulla intus Deum effigie, vacuam sedem et inania arcana [not a single image of a god, but an empty place and a deserted sanctuary]." In Rome, Cicero was consul, and Jerusalem was in Roman hands, but for most Romans, Jewish Jerusalem remained an absurdity or a mysterious threat. Juvenal mocked that Jews will sell you whatever dreams you like, for a small copper. Tacitus hinted at the legend, often repeated by the ancients, that the void in the temple of Jerusalem was a fraud, the Jews actually worshiped an ass's head in there. His only conclusion from all this was that Jewish Jerusalem was intent on living in a state of perpetual hostility with the rest of mankind.

Here, Isaiah cried in the wilderness and Jesus bore the crown of thorns and was killed with the thieves. A small band of Jewish sectarians — known as Christians — believed in Jesus. They gathered in this city after his death, furtively, and — in the name of hope — eventually took over the Roman Empire and the entire Mediterranean world. Here also, the eschatology — that is to say, the body of teachings about last or final things — of the Apocalypse and the millennium, of death and resurrection, seized human minds, never to let go again. Here, according to Moslem lore, Mohammed came on his night journey astride a winged white steed and climbed to heaven on a stair of light. From at least the twelfth century, Jews have come here to pray at the Western Wall three times daily, that they might "return in mercy to Your city Jerusalem and dwell in it as You have promised."

Here, in 1099, the Crusaders, contrite and knee-deep in blood, marched up the hill of Calvary. The weird combination (not for the first or the last time in the history of Jerusalem) of the vilest and most tender passions in man has been variously judged by philosophers and historians: by David Hume as easy and natural, by Voltaire as absurd and incredible. Perhaps, as Gibbon suggested, halfheartedly, the combination of godliness and bloodiness was too rigorously applied to the same persons and the same hour.

Four thousand years of history, innumerable wars, and earthquakes of the utmost severity — some involving the total destruction of buildings and walls — have left their imprint upon the topography of the city: twenty ruinous sieges, two intervals of total desolation, eighteen reconstructions, and at least eleven transitions from one religion to another.

The accumulation of historic rubble is enormous. Over the centuries, so many ruins have fallen down the steep slopes that the ravines around the Old City are quite clogged up with them. Within and without the old walls, every hollow, every nook and cranny, is choked with up to fifty feet of accumulated rubbish. If the huge mass of debris could be cleared away, the skeleton of the original city would come into view. The true shape of the site would, first and foremost, expose its natural disadvantage as an urban center, and the difficulty of defending it.

The ramparts did not protect. It is no wonder they were so often breached. The city walls were quite formidable in parts of the lower city, where Jerusalem first began, perhaps in the fourth millennium BC. But the impression of impenetrable strength is an illusion, especially in the north. The relatively low ramparts in the north were scaled in most of the city's famous sieges; hence Jeremiah's cry, "Out of the north an evil shall break forth." The city had political and religious significance, but little if any strategic value. Alexander and Napoléon, two great generals on their way to conquer the world, spurned Jerusalem; each marched past her in the near vicinity but did not consider her worth a detour.

It is not easy to see why this improbable site was picked as a stronghold, rather than one of several more natural hilltop rock fortresses nearby. Perhaps it was the proximity of water: a symbol of life and greenery on the edge of a dry desert. A natural spring stirred on the bottom of the deep eastern ravine. But water was available — more plentiful or secure — elsewhere too. Jerusalem may have been chosen because of the lure of some long-established local magic rite. Sanctity is always contagious and is passed on from one creed to the next. New creeds invariably take over the holy places of the old. Even at that, Jerusalem was only one of several holy mountains in the area. Among the others, to mention only the nearest, was Beth-el — where, we are told, Jacob met God in his dream and, upon waking, articulated the religious experience by describing one of its main attributes — *dread*. "How dreadful is this place! this is none other but the house of God, and this is the gate of heaven." The primitive mind pictured all force as personal and panicked in its presence. The earliest forms of religion were ritualized attempts to appease these dreadful forces.

Perhaps Jerusalem was chosen for reasons of tribal politics; perhaps because of a tradition passed on from pagan times that she stood on a holy mountain. Holy mountains were thought to be meeting places of heaven and earth. (In the flatlands of Egypt, people built artificial mountains — pyramids — to attain the same purpose.) Perhaps she was picked because of a tradition that the Stone of Foundation, the sacred rock under the temple platform, separated the world above from the primeval world below — chaos from creation. So powerful was this tradition that it has survived three thousand years from the Hebrews of the tenth century BC to the Moslem guardians of the rock in our own days. The cult of the world's "navel" is known in other holy cities as well. Ancient "navels" have been found in France, Iran, Ireland, and Greece (Delphi). In Mecca, as in Jerusalem, it survived the demise of one religion and passed on to the next.

The spring theory is not very convincing in any case. The spring, still visible today, was outside the city walls. In any event, it was sufficient for a limited population, of perhaps only two thousand or three thousand souls. As the city grew, water was channeled in from afar. The old aqueducts can still be made out on the sculptured slopes that flow one into the other in ever-expanding curves.

The site of Jerusalem was man-made, artificial and contrived. Jerusalem was the child of magic, a holy city already in pagan times. Far from existence conditioning consciousness, as in Marx's famous dictum, consciousness has conditioned existence in Jerusalem over the centuries. Unlike other great urban centers, Jerusalem had no easy access to the sea. The city was neither on a riverbank, nor on a crossroad, nor was it even easily defended. The Beth-el of Jacob's dream, a short distance north of Jerusalem and an old pagan sanctuary, would have made a better site on all counts, with its command of strategic roads along a trade route. Bethlehem, a few miles south, was in a district considerably more fertile. The improbable site on which Jerusalem grew afforded little pasture and only very limited wood for burning. The ground was too steep or broken up to allow the use of wheels; hence, in the ancient sources there is hardly ever a mention of chariots here. The site afforded no natural command of traffic or of trade. The nearest main trade routes lay forty miles away in one direction and fifteen in the other.

Jerusalem was the product of human effort and design, not of geographical configuration. Culturally too, she was always marginal to the great centers of the ancient world, in Egypt, Mesopotamia, in Greece or in Rome. Judaism and Christianity successively proclaimed her the navel of the earth. But at most times, people in Jerusalem must have felt themselves not at the world's center but at its end.

She has been holy — often at great human cost — to more than one religion, and has generated in perfectly interchangeable phrases the fear and the hope of the Apocalypse, not just once but three times, by adherents of several faiths, each equally hostile to the other. Judaism held reign until AD 70; Islam from 638 to 1099 and from 1187 to 1917. Christianity held the city from 300 to 638 and again from 1099 to 1187. Today, in almost equally interchangeable phrases, the raw, intense attachments of two mutually hostile nationalisms, the Israeli and the Palestinian, continue where the religions leave off. In Jerusalem, even the jackals at night are said to howl articles of faith and historical quotations at one another. In this respect, she hardly has a paragon. There is east, there is west, and there is Jerusalem, a world apart.

Marching up to Jerusalem in about 1000 BC, David found an existing sanctuary of considerable antiquity and renown. No one knows when that sanctuary was founded. As Salem, her name first appears on one of the still-mysterious Ebla tablets that were found north of Aleppo in Syria and are believed to be five thousand years old. Salem was the Canaanite god of the evening star. The Ugarit hymns contain a paean to Salem and Dawn, sons born on the same day to the god El by his two wives. The Salem of the book of Genesis is generally thought to be Jerusalem. A priest-king of Salem called Melchizedek (King of Righteousness) meets Abraham with bread and wine, and blesses him in the name of El-Elyon (most high God), "possessor of heaven and earth." David renamed the city Zion and took for himself the old priest-king's emblems of earthly and divine sovereignty. The memory of the ancient priest-king Melchizedek continued to hang mysteriously over the city; it entered Christian and Moslem lore as well. In Psalm 110, Melchizedek is at God's right hand and presides over the Last Judgment. In another account, Melchizedek was Shem, Noah's firstborn, who founded Jerusalem after the flood and reigned there as king and high priest.

These are legends, but behind them, like coins and clay shards in the sand, truth may well be submerged. The "most high God" may have been an early prototype of Jehovah. Abraham himself suggests this when he tells the king of Sodom, "I lift up mine hand unto the Lord [Jehovah], the most high God, the possessor of heaven and earth." The name of Salem, the Canaanite deity, later echoes mysteriously in that of Solomon (builder of Jehovah's first temple at Jerusalem) and of Suleiman the Magnificent, Mohammed's apostle, who like Solomon was said to control the winds and the spirits and know how to converse with animals.

A few shards of the Middle Kingdom (circa 1900 BC), accidentally found by an Egyptian peasant woman in the last century, brought forth for the first time the full name Urshamen, or

Urusalim: "Her heroes and fast runners . . . they shall all die."
Urusalim is almost identical with the Hebrew *Jerushalem* or
Jerushalaim. It means either "Foundation of the [god] Salem" or
"Foundation of Peace" (or "of Prosperity"), or both. The name
reappears in one of the so-called Egyptian execration texts that date
from roughly the same time (the twentieth to the eighteenth century BC). These were figurines, or fragments of pottery, inscribed
with the name of an actual or potential enemy. The ancient Egyp-
tians believed that by smashing these figurines — much like putting
pins in voodoo dolls — they were effectively breaking the power of
specific enemies. Some such enemy must have been one "Yaqar
Ammu, the ruler of Jerusalem, and all the retainers that are with
him," if we can believe one execration text.

Another accidental find, of a collection of cuneiform tablets at
Tel-el-Amarna in Upper Egypt, brought to light the royal archive
of Amenhotep III and his son Akhenaton. Among some four hundred dispatches on clay from princelings and chieftains in Palestine,
Phoenicia, and southern Syria were eight from one Abdu-Heba,
ruler of Jerusalem and an Egyptian vassal. The fascination of these
fragments is not only historical but human and dramatic as well.
Through the dark abyss of time, the scene suddenly lights up, revealing a few sober moments of intense urgency and crisis. Abdu-
Heba's crisis would prove to be of a recurrent kind in the history of
the city. His tone strikes a modern reader as almost contemporary.
He is threatened from all sides. He is concerned with image and
public relations. He is frustrated. He is annoyed. He conveys a
sense of fear and loneliness and a kind of cosmic depression that
Arthur Koestler, a future Jerusalemite, speaking of the mood of the
city more than three millennia later, defined as "Jerusalem Sadness"
— a local disease, like Baghdad boils, "due to the combined effect of
the tragic desolate beauty and inhuman atmosphere of the city."
Abdu-Heba's anguished letters are worth quoting. During the
thirty-three centuries between Abdu-Heba (circa 1400 BC) and
Arthur Koestler (1924), Abdu-Heba's bleak sentiments would re-
echo so often — in the same atmosphere of treachery and suspicion
— as to become almost the city's hallmark.

The dispatches are addressed to the pharaoh, "the King my Lord, the Sun God of the Lands." The vassal addresses his master with nauseating flattery. The pharaoh is the sun-god, who rises over the land day by day and gives life by his sweet breath. "Seven and seven times I fall at my king's two feet. I am the dirt under his feet, the ground which he treads. . . . The territory is being overrun by enemies and ruined." Abdu-Heba has written repeatedly for reinforcements, but they have not been sent. He has sent his couriers to the palace of the pharaoh, but they have returned empty-handed. He would like to come to Egypt, to "see the two eyes of the king, my Lord," but cannot since he has been unjustly maligned. In a postscript, he pleads for support among the king's courtiers: "To the scribe of the king my Lord. Thus Abdu-Heba, thy servant. Present eloquent words to the king my Lord. I am only a petty officer. I am more insignificant than thou. Send troops of archers." Without them, the land would be wasted "by the Habiru." The Habiru have already taken Rubada. "Shall we then let Urusalim go?"

Who were these Habiru? A connection between them and the ancient Hebrew remains a matter of speculation. Another letter from Abdu-Heba reports that traitors are conspiring against the king. The outlying territories have already fallen off. Even the Nubian slave troops of Egypt, stationed as a garrison in Jerusalem, have rebelled. They have burglarized Abdu-Heba's own residence and nearly killed him in his own home. "They attempted a very great crime. Let the king call them to account." If the king would only send the archers Abdu-Heba had requested in his last letter, let them "come up with an Egyptian officer . . ." The king must not abandon the city. "Behold the king has set his name in the land of Jerusalem for ever." This last injunction, addressed to Akhenaton, is the only oblique reference to the state religion — Aton worship — in the entire correspondence.

In a third letter, Abdu-Heba commiserates once again with his fate. Nature itself is conspiring against him. He is losing all hope. "I have been like a ship in the midst of the sea. . . . Twenty-one maidens, thirty captives I delivered into the hands of Shuba as a gift for the king my Lord." But the king has not sent him any troops. Thus "the land of the king is lost, . . . it is taken from me. There is war against me as far as the lands of Seir." If the king cannot send troops, let him fetch away Abdu-Heba and his clan that they might die before the king.

In yet another fragment, Abdu-Heba again bows "seven times at the feet of my Lord" and reports that more vassals of the king have fallen away. The king's other vassals have perished or betrayed him. "Why does not my king call them to account?" Even a town in the land of Jerusalem — Bethlehem — has gone over to the enemy. "Let my king send archers to recover the royal land for the king."

But Egypt's power was weakening. Egypt would soon lose its lordship over Canaan and southern Syria. When the Hebrews arrived two or three centuries later, Jerusalem was a small Jebusite citadel of little importance. At first, the Hebrews did not even bother to take it. When they finally did, under David, they made Jerusalem the high place of their invisible God. A deep irony ensued. Jehovah was a fiercely national, *tribal* deity. But, as Edmund Wilson pointed out, by choosing Jerusalem as the abode of this extraordinary moralizing God, the Hebrews gave the city — no doubt inadvertently — to all of mankind.

CHAPTER TWO

Holy City

So Jerusalem became holy and holy she has remained — for Jews, Christians, and Moslems — a city of never-ending solemnities. In her streets walked the men who claimed they had talked to God, moonstruck with holiness. Each revered the city for his own reason, or reasons. Within her walls, a sacred drama was forever enacted between the believers and their God.

There may have been one God, but there were several modes of worshiping him. In the ancient Roman world, as Gibbon said in a celebrated line of his *History of the Decline and Fall of the Roman Empire,* the various modes of worship were considered by the people as equally true, by the philosophers as equally false, and by the magistrates as equally useful. In Jerusalem, the various modes of worship essentially stood for the same cause but were equally hateful to one another. They never served as a unifying factor. Their adherents were equally manipulated by the clergies to regard the others as wicked infidels or idolaters. The centuries passed in constant pious agitation and in frequent religious wars. Jerusalem was the very epicenter of a turbulent country where empires, religions, and nationalities clashed so often that Armageddon (today Megiddo), a famous battlefield some sixty miles northwest of Jerusalem, gave its name to the Apocalypse, the End of Days, when the whole world shall be destroyed.

In the imagination of believers, Jerusalem became more than a city. She became a metaphor. Her name stood for holiness and peace — and at the same time, strangely enough, for their opposites. Faith and superstition frequently alternated and belief often degenerated into war, zealous fury, sectarian prejudice, and persecution.

The contradiction seemed embedded, somehow, in her name. In the Hebrew name *Jerushalaim,* the suffix *aim* implies a duality, a pair of things, as in *einaim* (eyes), *oznaim* (ears), *shadaim* (breasts). It was difficult not to read into this duality an implied parity between the heavenly and the earthly, peace and war, goodliness and sin. The parity even extended to her dramatic landscape. Jerusalem is poised between the barren badlands and the sown, exactly astride the borderline between the two. The harsh, stony mountains of arid desert that fall away on one side of her contrast sharply with the cultivated hills of wine, fig, milk, and honey on the other.

Since the earthly Jerusalem was so mean, brazen, and sinful, the saintly, sublime Jerusalem had to be raised to heaven. A duplicate city was said to hover above in the sky — eighteen miles up, according to the Jews, and twelve, according to the Moslems. The saintly would eventually rise up there to live within a kind of halo, woven of goodliness and splendor.

In the turbulent atmosphere of fantasy, there was a nightmarish, violent quality as well. Stones would "cry out." The slain were cast out and the mountains "melted with their blood." The sun stood still and time itself came to a stop. Men flew back and forth between heaven and earth. Dry bones came together, shaking, were covered with flesh and skin and lived to be "an exceeding great army." The heavens were "rolled together as a scroll." A virgin gave birth. The dead rose from their graves. Under the Temple Mount, dead souls were locked up in a well, said to be the entrance to hell.

The godhead had to be placated by living things. Children were thrown into open fires to placate a local deity named Moloch, in the Valley of Hinnom. A valley by this name still runs west of the city, under the ancient walls. Jeremiah called it "valley of slaughter." Plutarch reported that Moloch's priests would yell and drum to drown the child's crying. The valley lent its name to hell (Gehenna) in both the Hebrew and the Arabic tongues. In AD 1047, the "common people" in Jerusalem still claimed, according to the Persian writer Abu Muin Nasir-i-Khusrau, that at the brink of the valley — where a cinematheque now stands — "you may hear the cries of those in hell, which come up from below."

At a later stage, the godhead was appeased by animals. The animals were first bled, then burned in the belief that the living soul returned to its maker in pillars of sweet-smelling gray smoke. During the high holidays, according to Josephus, tens of thousands of animals were slaughtered on the altar every day. The great temple — or abattoir — must have been constantly engulfed in belching clouds of smoke. Solomon was said in the Bible to have slaughtered as many as 22,000 oxen and 120,000 sheep as "peace offerings" at the dedication ceremony of his temple. By way of poetic exaggeration, the biblical story attested at least to an assumption of the godhead's excessive appetite for blood.

Slaughter atoned for sin. As Norman Kotker has phrased it, "God Himself performed a sacrifice at Jerusalem to Himself, of Himself, the victim His own son."

> By the rivers of Babylon, there we sat down, yea, we wept,
>   when we remembered Zion.
> We hanged our harps upon the willows in the midst thereof.

Jewish exiles, pining in the Babylonian captivity for their lost city, first postulated the heavenly Jerusalem as a mystic alternative to the real. The so-called Jerusalem of the Upper World had her temple and elite of prophets and priests. A metropolis of the mind, her psychic empire extended to wherever Jews happened to live — Egypt, Mesopotamia, Persia, the city-states and isles of Greece, and the farthest reaches of the Roman Empire.

From this heavenly city, according to the messianic prophecies of Isaiah and Micah, the quest for perfection would go forth and the world be redeemed: "they shall beat their swords into plowshares." The rabbis imagined her, ideally, as a place where no woman ever miscarried and no one was ever stung either by serpent or scorpion, where the fires of the woodpile on the altar were never doused by rain and no wind blew the pillar of smoke over the worshipers, who stood pressed together and yet bowed themselves with ease. In Moslem lore too, the one God, the Almighty, the Merciful, the Compassionate, contemplated Jerusalem every night before he contemplated the rest of the world.

Christianity, a Jewish sect at first, assimilated these ideas into its radically new concept of human destiny — the body as a prison, the soul's afterlife in the kingdom of heaven, the New Jerusalem. Saint John saw the heavenly Jerusalem "coming down from God out of heaven, prepared as a bride adorned for her husband" in gold and precious stones; her gates would never shut, "for there shall be no night there," nor any sorrow or death or pain. This image of Jerusalem was carried a step further by Augustine after the sack of Rome, a momentous event that traumatized the ancient Roman world, as the destruction of Jerusalem had traumatized the Jews and produced similar apocalyptic dreams. Augustine's New Jerusalem was synonymous with the millennium, a vague time in the future when all flaws in human life will have vanished and perfect goodness will prevail. The heavenly Jerusalem captivated the mind as the physical city never did. It summed up the farthest boundaries of emotion in an imaginary whole.

From the early Middle Ages to the beginning of our own century, no other city approximated in intensity the symbol that was Jerusalem in the European mind. From the endless representations of the city in Romanesque and Gothic art to Lucas Cranach and Hubert van Eyck, Marc Chagall and Salvador Dalí, innumerable artists chose to depict Jerusalem as synonymous with Eden.

"Jerusalem, my happy home," lamented the anonymous author of a well-known Christian hymn,

> When shall I come to thee?
> When shall my sorrows have an end?
> Thy joys when shall I see?

Shakespeare's protagonists parted "sadly in this troublous world, / To meet with joy in sweet Jerusalem." William Blake gave her name to all that was tender in the human soul.

> I give you the end of a golden string
> Only wind it into a ball.
> It will lead you in at Heaven's gate
> Built in Jerusalem's wall.

Stylized, idealized Jerusalems of the mind proliferated in European poetry, painting, and architecture throughout the Middle

Ages and the Renaissance. Site and story of Jerusalem combined to produce a phantasmic geography of the mind. In the gothic cosmology of the Middle Ages, Jerusalem was the exact center of the universe. Wiping out the advances of classical geography, medieval mapmakers pictured Jerusalem as the center of a flat world dish, at the exact meeting point of Africa, Asia, and Europe. Long after the birth of modern cartography, maps of the earthly Jerusalem printed in the West remained, in effect, theological or philosophical ideograms. Bernard Breydenbach's famous, more or less realistic illustration of Jerusalem printed in Mainz in 1486 was a first of its kind. It was available to Albrecht Dürer, but in his painting Dürer preferred a Jerusalem of the imagination to the Jerusalem of the real world. Representations of real and imagined buildings in the earthly Jerusalem went up in Paris, London, and Rotterdam. There were Jerusalems-on-the-sea and Jerusalems-on-the-Rhine and Jerusalems-on-the-Dnieper. In the last century, northern Lombardy was still dotted with sacred hills known as New Jerusalems. A pop version of Jerusalem exists to this day in the Lombard town of Varallo. Situated on hills reminiscent of Jerusalem, it boasts all the routine pilgrim sites — a Holy Sepulchre, a via Dolorosa, a Mount Zion, a Tomb of Mary, a Garden of Gethsemane.

In the seventeenth century, plans were drawn to rebuild Moscow according to city plans of the ideal Jerusalem outlined by Ezekiel in the Old Testament. Such construction had actually been done five centuries earlier in faraway Ethiopia: the city of Lalibala was built to be an "exact" replica of Jerusalem in the secure fastness of Ethiopia's central highlands. It is still there today, carved in rock. A narrow river called Jordan runs through it; seven ancient olive trees stand in a little rock garden called Gethsemane. There is a miniature Holy Sepulchre and a Church of Golgotha.*

Jerusalem was invariably a feminine metaphor. Loves and terrors were projected on her. In the Hebrew Bible, Jerusalem was seen both "as a widow" and as a "harlot"; in the New Testament, she was a brilliant "bride" and "the mother of us all." The Divine Presence itself, the Shekinah — a kind of holy ghost, which according to

---

* When I was there in 1985, I was assured by a local priest that the ground plan of Lalibala corresponded exactly to that of the heavenly Jerusalem. "Isn't she beautiful, isn't she beautiful," he repeated in near-perfect English accents. Our conversation was interrupted by the sound of shooting between rebels and troops of the Marxist government in the nearby hills.

Jewish tradition never deserted the city but continued to brood over her ruins — was also feminine in gender. Perhaps she was some long-forgotten pagan mother-goddess that had somehow entered Yahvist lore. The kabbalists claimed they had seen the Divine Presence with their own eyes in the guise of a slim woman, dressed in black, weeping at the Wailing Wall. In Moslem lore too, Jerusalem was built by a woman. Language was playing odd tricks on the patriarchal East. Public statements are often rooted in private dreams. When men are mystified, they often resort to the female gender.

The real Jerusalem, in the meantime, continued through many ups and downs. Under one or another faith, destroyed or rebuilt, sacked or reconquered, under this or that foreign or local master, she remained, first of all, a city of multiple rites and religious agitation. Nothing in her story was ordinary. No other city in the ancient and in the medieval worlds provoked similar attachments and controversies. None had such fatal impact upon memory and imagination. Other ancient cities changed hands; none figured so decisively, for so long, in the daily lives of her exiles and their descendants.

Among the many cities in the ancient Mediterranean world, only Jerusalem refused to submit to the Roman yoke. For this, she was severely punished. It is still difficult to see why the all-powerful empire should have bothered so much over the disciplining of a remote people thought odd, if not crazy, in a remote city of no strategic importance. Why was Jerusalem worth such prodigious efforts? Why were even the handful of zealots who survived her destruction pursued all the way to Masada, where they posed no threat to any Roman? Why were they besieged there, at great cost, for more than a year?

The greed and mental sloth of the imperial bureaucracy excluded all possibility of compromise or exception. Rome's anger was intensified, wrote Tacitus, by the memory "that the Jews alone had not succumbed to her sway." The Romans must have been sick and tired of — or bored to death by — the Jewish zealots of Jerusalem.

Caligula offended them by insisting they worship him as a god in their own temple. Gessius Florus provoked them to their final insurrection and suicide. The surviving rebels were sold into slavery. The great temple was burned down, the walls were dismantled in AD 70. Some sixty years later, under Hadrian, the Jews rebelled once more to protest the establishment of another Roman shrine on the site of their former temple. The rebellion was brutally put down. The survivors were pursued at tremendous cost and effort to the remotest corners of the land and crushed, to the last man, woman, and child. The Romans besieged every wretched cave in which a few refugees hid. They would stop only, wrote Eusebius, when the Jewish cause is completely subdued. As you read the accounts of these wars and their aftermaths, you wonder again and again at the sheer incapacity of the Romans to suffer a few remote outposts of dissent. Jerusalem, or what was left of her, was plowed under. Even the name Jerusalem was erased by imperial edict. The Romans built a small garrison city on the ruins and named it Aelia Capitolina, after Hadrian. Jews were banned forever from entering it. The name of the country, Judea, was eradicated at the same time. Henceforth, in order to deny the Jews the last vestige of a national situation, it would be known officially as (Syria) Palaestina.

Among the many vanquished capital cities of the ancient world, only Jerusalem survived in the imagination of her exiles and in that of their descendants from generation to generation. By the fourth century, Hadrian's restrictions had been sufficiently relaxed, or forgotten, to allow Jews to visit the city once a year or look at her from an observation point on one of the neighboring hills, probably Olivet. Jerusalem by now was a Christian city engaged, under Saint Helena, the Roman empress dowager, in the rediscovery of Christian holy sites and relics. The edict forbidding Jews to resettle in Jerusalem seems to have been enforced for another two centuries. But the Jews had taken her memory with them into exile, as well as her Law — a tradition on wheels. As they wandered from land to land, they remained stubbornly a people of Jerusalem:

> If I forget thee, O Jerusalem, let my right hand forget her cunning.
> If I do not remember thee, let my tongue cleave to the roof of my
>   mouth; if I prefer not Jerusalem above my chief joy.

Jerusalem became their great Capital of Memory. Memory gave them their culture and their identity. Other peoples too had occupied lands and cities and then lost or abandoned them. The point was that they did not remember. The Jews did remember. They never forgot Jerusalem. Nothing remotely like this happened to any other vanquished people in the ancient Mediterranean world. Under the iron skies of northern Europe, the Jewish festivals remained tied to the seasons of the city. Passover and Yom Kippur services ended with the exhortation "Next year in Jerusalem." For centuries, Jews turned in prayer toward Jerusalem three times a day: "Return in mercy to your city Jerusalem and dwell in it as you have promised; rebuild it soon, in our own days. Praised are you, O Lord, builder of Jerusalem." The words of the Spanish-Hebrew poet Yehuda Halevi (c. 1075–1141) reaffirmed this devotion.

> Could I but kiss thy dust
> so would I fain expire.
> As sweet as honey then,
> my longing and desire.

Nor was the story of Jerusalem less extraordinary after the departure of the Jews. The Byzantines consecrated her to Christianity. The emperor Constantine dismantled a pagan temple on the presumed site of Golgotha and replaced it with the great basilica of the Holy Sepulchre. It was the finest in Christendom and would not be surpassed until two centuries later with the building of Saint Sophia in Constantinople, which Justinian, characteristically, would inaugurate with the words, "Solomon, I have surpassed thee!" The new Holy Sepulchre was only a few hundred yards west of the former Jewish Temple Mount. Eusebius rejoiced: "So . . . was the New Jerusalem built over against the one so famous of old." Of the latter, the old Jewish Temple Mount was deliberately left in ruins to confirm Christ's prophecy that "there shall not be left one stone upon another, that shall not be thrown down."

The Arabs, who took the city in the seventh century, removed the accumulated debris and garbage. They sprayed the platform with rose water, built the great Dome of the Rock that stands there today, and made Jerusalem the third-holiest city in Islam. Under their more tolerant rule, Christian worship in the city continued undisturbed. Jews were again allowed to settle in Jerusalem.

The Arabs, in turn, were ousted by the Crusaders in 1099. The Crusaders came armed with a thousand-year-old memory of their own, the memory of Christ. Driven by the alleged danger to his tomb, as well as by greed, the Crusaders were partly pilgrims, partly early forerunners of European colonialism. The first Crusader king Baldwin I consciously reinvoked biblical associations. He announced he was restoring the kingdom of David and had himself crowned in Bethlehem, David's city, on Christmas Day. The Crusaders were savagely intolerant of the other creeds. They massacred the surviving Moslems and Jews — crying out "Deus vult!" (God wills it) as they waded through what their own shocked chroniclers described as rivers of blood. The main mosques were stripped of their crescents and converted into churches. The Dome of the Rock on the old Temple Mount was renamed Temple Salomonis and became a Christian basilica.

A century later, the Moslems returned and the altars and crosses on the Temple Mount were ripped out again. The Holy Sepulchre and most of the other churches were not touched. Christian worship continued as before. The city now became a Capital of Memory for feudal Europe, too, as it had been for Jews. No other story so inspired the West during the late Middle Ages as that of the Crusaders' quest for the earthly Jerusalem. A special literary genre developed to tell and retell it again and again, the literature of chivalry and romance: from the *Gesta Francorum et aliorum Hyrosolymitanarum* by an Italian knight of the twelfth century to Torquato Tasso's *Gerusalemme Liberata* of the sixteenth. For centuries, Latin Europe remained obsessed with the story of Jerusalem and of the chiefs who had fought on her behalf: Tancred; Godfrey of Bouillon; Raymond, Count of Toulouse; Frederick Barbarossa; Richard Lion-heart; Saint Louis. Jerusalem represented the highest political ideal, one to which all European kings felt obliged at least to pay lip service: the recovery of the lost Holy Sepulchre. As late as the fifteenth century, European kings still felt virtually bound to set out and recapture Jerusalem by force. In 1422, as Henry V of England lay dying in France, in the middle of the Hundred Years' War, he interrupted the officiating priest reading him the last rites and declared that "if it had pleased God to let him live to old age" he would have marched on Jerusalem after the pacification of France. Having said this, he ordered the priest to continue, and died.

There were "Kings of Jerusalem" in Europe until well into the modern age. Centuries after the Crusaders were ousted from the city, the main princes of Europe still quarreled over the title. It was held, at times simultaneously, by the German emperors, the kings of Spain, of England, France, Cyprus, and Sicily, and by the dukes of Swabia. In the first half of the nineteenth century, the consuls of Austria and Sardinia in Jerusalem still regarded themselves not so much as representatives of foreign countries as envoys, or viceroys, of the true "King of Jerusalem" — a title claimed by both their sovereigns.

On a summer day, twenty years after the Crusaders were ousted from Jerusalem, three hundred Jewish pilgrims, many of them rabbis, arrived in the city from France and England. One was the Provençal Hebrew poet Al-Harizi. He stayed in Jerusalem for a month and reported home that time was passing most agreeably. One day, he and his party gathered on Olivet for prayers. They were struck by the famous view of the temple platform below: "What torment to see our holy courts converted into an alien temple! We tried to turn our faces away."

Those unable to go on pilgrimage were assured by the Jewish sages that through piety and prayer they were "building Jerusalem daily." One adds a row, "another only a brick. When Jerusalem is completed redemption will come." The rabbis developed elaborate rules and rituals to keep Jerusalem alive in the memory of her exiles. No home was to be without a *zecher lakhurban* (reminder of the destruction) — that is, a piece of wall left unfinished or without paint, and a plaque, often with a sketch of the Western Wall, indicating the direction of prayer. In another common Jewish rite, ashes were pressed on the forehead of a bridegroom on his wedding day — to remind him of ruined Jerusalem.

As the centuries passed and Jerusalem gradually lost her attraction for the popes of Rome and for the younger sons of the feudal aristocracy of Europe, and as the power of Islam was sapped by overextension and a proclivity for voluptuous living, Jerusalem became an impoverished, plague-ridden, provincial city on the fringes of the declining Ottoman Empire. A seventeenth-century Ottoman imperial edict described Jerusalem as a remote outpost "on the frontier of Arabia, where rebellious Bedouins disturb the peace." The great Christian churches and religious orders in the city survived Ottoman rule, or misrule, through bribery and the influence of the European powers. So did the few Jewish synagogues and institutions of religious learning. The Jews — most were wretchedly poor and living on alms — huddled in their separate quarter. "This luckless people," the German traveler Ulrich Seetzen observed in 1806, "which here as elsewhere is among the most despised, is much like Tantalus, who is always so close to what he so deeply yearns for and yet will never be able to attain."

Nor was the lot of the Moslems very much better. Most visitors were aghast at the misery rampant everywhere in the Moslem quarter. François René de Chateaubriand, in Jerusalem the same year as Seetzen, and with scarcely less rage at the misery and oppression he witnessed, wrote: "The only thing you hear in this country, the only justice is: 'He will be given five hundred lashes. He will be beheaded.' "

The city's physical aspect became equally discouraging. It must have deteriorated considerably in the final centuries of Ottoman rule. "To see its destroyed walls, its debris-filled moat, its circuits choked with ruins, you would hardly recognize this famous metropolis which once defied the most powerful empires in the world," the Comte de Volney noted in 1784. "For a moment [it once] held even Rome at bay. . . . By a bizarre twist of fate [it] gains honor and respect in its disgrace." Gustave Flaubert called Jerusalem "un charnier entouré de murs" — a charnel house surrounded by walls.

Eighteenth- and early nineteenth-century Jerusalem was a much less secure place than it had been two hundred or three hundred years earlier. The situation gradually improved only after 1831, as a result of the Egyptian occupation of the city in that year. The "westernizing" Egyptian general Ibrahim Pasha relaxed the restrictions on foreigners and on local Jews. Christians were given permission to ring their church bells for the first time in five centuries.

Ibrahim Pasha's regime was short-lived. Ottoman rule was restored in 1840. But under pressure from the European powers, the increased security and tolerance that Ibrahim inaugurated survived his demise.

Between 1800 and 1870, the population of Jerusalem tripled to about 30,000. Few houses yet existed outside the medieval walls. The desert reached to the city gates, which were closed at sunset and on Fridays from eleven in the morning till one in the afternoon, while the Turkish garrison were at their weekly prayers in the mosque. In the last three decades of the nineteenth century, the city began to spread beyond the walls to the western and southern hills; but for security, most settlers outside the walls still built their new houses within walled compounds that were locked at night.

By 1914, the population had grown to an estimated 80,000; more than half were Jews. Ottoman rule ended in 1917. The British occupation of that year — the British marched up from Egypt — found a famished city, its population reduced by a third. Under British rule, the population soon grew again, mostly through Jewish immigration from central and eastern Europe. By 1946, on the eve of British withdrawal, Jerusalem was a mixed city of about 100,000 Jews and 60,000 Arabs. In 1948, the city was a battlefield. The Jews of Jerusalem — by now they were called Israelis — came under siege by Jordanian troops and Palestinian guerrillas. The small Jewish quarter within the walled Old City was cut off, a siege within a siege. Its population (mostly old men and women) suffered heavy losses and surrendered. The ancient synagogues were razed or burned down by the Jordanian troops or by the mob.

The New City, outside the medieval walls, remained under siege. Its population amounted to some 99,000 Jews. They suffered heavy artillery bombardment. After six weeks of street-to-street fighting with only limited quantities of ammunition, fuel, water, or food, the Jewish population found relief: forces from the main Israeli territory in the coastal plain finally pushed a corridor through the mountains and lifted the siege. The battle lines established between the two sides during weeks of heavy street fighting froze, to become an international frontier. The Jews retained control of the New City south and west of the medieval walls. The Jordanians held on to the Old City and the suburbs in the north. Neither side was able to reach its main hospitals and cemeteries. The Hebrew University campus on Mount Scopus remained an inaccessible enclave surrounded by Arab territory.

The years 1948 through 1967 saw Jerusalem divided by trenches and barbed wire. The frontier between Jordanian-controlled East Jerusalem and Israeli-controlled West Jerusalem ran erratically through gutted houses and deserted streets. Great scars of no-man's-land marred the city center. Sappers of both sides roamed the ruins, mining and countermining. The rusting remains of wrecked armored cars lay against walls — pockmarked by artillery hits — that blocked the prewar thoroughfares. An Israeli-Jordanian armistice signed in 1949 stipulated that Jews would have free access to the university on Mount Scopus and to the Western Wall. The Jordanians never honored this commitment. The so-called municipal line often flared up in bursts of machine-gun fire. Only diplomats and a few privileged foreign tourists were allowed to cross from side to side. The crossing point was a roadblock flanked by two huts and fierce-looking guards who hid behind sandbags. It was called Mandelbaum Gate: the bombed house next to it had belonged to a man by that name. All tourists were required by the Jordanians to produce baptismal certificates. The Jordanians seemed almost biologically unable to utter the word "Israel." They pretended the tourists were coming in from the void and did not allow them to cross back into Israel.

These were years of fear and nostalgia on both sides. Pious Jews gazed from their rooftops, across minefields, toward the lost stones where they could no longer worship. Arabs, likewise, stared across in the opposite direction at the old homes in West Jerusalem they had been forced to abandon during the fighting, which were now occupied by new Jewish immigrants. A beautiful new university campus was erected on the Israeli side to replace the one on Mount Scopus; many new residential quarters were built, as was a great administrative center for the new Israeli government, which had made the half-city Israel's capital. But Jerusalem remained a somber city on both sides of the great divide. In daytime, snipers lay in wait behind sandbags on abandoned rooftops. At night, the dogs of both sides barked through the dark, as though when their masters rested they took up the fight and yapped at one another till morning.

By the time the next Arab-Israeli war broke out in June 1967, the population on the Israeli side had doubled to almost 200,000 inhabitants. On the Jordanian side, it was just over 70,000. Hostilities began on June 5. The Jordanian attack was entirely unprovoked. Israel — already at war with Egypt on that day — sent an urgent message to Amman, via the United Nations, urging the Jordanians to stay out and guaranteeing the territorial integrity of their zone. King Hussein of Jordan received the message and ignored it. He had just been assured by Egyptian president Gamal Nasser that Egypt's forces were winning on all fronts.* The Israeli part of the city quickly came under Jordanian artillery fire. "Bring about Israel's end," Radio Amman admonished Jordanian soldiers at noon, "strike her everywhere, until victory!" Israeli forces counterattacked in the evening. In forty-eight hours of heavy fighting, they took the entire city (and the whole West Bank area of the river Jordan as well).

When the fighting ended, General Moshe Dayan, defense minister and wildly acclaimed hero of the war, crossed the lines into Arab Jerusalem. Upon reaching the slopes of Mount Scopus, his first words, reportedly, were: "What a divine view!" Coming from so secular a man, this was a compliment of sorts. The minister and his party, in steel helmets with camouflage nets, then went through the Lions' Gate into the Old City to inspect the mosques on the Temple Mount and the Western Wall. It was the eve of Shabuoth — the Feast of Weeks — in ancient times one of the three annual days of Jewish pilgrimage to the city. During the following days, hundreds of thousands of Israelis swarmed through the narrow alleys of the Old City, exploring every historic nook and religious cranny.

The Arab population was in shock. The Israelis were met with a mixture of fear, curiosity, and hope that their presence in East Jerusalem would be brief. The Israelis made it clear they had come to stay.

East Jerusalem was formally annexed by Israel almost immedi-

---

* The Israelis tapped the bizarre telephone conversation and later played it back to the press.

ately. The crowds continued to stand in awe in the vast, newly cleared plaza facing the Western Wall. To accommodate them, an entire Moslem quarter was razed by bulldozers overnight, then leveled by heavy compressors. The Arabs protested the annexation and the dissolution of their own municipality in East Jerusalem. The Arab mayor of East Jerusalem and his councillors refused an invitation to join the Israeli municipality of West Jerusalem as "advisers." The former Arab mayor was expelled to Jordan on a charge of "incitement"; his councillors continued to protest the occupation. Most Israelis saw the city not as occupied but as liberated. A few, perhaps too conveniently, said it was reunited. The effective reunification of the two parts became the burning ambition of Israelis of all political classes. David Ben-Gurion, Israel's first prime minister (by now in his eighties and retired), scandalized urbanists and aesthetes by calling, perhaps facetiously, for the razing of the Old City walls to forge the two city halves into one. Ben-Gurion, a secularist, who like many other Zionist leaders had never warmed to Jerusalem in the past, called on tens of thousands of Jews to settle in East Jerusalem immediately, if necessary "in huts, helter skelter . . . to make it clear to the world that it would never be taken from us again." In the former Jewish quarter of the Old City, Arabs were evicted from houses occupied by Jews before 1948. But Arabs in the united city were not allowed to repossess property across the former dividing lines that they had been forced to abandon in 1948. Nor would most of them submit formal claims for compensation. The majority of Jerusalem Arabs continued to boycott official Israeli institutions.

Jerusalem was but a small part of the territories Israel gained in the Six-Day War. Israelis would henceforth be divided — as they are today — into hawks and doves. The former saw the newly gained territories as permanent acquisitions; the latter saw them as temporarily held bargaining chips for peace. Both groups were united in opposing a compromise on Jerusalem. Her two parts were solemnly declared the capital of Israel "for ever and ever."

For a few days, even as streets were still partly blocked by the debris of war and as refugees from the Arab city, in blind and irrational fear, were fleeing east across the river to Jordan, there was an extraordinary intermingling of peoples in the reunited city. Miles of barbed-wire fences were rolled back. Battlements and minefields were dismantled. Old acquaintances between Arabs and Israelis were renewed. The euphoria was one-sided and short. The physical scars of war were removed and the two halves of the city rejoined in a common whole, but the city remained divided, like Ulster in Ireland, by the festering wounds, the hatreds and fears generated in the continuing clash of nationalities and religions.

For the first time in almost two thousand years, Jews controlled the whole historic city. Benjamin Disraeli, a romantic acutely aware of the power of memory, had foreseen this possibility in the nineteenth century: "A people that celebrate the wine harvest even when it does not reap grapes any more, will regain its vineyards." But history had come full circle in another sense too. The fall of Jerusalem to the Jews aroused and fanaticized the Arab world as had no other event since the Crusades. Among Palestinians, a new kind of awareness grew, a mirror image of Zionism, a zeal, a violent passion highlighted by indiscriminate terror. "If I forget thee, O Jerusalem" now became the war cry of Arabs and Moslems from Syria to Saudi Arabia and from Morocco to Iran.

Since then, the city has grown immensely, tripling in size and nearly doubling in population.* The victors live side by side with the vanquished. They are still as divided and bitter as before. Before 1967, West Jerusalem had been the dead end of a narrow corridor from the sea. East Jerusalem had been no less isolated and provincial in a remote and neglected corner of the kingdom of Jordan. The two formerly divided parts soon became a dynamic, thriving city, often overcrowded with tourists. Politically, Jerusalem remained as fragmented as before. Twenty-two years after reunification, she was plagued by Palestinian strikes and riots and occasional counterriots.

Jerusalem spreads out today to the outskirts of Bethlehem in the

* The municipal area in 1989 was approximately 26,000 acres, as opposed to 9,390 acres in 1967. The population was close to half a million, versus 267,000 in 1967. The lines of annexation were drawn in 1967 to take in a maximum of territory and a minimum of Arab population. In 1967, 73 percent were Jews. The last available figure (1987) was 71 percent.

south and Ramallah in the north. The city proper holds perhaps the same number of inhabitants as Florence — a middle-sized municipality of about half a million. Together with the surrounding, relatively dense, built-up area, the population of Greater Jerusalem now reaches over 600,000.

The new residential quarters have caused dramatic changes in the landscape. The old dividing line between city and pastoral countryside, which had been a striking feature of the city in the past, has almost disappeared. High-rise buildings have been erected and multilane highways cut into the hillsides. In the rush and flurry to build a capital of the future after 1967, the municipality solicited the advice of some of the best-known architects and city planners from all over the world. They were invited to comment on some of the more grandiose projects. The results came as a shock to an establishment keyed up to high expectations of near-universal approval for its plans. The experts were almost unanimous in their criticism of what had already been built and of what was planned for the future. Much of the criticism had to do with scale. The American urbanist Lewis Mumford advised the mayor to take his clue from Ps. 122:3 — Jerusalem as "a city that is compact together" — rather than from the Paris of Baron Haussmann with its strategic network of axial boulevards designed to put down popular uprisings. The advice was heeded only partially. With the exception of the new parks, much of the urban planning after 1967 was shortsighted. A good deal was politically motivated. The Jewish quarter in the Old City was rebuilt and repopulated. But on the bulldozed hilltops around the city, the new suburbs have buried under poured concrete what had seemed, only a few decades ago, a near-pristine landscape.

The new suburbs — intended exclusively for the growing Jewish population — were heavily subsidized by the central government and built on expropriated Arab land. Little public housing was made available to the Arab population, which grew at almost the same rate. The fact that most Arabs continued to boycott the municipal elections contributed to the disproportionate appropriation of public funds. The municipality, headed by the popular mayor Teddy Kollek, would have preferred less politically motivated ostentation at the fringes and more development in the old urban core and the central business district. Kollek also would have liked to do more for the Arab population in the former Jordanian sector. But the municipality had little to say in a situation dominated since 1967 by political demagoguery and by the bureaucracy of a central government eager to consolidate the Israeli presence by establishing political facts in the periphery. Next door to the luxuriously restored and "gentrified" Jewish quarter in the Old City, the Moslem quarter was barely touched and remained a slum, perhaps the worst in all Jerusalem.

In Jerusalem after 1967, form did not follow function; it followed ideology and politics. The politics of town planning and of housing in this period were the politics of demography and annexation. Suburbs and satellite towns are usually built because the city proper cannot meet the demand for homes: *needs are satisfied.* The new suburbs and satellites of Jerusalem were built not because housing needs could not be satisfied within the city but to populate the Arab countryside with Israeli suburbanites: *needs were induced.*

The building style of Jerusalem remained an odd potpourri. Her style has always been highly eclectic. With her long history of inimical creeds and warring sects and nationalities, Jerusalem never had a common cultural or social base; and so she never developed a distinctive building style either. The ancient Hebrews were not known for their material culture; they were noted for their achievements in other fields. The building materials, the architects, and the style of Solomon's first temple and royal palace were imported from neighboring Phoenicia. Solomon's city must have been an amalgam of Egyptian, Phoenician, and Mesopotamian tastes. The Jerusalem of Herod or of Jesus was a mix of Ptolemaic-Egyptian and classical Greek. (Little else has come to light in the extensive excavations of the past fifty years.) Hadrian, in AD 132, rebuilt Jerusalem as a regular Roman garrison town, not much different from Cologne and probably much more modest. Justinian's Jerusalem of the sixth century was elaborately Byzantine. The Arabs superimposed on this laborious foundation the austere lines of desert architecture and geometric decoration. The Crusaders imported the Romanesque. The Mamluk sultans of Egypt added a number of superb medieval Cairene townhouses. Everything was enclosed in 1540 within an excellently built new wall, designed by a great Ottoman military architect, perhaps the famous Sinan, builder of the Blue Mosque of Istanbul.

The eclectic mix of Jerusalem's current styles, most of them imported, reflects the shifting tastes of national and religious groups, the conquerors, pilgrims, priests, and settlers of the past twenty centuries: Romans, Byzantines, and Arabs; Crusaders and Armenians; Persians, Mamluks, and Turks; Jews from all corners of the earth; Ethiopians, Copts, Greeks, Spaniards, Germans, Swedes, Englishmen, and Americans. Early in this century, the main colonial powers — France, England, Russia, Italy, and Germany — went on a great building spree in Jerusalem, partly for political reasons, constructing churches, hospitals, and hospices — like flags planted in the ground — each in its own "national style." The confusion, which elsewhere the connoisseur would spurn as shallow, seems justified here, even attractive and charming. Consider some of the more conspicuous landmarks:

- The replica of an Oxford quadrangle in the Anglican bishopry on Nablus Road.
- A Mamluk fountain on the Temple Mount esplanade, in the best style of fifteenth-century Cairo, donated by an Egyptian sultan to quench the thirst and please the eye and the feet of the visiting pilgrim.
- The seventh-century Dome of the Rock, the noblest building in Jerusalem and perhaps in all Islam, built by Syrian masons in the Christian-Byzantine style of the time; its octagonal exterior is covered with lovely seventeenth-century Persian tiles.
- A modest little synagogue in Mea Shearim that seems to have been moved to Jerusalem two hundred years ago from a Jewish shtetl somewhere in northeastern Europe.
- A nineteenth-century Greek windmill, overlooking the Valley of Hinnom, as though transplanted to Jerusalem from some Aegean island.
- The onion-shaped domes of a Russian Orthodox church in Gethsemane, strongly reminiscent of one in Moscow.
- The soldiery face of Mishkenot, the municipal guesthouse

for visiting artists and intellectuals, built in the last century
by an English philanthropist, Sir Moses Montefiore. With
its regularly spaced windows and pseudobattlements above
delicate cast-iron balustrades and verandas, it might have
been an English officers' mess in Malta or Lahore, a bonded
warehouse in East Africa, or a customhouse in Bermuda.

- The former hospice, endowed by a German kaiser and distinguished by the gothic outlines of a castle on the Rhine,
that dominates the city's skyline on Mount Scopus.
Wilhelm II is depicted in the chapel's murals as a Byzantine
emperor holding on his knees the architect's model of this
hospice. It was built in 1908, in anticipation, it was ru-
mored, of a German conquest of Jerusalem.

- The neo-Teutonic Church of the Redeemer in the Old City,
by the German patriotic architect Bruno Schultz — inaugurated by Wilhelm II in 1898 — which like the Paris Opera
so fascinated the young Adolf Hitler he filled a whole
notebook with sketches of it. (The same architect later built
the Völkerschlachtdenkmal at Leipzig to commemorate the
hundredth anniversary of the victory over Napoléon.)

- The copy of the tower of Florence's Palazzo Vecchio atop
the former Italian hospital and church, a building that now
serves yarmulke-wearing Orthodox officials of the Israeli
ministry of education.

- The south-German village architecture in the former German colony built in the last century south of the Old City
by pious Protestant settlers from Baden-Württemberg.

- The gaudy club building on King David Street, with its tall,
phallic tower — not surprisingly, America's contribution to
the ensemble (it is the local YMCA and by the same eclectic
architect who built the Chicago Tribune Tower for Colonel
Robert McCormick).

- The pure, twelfth-century Romanesque arches of the
French Church of Saint Anne on the via Dolorosa.

- The clean, functional lines of a bank on the Jaffa Road and a
hospital on Mount Scopus built in the 1930s in the best
Bauhaus style.

A certain uniformity of texture, color, and material bridges the greater extremes of taste, nationality, and religion, mellowing the contrast between old and new, European and Levantine, poor and rich, Palestinian and Israeli, Moslem and Jewish. This is so, largely, because of the ubiquitous Jerusalem stone. Throughout the centuries, Jerusalem has been, literally, a city built of rock. In whatever style, whatever period, the clear, white stone, quarried locally, which cuts soft but dries hard and weathers into blue-gray, pink, or amber, has been Jerusalem's only building material. Its use is dictated by law. Sir Ronald Storrs, the first British military governor of Jerusalem, promulgated this law in 1917 — one of the finest contributions any British colonial administrator ever made to the aesthetics of a historic city. It was upheld, more or less religiously, by all succeeding administrations, and, between 1948 and 1967, on both sides of the barbed wire.* All new buildings in Jerusalem must still be built of, or at least faced in, stone. The result is often very pleasing. But although the new, rather monstrous hotels and office buildings have been faced in stone, the low skyline and human proportions of days past have been irretrievably lost.

For the most part, the two main communities, Palestinians and Israelis, still work and live apart from one another, in separate quarters, much as though the city were still divided by minefields and barbed wire. Tension is never far beneath the surface. Though Jerusalem has been one municipality since 1967, the city remains a breeding ground for ghettos. People on one side of the great political and religious divide are ignorant of daily life on the other. The Palestinians have their own Arabic newspapers, which, like the Hebrew newspapers on the Israeli side, report events behind the divide exclusively in terms of conflict.

There are two distinctly separate downtown areas — that is, two business-and-entertainment centers — one Palestinian and one Israeli. Welfare policies in the two sectors are governed by different

* A citation in Storrs's memoirs recalls the medieval hymn "Jerusalem is built in heaven / Of living stone." Storrs was a vicar's son. Perhaps he had in mind the ancient idea that the earthly Jerusalem should be a replica of the heavenly.

criteria. Each community is still served by its own fire department, hospitals, and medical-emergency crews. Schools are entirely separate. There are two urban and interurban transportation systems, often serving the same routes; two electric power grids (administered, respectively, by an Israeli and a Palestinian company); and two price scales for real estate. Jews will not use Arab electricity, if they can avoid it, and Arabs, if they can help it, will not put their money into an Israeli-owned bank. The new Jewish suburbs across the old demarcation line are often isolated, high-density enclaves encircled by low-density, semirural areas inhabited by Palestinians. An ingenious new road network enables Israelis in the new suburbs to travel back and forth almost without seeing an Arab.

The hills and valleys around the Old City are still known by their ancient ghostly names — Hill of Evil Counsel, Hill of Offense, Valley of Hinnom (Hell's Valley). Their physical aspect has dramatically changed in recent years. Returning residents who have been away from Jerusalem since the early sixties scarcely recognize her environs. Great barren folds are green now. Fine lawns and trees have been planted in new public parks surrounding the Old City. Against this unexpected green foreground, the newly excavated and restored ramparts stand out majestically in the sun. The debris of centuries has been dug up and carted away. The old walls are scraped, weathered gray and heavy with towers. For the first time since, perhaps, the eighteenth century, they are now fully exposed. Rows upon rows of first-century Herodian and later Crusader ashlars have been carefully laid free at the base. Here and there, the walls are still marked by bullet holes. Most other scars of war have disappeared. The walls are lit up at night. The staged blue lighting, entirely frontal, gives the feeling, sometimes, of a Hollywood film-set — as though the backs dissolve into paper and hot air.

Below the ancient ramparts, ruins of the original Jebusite, Davidic, and Hasmonaean city have also been dug up in recent years. The archaeologists had to brave violent ultra-Orthodox demonstrators who felt the excavation violated ancient Jewish tombs. Within the walls, archaeologists have laid free a number of extraordinary "burnt houses," black with historic soot, said to have been sacked by the Roman legions in AD 70, the year they burned Jerusalem to the ground and carried her people into exile. Elsewhere, in the New City, are other gracious new parks, new theaters, new concert halls and museums, all opened after the reunification of 1967. The new campus of the Hebrew University hovers on Mount Scopus. Its great stone mass — foreigners often mistake it for a fortress — mirrors the walled city below.

Above all, even the casual observer will note almost everywhere the visual manifestations of a new sovereignty not yet entirely sure of itself because of the unresolved international status of Jerusalem. They are designed to reemphasize Jerusalem's status as Israel's capital city: new ministries set up beyond the old demarcation lines (some foreign leaders and diplomats still boycott them, to protest the annexation by Israel of East Jerusalem); flagpoles along the main highways; motorcycle escorts — and mind-boggling traffic jams — that mark the occasional state visit by a foreign potentate. State visits in Jerusalem — the most notable since 1967 was that of President Anwar el-Sadat of Egypt — are all the more remarkable here since Jerusalem is not yet universally recognized as Israel's capital city. Most foreign diplomats still drive up daily from their embassies in Tel Aviv.

The United States, Britain, Italy, Belgium, Greece, Spain, and France maintain only consulates in Jerusalem. They are headed by diplomats who often carry ambassadorial rank but are not accredited with the Israeli authorities. Nor are they subservient to their embassies in Tel Aviv; they report directly to their foreign ministries. The consuls attend mostly to the Arab population in East Jerusalem and in the occupied West Bank; they are, in effect, ambassadors to the Palestinian people. Only the United States consulate will invite Israelis and Palestinians to the same functions — though Palestinians in recent years have tended to boycott those. The others give separate parties to celebrate national holidays — one for Israelis from West Jerusalem, and one for Palestinians from East Jerusalem. An apostolic delegate represents the Vatican in Jerusalem, but it is difficult to see how or to whom, since he, too, boycotts the Israeli government. The Vatican, partly for reasons of theology, has never recognized Israel, not even within its pre-1967 borders. In the end, everything in Jerusalem becomes an article of faith. The reformers face the counterreformers. The Israelis emphasize and reemphasize the role of Jerusalem as their capital. The speechmaking, the state ceremonies enacted with much care and solemnity, the schoolchildren conducted around the city, the emblems, the flagpoles, the military displays, the endless pomp and circumstance are a kind of civil religion. They recall another famous holy city, Banaras, where the chief object of veneration in one of the great temples is a map of Mother India.

The New City spreads out nowadays over the hilltops. The valleys are left green. In the new residential areas, the streets are wide and spacious between the compactly built public-housing units. In the Old City, the streets are narrow, steep, and stony. Many are covered. Everything is tight and crowded, old, ruined, and intertwined. Under a stone parapet placed there by a British engineer after World War I lies a Mamluk doorway, which was built over a Crusader tower that rests on foundations from the time of Herod. A Roman arch of the first century spans an early Israelite pavement that connects the apsis of a Byzantine church with the top of a Hellenistic column. An eighteenth-century Arab caravansary stands partly on a Roman tower dating from AD 200 and partly on a Jewish fortress that antedates Nebuchadnezzar's destruction of Jerusalem by nearly twelve decades. The fortress, in turn, was built over a foundation from the time of the Jebusites. This, we are told, rests on the bedrock. But wait! On the bedrock, scattered implements have been found that can safely be dated back to the early Bronze Age. And, finally, the front wall of the caravansary itself is covered with recent graffiti extolling the virtues of the Palestine Liberation Organization.

Walking through the narrow lanes of the Old City, you sometimes feel as though you are inside a prison or a fortress, but also that you are on the edge of a precipice. A sense of being uplifted to a high place comes overwhelmingly as you climb the Temple Mount. You can stand atop the Herodian walls and lean on narrow slits in the stone through which medieval archers pointed their arrows and soldiers poured down boiling oil. Outside, the silted banks fall off steeply down the ravine, entirely covered with tombs.

The great Turkish fortress ("David's Citadel") outside Jaffa Gate spans the ages. Its great towers predate the Roman destruction.

They were built by the mad Herod and stand on Hasmonaean or early Israelite remains of the seventh century BC, the age of Isaiah and Jeremiah. According to Josephus, the citadel was Herod's royal palace — and "so wondrous," he wrote, that it exceeded "all my ability to describe it." The palace had splendid ornaments and banquet halls, reported Josephus, and "large bedchambers, that would contain beds for a hundred guests apiece." Three decades later, the citadel was the Praetorium of Jerusalem, where Pontius Pilate sat in judgment of Jesus. Here, the Roman soldiers platted a crown of thorns and put it on the Nazarene's head. The real via Dolorosa, if there was one, ran down from here through the bazaar. When the Roman general Titus razed the city in AD 70, he left standing the citadel's three gigantic towers as a monument to his victory, "to demonstrate to posterity what kind of city it was," wrote Josephus, "and how well fortified, which the Roman valour had subdued." The beautifully cut and proportioned stones impress even today. They are more massive than anything seen in Rome or Greece (though not in Egypt). The main tower served in the twelfth century as the residence — château fort — of the Crusader kings, and appears on medallions of the period. Today, it forms part of the new Historical Museum of Jerusalem.

From this tower, in October 1187, Saladin watched the two separate files of defeated Christians leave the vanquished city — one going to slavery, "the other [those who could afford to pay the ransom he demanded] to freedom." Saladin was shocked to see so many Christians march to slavery while Heraclius, the Latin patriarch of Jerusalem, having paid his ten dinars' ransom, left the city bowed down "by the weight of the gold he was carrying, followed by carts laden with carpets and plate." The far end of the citadel is marked by another tower, the so-called Tower of David. In reality, it is the seventeenth-century minaret of a Turkish military-garrison mosque. Nevertheless, the tower became the main emblem of the nascent Zionist movement in the nineteenth century, reproduced endlessly on colored plates, stamps, paperweights, embroidered carpets, and other tourist bric-a-brac, eclipsing in popularity even representations of the Wailing Wall.

The city wall is breached between the citadel and the Jaffa Gate and permits the entry of motor traffic. The breach was ordered in the last century by the Ottoman sultan Abdülhamid II to enable the German kaiser Wilhelm II ("I come as a knight of peace and labor, interested not in riches but in the healing of souls") and his suite to enter the Old City without dismounting their horses and carriages. From the breach, you walk down David Street, the traditional access route, through the medieval bazaars, to the holy places of the three main faiths. The fifteenth-century historian Mujir al-Din, a resident of Jerusalem, believed the street was so called because the Hebrew king had excavated a tunnel under it to enable him to move unobserved from the citadel to the Temple Mount. The underground passage exists to this day; but its construction seems to be Byzantine, or early Arab.

David Street is a crowded bazaar, filled with tourists and pilgrims and shops with the usual printed T-shirts, fake antiquities, crucifixes in carved olive-wood frames with built-in barometers, battery-lit menorahs, plastic shields of David, chess sets with wooden figurines representing Arab and Israeli soldiers, and packs of playing cards wrapped in cellophane. Card games make irresistible metaphors for writers on Jerusalem. "Whoever shuffled Jerusalem had a wicked pack of cards," Dennis Silk wrote in his introduction to *Retrievements,* an anthology of odd and fascinating texts on Jerusalem; "a good many hands have been dealt and the vicious game still goes on." In Edward Whittemore's hilarious novel *Jerusalem Poker,* a Jew, an Arab, and an Englishman sit playing poker in the back room of an Old City café. The game has been going on for decades. The stakes are nothing less than the control of Jerusalem, winner take all.

On David Street, the creeds sort themselves out in three neatly divided human flows. Halfway down, Christians turn left to the Holy Sepulchre. Moslems continue straight on to the mosques on the ancient Temple Mount. Jews, when not dodging stones thrown at them by Palestinian militants, turn right to the Western Wall. There are frequent processions along the street; and on the busiest days, two sounds rise ceaselessly above all others: the peal of bells and the call of the muezzin. Both come periodically and unsynchronized from dozens of towers and minarets. The muezzin nowadays is most often a tape amplified by powerful loudspeakers. At times of tension between Moslems and Jews, the volume is increased; after a few days of calm, it is turned down again.

Every Christian sect has its own bells. You learn to recognize their different tolls as they reverberate off the chiseled limestone in the narrow alleys: the deep boom of the Greek Orthodox in the basilica of the Holy Sepulchre; the clank-clank of the Ethiopians on the rooftop above the basilica (to which they have been banished by their longtime antagonists, the Copts); the growling peal of the German Lutherans nearby; the low, sepulchral knell of the Armenians, as though coming from another world; the mellow clang of the White Fathers on the via Dolorosa.

The crowds fill the mosques, the synagogues, and the churches on their respective Sabbaths and holidays. The faithful seem driven by a need to be close to their particular ideas of God and to their fellow believers, not only spiritually, but in space, too — a desire that in all three religions has occasionally been questioned theologically. What are they in search of? First and foremost, it seems, they are in search of continuity.

Everywhere in Jerusalem, ritual is enhanced by repetition. Day in, day out, the same liturgies, the same formulations, the same tunes, the same invocations are endlessly repeated. The same gestures are executed in the same vestments, in the same sacred spaces as hundreds and hundreds of years ago. Nothing changes. Again and again, morning, noon, evening, night, the endless repetition confers a kind of reality to the unreal. It is the same in most synagogues, churches, and mosques. Nothing gives as much reassurance as repetition. Perhaps this is so because the reiteration harks back to an archetype, a primeval, subconscious memory — by now, almost a genetic code. Through repetition, time is brought to a standstill, as the sun was at Gibeon. At the very least, as Mircea Eliade has suggested, time's virulence is diminished.

Much of the color of the city still comes from this endless repetition — from the centuries-old rituals in the holy places of the faiths and from the great variety but unchanging order of their festivals and processions. It is reflected in the simple dedication of Greek and Cypriot peasants kneeling among the old and gnarled olive trees in Gethsemane; and in the devotion of ultra-Orthodox Jews who brave the great heat and the blinding light in their seventeenth-century eastern-European black overcoats, heavy fur hats, woolen knickers, and white stockings as they pray at high noon at the Western Wall. It comes from the sight of thousands of bowed backs on the temple platform as the observant recite Friday prayers in the forecourts of the mosques; from the splendor of seventh-century Moslem architecture; from the barbaric treasures of the Eastern churches and the elaborate Byzantine or Armenian vestments of their clergy, unchanged since the sixth or seventh century. Every brocade collar, every gold button, every white scarf is still exactly where it was when Armenia extended from Mount Ararat to the Mediterranean Sea, when Justinian and Theodora officiated under the great dome of Saint Sophia. Their canopies and miters are those seen on the mosaics of Ravenna. The same deep blues, greens, and golds dominate the scene. The same relics are encased in the same gold and silver capsules studded with precious jewels — a strain of hair from Mohammed's beard, bits and pieces of the true cross, fragments of a saint's bone in sparkling glass spheres. The walls are hung with lovely rugs and icons.

In every synagogue, the same priestly benediction is intoned daily, in exactly the same words as in Jerusalem almost three thousand years ago: "The Lord bless thee, and keep thee . . . make his face shine upon thee . . . lift up his countenance upon thee, and give thee peace." The very same text (based on Num. 6:24–26) was found in 1979 in a Jewish tomb of the first-temple period. Carved in ancient Hebrew script on a tiny silver cylinder of the sixth or seventh century BC, it is the oldest biblical inscription found anywhere — a remarkable, perhaps unique instance of uninterrupted continuity. (The cylinder, which predates the Dead Sea Scrolls by about four hundred years, is now on permanent display at the Israel Museum.)

The organ music of the Latins and the Lutherans resounds under barrel vaulting and pointed arches that have preserved through the centuries a hallowed and unforgettable tradition. The same incense still billows through the dim-lit choirs. And throughout the Old City, crowding against one another: the priests of all faiths — ulemas, rabbis, and Protestant ministers and monks in their white, brown, gray, or black habits with cocked or cowled hoods — and hermits on short leave from their monasteries in the Judean desert.

Earlier in this century, hermits were more numerous. They were a lonely race; some inhabited caves cut into the desert rock by their precursors, the Essenes of the first century (authors of the Dead Sea Scrolls), whom Pliny the Elder described as "strangest among the inhabitants of the world, . . . a race [without women] which exists perpetually and in which no one is born for it is propagated by other men's dissatisfaction with life."

Jerusalem may not be as old, perhaps, as Babylon or Memphis. But in Jerusalem, the same religion is still practiced as was practiced twenty-five hundred years ago; and the same language is spoken today that was spoken by David and Isaiah. In Jewish Jerusalem — unlike in Rome, Athens, Cairo, or Baghdad — language and religion unite rather than separate the modern nation and its distant past.

The forces of the past seem so strong here that the city sometimes fails to have a present. Time sequences are scrambled. Everybody finds his or her own most convenient precedent. "A thousand years . . . are but as yesterday," said the psalmist. When the British general Edmund Allenby entered the city in 1917, he proclaimed, as a matter of course, the reestablishment of Crusader rule in Jerusalem after an interval of 730 years. Similarly, in the aftermath of the 1967 war, Israelis linked their successes to the victories of Joshua over the Canaanites. The Arabs, in the same manner, cited Saladin's victory of 1187 to belittle the Jews' prospects of holding on to their unexpected conquests.

In the Old City today, prints of the victorious caliph Omar riding into Jerusalem in AD 638 are on sale in Arab shops; Jewish shops offer prints of the Temple Mount with the mosques wiped out and a great Jewish temple built there instead. In the crush of one memory against the other, time is squeezed — as in some science fiction novels. News, the modern commodity most dependent on time, is directly affected. Local news events in Jerusalem reach the wider world with greater regularity than the local news of other capitals larger and more mundane. A stone thrown at a passerby in Jerusalem is reported in the world press; great disasters elsewhere might not be reported at all. Jerusalem has one of the largest contingents of foreign correspondents in the world. Every Sabbath, every holiday — and in every riot or war — Jerusalem is the world's *largest* little town.

A story is told of George Adam Smith, the Scottish historian and Bible scholar, whose familiarity with every detail in the life of ancient Jerusalem was phenomenal. Shortly before he died in 1942, he is said to have given a lecture at Aberdeen on the topography of Jerusalem. When the lecture was over, a young relative arrived to take him by the hand and lead him back home. George Adam Smith knew the location of every important site in ancient, medieval, and modern Jerusalem but needed help to find his way home in the city where he had lived for more than forty years. The story may be apocryphal, yet it sums up, as such stories sometimes do, the central facts of the case: Jerusalem's extraordinary hold over the imagination. In nineteenth-century England, the cult of Jerusalem was tied to the evangelical revival. Eighteenth-century rationalism was giving way to revelation, and Hellenism to Hebraism. The challenge of Darwinism served as an added impetus for many to explore and excavate Jerusalem and prove the Bible true.

Christian, Moslem, and Jewish interest in the earthly Jerusalem derived from conflicting sources. Christians upheld her sanctity as the place of Christ's ministry, passion, and resurrection. Christian piety, for the most part, insisted that pilgrimage — moving the body to Jerusalem — was almost as important as moving the soul there. Pilgrimage was sometimes of the crude, crusading kind; at other times, it was purely speculative or spiritual. Actual pilgrimage was not always held in high regard and was sometimes seen as mindless fetishism. Gregory of Nyssa admonished the pious to ascend from the flesh to God, rather than travel from Europe to Jerusalem. Jerome insisted that the "heavenly sanctuary is open from Britain no less than from Jerusalem, for the Kingdom of God is within you." And yet, Gregory himself went on pilgrimage to Jerusalem and Jerome spent most of his life in nearby Bethlehem.

Moslems venerate Jerusalem as the city of Abraham, Solomon, and Jesus — prophets of Islam — and, of course, as the city where Mohammed stopped on the *isra'* — his celebrated nocturnal flight to heaven — to behold the celestial glories. The belief in the *isra'* rests on a single line in the Koran that does not specify Jerusalem by name but refers merely to an otherwise unidentified "Far-Away" mosque: "Praise to be Allah who brought his servant at night from the Holy Mosque to the Far-Away Mosque the precincts of which we have blessed." There has been much tedious doctrinal argument about whether the *isra'* was a real or an ecstatic (that is, visionary) experience. It has been argued that early Islam simply incorporated Jewish and Christian notions of the heavenly Jerusalem. Others have maintained that, for practical reasons, it is highly unlikely Mohammed himself actually visited Jerusalem — as though the concrete facts in this case weighed heavier than they did in the case of the Immaculate Conception or the parting of the Red Sea. The lasting power of such legends is in the metaphors they evoke in the religious traditions and in the readiness to believe them.

It might well be that Jerusalem became holy in Islam for political reasons as well. The eighth-century Umayyad sultans of Damascus may have wished to divert the lucrative pilgrim trade from Mecca. But in the history of Jerusalem, politics and religion have always overlapped. The Jewish and Israeli attachment to Jerusalem is equally an amalgam of religious and political sentiments. Even if Islam linked itself to Jerusalem only in the eighth century, the legend of Mohammed's ascent to heaven from the Temple Mount of Jerusalem is by now as central an element in Islam as the Exodus is in Judaism and the cult of Mary is in Christianity. The cult of Mary was unknown in the first centuries after Christ. It seems to have fully matured only during the Crusades, for whatever reason or reasons — religious, political, or psychological. The doctrine of the Immaculate Conception was pronounced only in the last century.

The literature on the role of Jerusalem in Islam is immense. Mohammed himself may not have visited the city. Her religious and eschatological associations with his ministry, however, and with the End of Days seem as important to practicing Moslems today as the parallel associations are to most practicing Jews and Christians. Why and how Jerusalem came to figure so importantly in Islam is by now almost a moot point. Drawing on a modern

metaphor, R. J. Z. Werblowsky, a Jerusalem professor of compara-
tive religion, has quipped: "There are no direct flights from Mecca
to heaven; you have to make a stop-over in Jerusalem."

On the Day of Judgment, according to Moslem lore, the Kaaba,
the shrine that houses the holy black stone of Mecca, will be transported to Jerusalem and placed on Mount Zion. In modern times,
nationalism has joined religion in Jerusalem to produce among
Arabs a mixture as explosive as that among Jews. One fanaticism
rooted in religious memory fans another fanaticism rooted in another religious memory. The claims overlap and sanctity is invariably conceived as exclusive. Thus, Mohammed is now said to have
tied his winged steed al-Buraq to, of all places, the Western Wall of
the Jews. Hence the persistent and sometimes bloody struggle between Moslems and Jews, since the middle of the last century, over
control of the wall area.

The original qibla (direction of prayer) was not toward Mecca. In
the early days of Islam, Moslems, like Jews, said their prayers facing
the direction of Jerusalem. The qibla later changed to Mecca, but
Jerusalem remained the third-holiest city in Islam, after Mecca and
Medina. Over the centuries, an immense body of Islamic literature
has grown up extolling the merits of Jerusalem. This lore takes the
form of hadiths, traditions attributed to the prophet Mohammed.
Jerusalem hadiths proliferated especially after lost wars. They first
assumed great prominence after the fall of the city to the Crusaders
in 1099. These hadiths were an early kind of "Moslem Zionism."
According to one such hadith, a sin committed in Jerusalem is
worse than a thousand committed elsewhere, while a good deed
done there is equal to a thousand in another place. Other well-
known hadiths dating from the Crusader period are cited to this
day: "He who lives in Jerusalem is considered a warrior in the Holy
War"; "To die in Jerusalem is almost like dying in heaven"; "He
who lives in Jerusalem for one year, despite the inconvenience and
adversity, for him God will provide his daily bread in this life and
happiness in paradise."

The worship of Jerusalem for more mundane reasons antedated
in Islam the loss of the city to the Crusaders. In the tenth century,
the Arab geographer Mohammed ibn Ahmad al-Muqaddasi, a native of Jerusalem, boldly claimed that the city united the pleasures

of this world with those of the next. Muqaddasi was inexhaustible
in his praise of the city. It is easy to dismiss his enthusiasms as the
product of religious fervor (he lived around AD 1000). But he was
an observant reporter and something of a gourmet, too; and he
readily admitted the city's many faults — her baths and inns were
dirty, overcrowded, and expensive; justice was badly administered;
and water was short. Above all, according to Muqaddasi, there
were too many Jews and Christians. Still, he insisted, Jerusalem's
climate was the best on earth. Reverting to even higher reasons, he
reminded his readers that on the Day of Judgment, Mecca and
Medina will come to Jerusalem and their excellencies shall be
united.

The merits-of-Jerusalem literature proliferated once again in the
aftermath of the Six-Day War of 1967, and the tradition continues.
A particularly enticing hadith comes from the twelfth-century historian Ibn Asakir: he defined happiness as "eating a banana in the
shade of the Dome of the Rock."

In Jewish tradition, the sanctity of Jerusalem derived from the temple. The temple was God's abode. "God is in the midst of her," the
psalmist sang, "she shall not be moved." The Jewish (and Moslem)
view of a holy place was spatial: a hallowed, sacred enclosure. It was
very different from the Christian conception of holy individuals or
their bodies, which remained sacred even after death. Yohanan ben
Zakai, the first-century Jewish sage who was smuggled out of embattled Jerusalem in a coffin during the Roman siege of AD 70 and
founded the great postexilic center of learning at Yavneh, assumed
that the Jews would have no further need of the earthly Jerusalem
— henceforth they would have the Almighty and his sacred law,
and these would suffice; but it was not to be. After the destruction
of the temple, the city as such assumed its sanctity. God's living
presence was said to brood over Jerusalem's ruins. As a ruin,
Jerusalem became even more sacred than before. As a Byzantine
town and then an Arab one, she remained a Jewish icon. Her
memory highlighted the continuing vitality of an exiled, dispersed,
persecuted people who never despaired of the possibility of return,
even if only at the End of Days. The power of memory in the grip

of the religious imagination forged links as strong and as passionate as those of settled peoples to their land.

In Jewish lore, even the celestial Jerusalem had a curious, down-to-earth, almost corporeal touch. The celestial city of the Christians was more ephemeral. It had no need for sun or moon, "for the glory of God did lighten it." By contrast, the heavenly Jerusalem of the Jews was said by the rabbis to be the exact physical replica of the earthly one. They did not go as far as Samuel Butler, who predicted that the New Jerusalem would so resemble the old as to stone its prophets freely.

As the centuries passed, the attachment of Jews to Jerusalem became a compelling bond. Without this mystic lure, they and their religion might not have survived. Jerusalem was there every day of the week, every Sabbath, and every holiday, in every religious rite and prayer, morning, noon, and night. No matter where in the world Jews found themselves, they invoked the memory of Jerusalem — when completing a meal, when marrying, when a son was born, when he came of age, when someone died and was buried. No other religion exacted a similar emotional commitment to a specific place. Nor was it purely religious sentiment. Yehuda Halevi, the medieval Hebrew poet in Arab Spain, wrote:

> My heart is in the east, and I in the uttermost west
> How can I find savor in food? How shall it be sweet to me?
> How shall I render my vows and my bonds, while yet
> Zion is in the fetters of Edom, and I am in Arab chains?

The Jewish dispersion was a spiritual empire with Jerusalem as its capital. Jews turned to her in prayer and in song, and even as they became assimilated to the ways of the Greeks, the Arabs, the Spaniards, or the Germans, they did not forget her. In czarist Russia, in North Africa, or in the farthest corner of Iran, they remained residents of an imaginary Jerusalem through their rituals. Nothing remotely like this sentiment surfaced among any other exiled people or lasted so long. In his memoir *Kindheit im Exil* (*Childhood in Exile*), Shmaryahu Levin recounted how the ninth of Ab (the anniversary of the destruction of the temple of Jerusalem) was marked in the 1880s, more than eighteen hundred years after the event, at Swislowitz, a little town near Kiev, where Levin was born. In his mother's telling of the story, he wrote, there was so much freshness, so much passion, so much personal indignation "that the sense of time was wholly destroyed"; it was as though the Romans had crushed "*us*," as though it had been "*our*" house that they had brutally destroyed, as though "we, our family, our relatives and friends had lived in glorious Jerusalem, and only yesterday the villain Titus had banished us to Swislowitz," where, instead of the golden temple and the high priest, there was only a rickety old wooden synagogue and an old fool as a rabbi.

Samuel Joseph Agnon, whose modern Hebrew novels echo the life and death of Eastern European Jewry (he has been compared to Kafka), expressed a kind of transcendental truth when he said in his speech accepting the 1966 Nobel Prize in literature: "Through a historical catastrophe — the destruction of Jerusalem by the emperor of Rome . . . I was born in one of the cities of the diaspora. But I always deemed myself as one who was really born in Jerusalem."

In the Jewish tradition, Jerusalem came to be almost synonymous with the Jewish people. Modern Jewish nationalism took its name from Zion, a synonym for Jerusalem. This was no coincidence. The term Zionism first cropped up, spontaneously, among secular Jews in Vienna in the early 1890s. It was immediately adopted by friends and foes alike. The early Zionist hymn "Hatikva" ("The Hope"), today Israel's national anthem, speaks neither of Jewry nor of Israel but of the "hope to be a free people in the land of Zion and Jerusalem."

In the past, religion was the great legitimizing language in Jerusalem for Arabs and Jews. Today, there is nationalism, too. The traditional Moslem in Jerusalem knew Jews only as a docile minority, devoid of all political ambition, grateful for the protection they received at various times by Arab or Ottoman rulers. The new nationalism of the Jews came as a shock to most Moslems (a shock from which they have not recovered). The idea of an Israel *revidivus* in Jerusalem was theologically problematic, if not downright embarrassing, for conservative Catholics, too. Other Christians, fundamentalist Protestants mainly, saw a rebuilt Jewish Jerusalem much as most Orthodox Jews do, as the fulfillment of prophecy, even as heralding the End of Days. The borderlines between politics and religions in Jerusalem were always blurred. As in India or Northern Ireland, politics were embittered by theological rancor. In political discussions, Arabs and Israelis today freely resort to religious images and catchwords. Even when couched in secular terms, the arguments draw their vitality from religious roots. Crude ambitions sometimes pose as spirituality; hatred, as love. The tone is occasionally Orwellian and there is none so far to reconcile the jarring interests of piety and reason.

Jerusalem, Yehuda Amichai wrote in 1967, is a city where "all remember they have forgotten something." A decade later, he observed:

> The air over Jerusalem is saturated with prayers and dreams
> like the air over industrial cities.
> It's hard to breathe.

Hatred is also a form of prayer, as is fear. This has always been true in Jerusalem, and never more so than when the stones start flying, and the knives are pulled, and the bombs go off.

CHAPTER THREE

Cruel City

A CRUEL CITY, a city of contention and strife. Her existence has always seemed temporary and precarious, as though she were standing in the eye of a cyclone. Graham Greene said that she was the "great survivor of the world." Aldous Huxley called her the great "slaughterhouse of the religions." This was in 1953, when the city was still cut in two parts. There was no communication between the two sectors other than by bursts of rifle and machine-gun fire. People on both sides were shot dead by snipers on the walls.

Huxley visited the Arab side only. He remarked on "the hopelessness of the inhabitants of Jerusalem, for whom the holiest of cities is a prison of chronic despair punctuated by occasional panic when the hand grenades start flying." He had never before, he wrote, felt such a sense of the "tragic nature of the human situation" as he experienced here. He felt overwhelmed by an obscure, immediate sense of it — an organic realization.

> These pollulations among ruins and in the dark of what once were sepulchres; these hordes of sickly children; these mortal enemies behind the dividing walls; these priest-conducted groups of pilgrims with their vain repetitions, against which the founder of their religion had gone out of his way to warn them — *they were dateless, without an epoch.* In this costume or that, under one master or another, praying to whichever God was temporarily in charge, they had been here from the beginning . . . in the same brown squalor, alternately building or destroying, killing and being killed, indefinitely.

Arthur Koestler remembered the city no less bitterly. He was not
a transient visitor; Koestler lived in Jerusalem for a few years in the
late 1920s. "Tragedy without catharsis," he wrote. "The angry face
of Yahweh is brooding over the hot rocks which have seen more
holy murder, rape and plunder than any other place on earth. Its
inhabitants are poisoned by religion."*

Was the land itself somehow the effect rather than the cause of its
legends? Could it be that its desolation was a result of the fatal
embrace of the deity? Would it have been so desolate if three religions had not fought over its ruins for so long? Koestler was
haunted by these questions. He may have been overreacting to the
austere landscape. In the twenties, the immediate surroundings of
the city were still almost as despondent and severe as the moon. In
the harsh daylight, Koestler reported, they made you feel suicidal.

Fifty years earlier, the hills around Jerusalem must have seemed
even more austere. They struck many a European as perfectly mor-
bid. Selma Lagerlof, the Nobel Prize–winning author of the international best-seller *To Jerusalem,* insisted that many people were not
strong enough to live there. The city "depresses and weighs upon
them, or else they go out of their minds — ay, it can even kill them
outright." The Roman Catholic, she reported, spoke evil of the
Protestant, the Methodist of the Quaker, the Lutheran of the Reformed Church, the Russian of the Armenian. "Here — no mercy is
shown [and] one hates one's fellow man to the glory of God."

Even clerics occasionally sensed the destructive power of the
place. The fifteenth-century Dominican pilgrim Felix Fabri con-
tended that in reality Christians and Moslems cared little about who
ruled Jerusalem as long as they could freely worship at the holy
places. But since their leaders could not reach agreement on this
matter, "unhappy Jerusalem has suffered, does now suffer and will
hereafter suffer sieges, castings down, destructions and terrors beyond any other city in the world." In Fabri's days, pilgrims were
harassed on the highways and taxed at the city's gates. They paid
another fee to the Moslem doormen each time they wished to enter
the Holy Sepulchre.

The vision of one God united the different religions in Jerusalem,

* Koestler had just invented the modern Hebrew crossword puzzle. It was called "brain
acrobatics" to avoid giving offense: the rabbis might have resented the reference to a cross.

but the practice of that vision divided them bitterly. Even the good brother Fabri had nothing but contempt for Moslems and Jews, and sheer loathing for all Christian sects other than his own. "The following nations dwell in Jerusalem at this day [1480–1483]," he wrote:

- The Saracens, "who are Mohammedans befouled with the dregs of heresies, worse than idolators, more loathsome than Jews. . . . [From their minarets,] they shout and howl day and night according to the ordinances of their accursed creed. . . . They practice sodomy."
- The Greeks, "who in the olden days contained men of exceeding great learning [but who are now] monstrous heretics and schematics. . . . They do now believe that the Holy Spirit proceeded from the son. . . . [Worse still,] they say that simple fornication is no sin."
- The Syrians, "who in truth are not Christians but children of the devil, liars, thinking nothing of theft. . . . They are womanists and totally useless for war."
- The Jacobites, who live in dark mischief "and circumcise their children."
- The Nestorians, "who are led astray by errors of the worst kind [regarding] the Mother of God and her Son."
- The Armenians, "who are sunk in diverse errors. . . . They eat meat on Fridays . . . and share the errors of the Jacobites concerning Christ."
- The Gregorians, "who are merely called Christians and are tainted by almost all the errors of the Greeks."
- The Maronites, "who are heretics and believe that Christ had only one will and one energy."
- The Beduins, who are the most evil and "worship the sun."
- The Turkomans, who are "wandering savages."
- The Mamluks, who are hateful because they are "renegade Christians."
- The Jews, who "among all these, are held to be accursed insomuch as the [deserved] misery and contempt which they undergo greatly dulls their understanding [of the true faith]."

Jerusalem was the civic embodiment of contentious faiths. Her monuments had a rhetoric of their own, which each religion interpreted differently. Her names, forever changing from Hebrew to Greek to Latin to Arabic, echoed the conflicting claims of creeds and clashing nationalities. In the Bible, she was YRSLM. We cannot be sure about the ancient pronunciation since the vowel points for *e, u,* and *a* were inserted into the Hebrew Bible only in the tenth century. It may have been "Yerushalem"; or "Yerushalaim." As "Ierusalem," the name first appears in the earliest Greek translation of the Bible, the Septuaginta (so named from the legend of its composition by seventy translators, each secluded in his cell, but all seventy versions miraculously identical, so that they were said to have been inspired by God).

On coins dating from the first Jewish revolt (AD 66–70), she is called Jerusalem the Holy. Saint Matthew echoed this in the New Testament; he dubbed her Hagia Polis (Holy City). The emperor Hadrian renamed her after himself, Aelia Capitolina (the third-century church father Philostronius claimed that he did so to eradicate any connection whatsoever to the accursed Jews). In the fourth century, Saint Jerome spoke of the City of Three Names. In the seventh century, the Arab conquerors added three more: Iliya (a corruption of Aelia, to which they attached a fantastic biblical etymology), al-Balat (the Palace), and Beit al-Maqdis (Holy House), later abbreviated to al-Quds (the Holy One). The Crusaders in the eleventh century revived the name Jerusalem (Christians had never called her by any other). In the twelfth century, Saladin reinstated her as al-Quds. By this name she is known to this day to Moslems throughout the world.

The disputes over the love of the city have kindled so much animosity that up to the modern age there were scarcely any Jerusalemites, as there were Londoners or Venetians. The Venetians had a way of describing themselves even in the Middle Ages as "Veneziani, poi Christiani" (Venetians first, then Christians). In Jerusalem, one has always been a Moslem, a Jew, or a Christian first, a Jerusalemite afterward.

In addition to the larger quarrels and wars, there were subsidiary quarrels and, sometimes, wars within the religions themselves. Since the early Middle Ages, the various Christian denominations and sects have lived in a state of constant rivalry and strife. Most conflicts between the sects centered on the Church of the Holy Sepulchre. To this day, the church is not only the heart of Christian Jerusalem but its battlefield.

Sectarian conflict within the Jewish community was no less bitter. Sadducees clashed with Pharisees, Hellenizers with Maccabees, Zealots with Sicarii. In our own days, Orthodox, ultra-Orthodox, non-Orthodox, and secular Jews disagree on almost every tenet of daily life — often violently. Orthodox and ultra-Orthodox Jews reject one another as dissidents and idolaters. Both condemn Conservative and Reform Jews as renegades or heretics. All disdain secular Jews as sinful and godless. Cars passing through certain quarters inhabited by ultra-Orthodox Jews on the Sabbath are likely to be stoned, as are Jewish-owned restaurants and cinemas open on the Sabbath anywhere in the city. On their way to the Western Wall, the ultra-Orthodox walk through the busy Arab bazaars of the Old City in complete equanimity: it is the non-Orthodox Jews whom they are determined to save from themselves, from sin — if need be, with brute force. Rioting yeshiva students regularly clash with non-Orthodox Jews, and with the police, in ugly street battles. Nonkosher restaurants and butcher shops are vandalized. Bus stations are burned down. Archaeologists are attacked for desecrating holy ground. There is violence among the several sects within the ultra-Orthodox community as well. This has been so almost since the beginning of this century, and the end is not yet in sight.

Christian rivalries in Jerusalem are a result of the so-called heresies of the fifth and sixth century, which saw the rise of Monophysitism and of the historic estrangement between Eastern and Western churches. The Monophysites held that Christ had not two but one composite nature, at once human and divine. Eastern and Western Christians, Latins, Greeks, Copts, Jacobites, and other Christian sects have since anathematized and excommunicated one another as schismatics and heretics. The reasons were partly political or geopolitical, and partly theological: rivalries between East and West — Constantinople and Rome — or controversies over such questions as whether the Holy Spirit proceeded from the Father only or from the Father and the Son. The Monophysites broke away to establish the separate churches of the Ethiopians, the Copts, the Armenians, and the Syrian Jacobites. When the Arabs conquered Jerusalem in the seventh century, they found a church already divided into at least five rival sects. There was still only one patriarch, Sophronius, who negotiated the surrender of Jerusalem to the caliph Omar. Today, there are three patriarchs (Greek, Latin, and Armenian) in Jerusalem and the titular heads (archbishops, bishops, and deans) of thirty-two other independent Christian churches and sects.

The final break between the Eastern and the Western churches in Jerusalem was a result of Christian, not Moslem, supremacy in the city. It came about during the First Crusade, which expelled the Greek Orthodox hierarchy from Jerusalem and appointed a Latin patriarch instead. "We defeated the Turks and the pagans," the leaders of the First Crusade reported to Pope Urban II, "but we could not defeat the heretics — the Greeks and Armenians, Syrians and Jacobites." This task was achieved, a century later, by the knights of the Fourth Crusade. Instead of moving against the Moslems to recover Jerusalem, they attacked the center of Eastern Christianity. Constantinople was looted and destroyed in 1204 with all conceivable cruelty and horror. The pillage and slaughter lasted for an entire week. "Since the world was created, never had so much booty been won in any city," exclaimed Geoffroi de Villehardouin, who described the glories of Constantinople before her fall as Josephus had chronicled Jerusalem's. The sack of Constantinople so poisoned Latin-Orthodox relations that it was still a living memory for the Greek Orthodox in Jerusalem seven centuries later. In 1912, boys at a Greek Orthodox primary school in Jerusalem were still made to recount lurid tales of those horrors, much as though they had happened the day before. "[Latin hatred] of the Orthodox faith is boundless," proclaimed one school primer, "and has barely diminished over the centuries."

As late as 1876, Baedeker's guidebook to Jerusalem noted the "humiliating fact" that armed Moslem guards were posted in the vestibule of the Holy Sepulchre. But it went on to explain that this was "absolutely necessary" in order to keep order between warring Christian sects: "So completely do jealousy and fanaticism [in Jerusalem] usurp the place of true religion." Nowadays, armed Israeli policemen are on duty outside the basilica. The keys to the Holy Sepulchre are in the custody of a Moslem family in order to prevent disputes between the various Christian sects over their possession.

The history of Christianity in Jerusalem during the four centuries of Ottoman rule (1516–1917) was a series of interminable disputes and of occasional violence among inimical sects. Greek or Armenian churches were sometimes favored by the Turks as "Eastern" — that is to say, as indigenous churches. The European powers were divided as to which churches to support. The French traditionally favored the Latins. The Russians sided with the Greeks. The English and Germans made efforts to establish themselves on the margins of religious life by protecting Armenians or Jews. The Turks and their local satraps were, as a rule, eager to make the most, politically and financially, of the dissensions among the Christians. Holy places were often sold to the highest bidder.

Between 1625 and 1637, the Ottoman sultan Murad IV issued no fewer than twelve contradictory edicts concerning the "ownership" of Christian holy places in Jerusalem. In the eighteenth century, Latins and Greek Orthodox alternated at least five times as sole owners of the Holy Sepulchre. Most changes were short-lived, the result of pressures applied by the European powers, of bribes paid to Ottoman court officials, or of both. In the nineteenth century, European rivalries in Jerusalem came to a head. In the words of one historian, "the scenes of our Lord's life on earth became a political shuttlecock," and eventually one of the causes of the Crimean War.

In 1808, a fire swept through the Holy Sepulchre, destroying the Rotunda of the Anastasis. The great dome collapsed, causing great damage to the tomb itself. Latins, Greeks, Copts, and Armenians accused one another of criminal negligence or even of causing the fire by deliberate means (a drunk Armenian monk was said to have poured aquavit on the flames, instead of water). The restoration of the gutted basilica was held up for years. Latins and Armenians feared that it would result in more Greek control of ownership over the entire edifice. Several ministerial palms were greased by French and Russian gold in the hope of securing advantages to one or another church. After much diplomatic to-and-fro, the Ottoman government authorized the Greeks to restore the church (allegedly after payment of a bribe of 2½ million Russian rubles, almost twice the cost of the restoration itself).

The actual work only increased the tensions among the sects. Apart from building a particularly ugly new structure over the tomb of Christ — more like a gaudy newspaper kiosk in Salonika, in the words of one modern Franciscan author — "the sacrilegious hammer of the Greeks followed no other design than that of erasing from the edifice of the Crusaders every vestige and record of Latin civilization and Catholicism. . . . The basilica emerged more damaged than was possible by the destructive flames."

Be that as it may, the Greeks did efface the remaining sarcophagi of the Latin kings, Godfrey of Bouillon and his two successors, which Chateaubriand had still seen intact and copied two years before the fire. They disappeared completely and have not been found since. Six Christian communities shared the Holy Sepulchre: Greeks, Armenians, Latins, Copts, Syrians, and Ethiopians. In the aftermath of the fire, scuffles between them became more violent and more frequent. They reflected the growing rivalries between the main European powers. Throughout the first half of the nineteenth century, clergymen of all denominations made it a habit to show visitors scars and fresh wounds they claimed to have suffered during one of the scuffles in the church. Nor were the fights confined to the basilica itself. In 1854, Greek monks broke into the residence of the newly appointed Latin patriarch of Jerusalem — the first in the city since the defeat of the Crusaders — and threw him out, then brought a herd of camels to house in his rooms. When the first Anglican bishop — Dr. Michael Alexander, an ex-rabbi and recent convert to Christianity — was appointed, he was advised (wisely, it seems) to assume the title of Anglican bishop *in* Jerusalem, not *of* Jerusalem, to avoid giving offense.

In 1856, fighting broke out between Armenian and Greek monks inside the tomb of Christ during the Easter ceremony of the Holy Fire. Ten men were injured, four seriously. The Greeks had been "provided with sticks and cudgels which had been previously con-

cealed [the Armenians claimed] behind the columns and in dark
corners." The communities would come to blows over the mere
moving of a rug or the lighting of a candle at the wrong time. Even
cleaning the basilica became a cause. The slightest digression of a
broom or hammer beyond the territory assigned to each community could result in bloodshed. If from excessive dusting a nail in the
wall worked loose, difficult and prolonged negotiations followed
and sometimes armed police might be needed to put it back in
place.

Christian squabbles in Jerusalem were often attributed to the fact
that Jerusalem was under the dominion of a non-Christian power.
But when Christian rule was restored under the British in 1917,
the rivalry between the sects reached a new high. It was vividly
described by Sir Ronald Storrs, the first British governor of
Jerusalem. In his memoirs, he cited some of the bizarre communi-
cations he regularly received from prominent Christian clergymen.
"Excellency," the Greek patriarch wrote, "I have repeatedly called
your attention upon the insufferable arrogance of the Copts."
"Your excellency is well aware of the unbearable transgression of
the Ethiopians," wrote the Copts. The Armenian bishop appealed
for intervention against Greek Orthodox "greed and hypocrisy."
The latter had moved a rug a few inches beyond the proscribed line.

Copts and Franciscans were also at loggerheads. The Copts had a
little shrine in the back of the aedicula of the Holy Sepulchre, a
niche so small it could contain but one person. The Coptic priest
was obliged to celebrate the mass kneeling with his congregation
outside, in the circular passage around the tomb. The Franciscans
would insist on asserting their right of way in this narrow passage
by lugging benches through the worshipers "with a zeal," Storrs
noted, "which would hardly have won the approval of St Francis."
The Copts retaliated in their own fashion. They had a convent
overlooking the via Dolorosa, at the ninth station of the cross, and
they emptied "their slóps out of the windows on the exact spot
upon which the Friday procession of Franciscans was accustomed
to kneel."

The one agreement achieved in Storrs's days between the warring
Latins and Greeks over some long-overdue structural change in one
of the joint holy places was reached only through subterfuge. Storrs

first persuaded the Latin patriarch to sign the agreement by assuring him that the Greeks were opposed to it. Then he induced the Greek patriarch to sign by saying that the Latins disliked it very much. His trickery won Storrs the nickname "Oriental Stores," an allusion to a rather dubious souvenir shop of that name in the bazaar.

The basilica, meanwhile, was crumbling of old age. It was further damaged by an earthquake but could not be repaired because the sects were unable to reach an agreement. The British were unwilling to enforce one. Emergency steel scaffolding held up the facade for decades. The entrance hall, below Calvary, was so encumbered it was like a tunnel leading into an underground mine. A mixed commission to sort out the rights and claims of the various communities was called for under Article 14 of the League of Nations' Mandate for Palestine. It never met. One sect always objected to the participation of another. When the sole surviving Crusader tombstone in Jerusalem — that of the Englishman Philip d'Aubigny, a signer of the Magna Carta — was unearthed under the main door leading into the Holy Sepulchre, Storrs had to call in a platoon of British soldiers to excavate and protect it. Greek priests thronged the roofs, terraces, and battlements, "contemplating with mournful anger the preservation [in their midst] of a Latin monument."

In his first proclamation the day his forces occupied Jerusalem in 1917, the British general Edmund Allenby had promised to maintain and protect the status quo at all holy places "according to the existing customs and beliefs of those to whose faith they are sacred." This was more easily said than done. The status quo proved a difficult code to apply. It was one of the most fluid and imprecise in the world. The status quo was defined as the situation that had prevailed in the basilica in 1757. But there was no general agreement exactly which rite had enjoyed "preeminence" at which altar, rug, shrine, tapestry, picture, door, curtain, passageway — or parts thereof — at that remote date. Some belonged to two or three sects. Within one sect, there were several conflicting customs.

A Moslem power at last succeeded where Christian power or goodwill had failed for so many centuries — though not without the added impetus of several crumbling buttresses and ceilings. In 1958, King Hussein of Jordan finally induced the various com-

munities to cooperate on an agreed scheme of restoration. Rivalries
and suspicions diminished only partially as a result. The agreed
scheme was repeatedly violated by one or more of the warring sects.
A typical incident occurred in 1964 shortly before the pope's visit to
Jerusalem. Paul VI had expressed a wish to pray in a part of the
Grotto of the Nativity in Bethlehem controlled by the Greeks. Latin
emissaries approached the Greek patriarchate and were given to
understand that there would be no problem. They were advised to
apply in writing. The Latins applied and were promptly refused.
Years later, the Greek patriarch admitted that he had purposely
asked for a written request to have proof, written by representatives
of the pope himself, that the Greeks enjoyed prior rights in the
grotto.

The religions were islands unto themselves. To be sure, they held
certain beliefs in common: they believed in a single God, in a
similar ethical code, in the efficacy of prayer, and in the Last Judgment. They even agreed on the exact site where the Last Judgment
would take place — among the tombstones in the ravine between
the city wall and Olivet. But over the centuries, they were not, as a
rule, involved with one another, except negatively — in scorn, discord, recrimination, or in war.

Even at their most tolerant, they were obsessed by a kind of
narcissism of small differences. Catholics teased the Eastern Orthodox sects that they differed among themselves about a single
letter. Greeks or Armenians retorted that the difference between an
atheist and a theist also consisted of a single letter. Voltaire, antici-
pating the insights of modern psychology, was probably the first to
point out that the persecution of one religion by the adherents of
another was tantamount to rebellion against one's own God. At the
apex of their power and influence, the ruling religions of Jerusalem
seemed to feel a deep need to spite or disparage all others.

The Golden Gate, also known as the Gate of Mercy, is a Byzantine or early Arab opening in the eastern wall of the Temple Mount.
The most beautiful, perhaps, of the city's gates, it has been the
subject of many traditions and legends. Jews and Christians shared
a belief that through this gate the messiah would return in judg-

ment. Hence, in the thirteenth century, the Moslems decided to block it permanently. The gate was first sealed and then walled up. A cemetery was planted outside in the belief that the savior would hesitate to stumble over alien tombs.

In the fourteenth century, the Romanesque bell tower of the Church of the Holy Sepulchre was ordered cut down to make it lower than the nearest minaret. Since the churches were now forbidden to ring bells, the pious had to be summoned to prayer by wooden rattles, such as can still be seen outside the Armenian Cathedral of Saint James. Until the middle of the nineteenth century, churches and synagogues could not be built taller than mosques. Soon after the new Hurva Synagogue was consecrated in the Old City in 1858, a Moslem minaret taller by a few feet went up right next to it.*

Moslems ridiculed Christians for pretending that God could have a son by a mortal woman. Christians considered it preposterous that the archangels had dictated the whole truth about God to an illiterate tribesman from an obscure town in Arabia. Jews scorned both for their implausible legends, unmindful that it might seem just as implausible that God had made a special covenant with them only, leaving the rest of mankind in darkness. Christians believed in the Eucharist but regarded as absurd the refusal of Moslems and Jews to eat pork.

All disdained one another, with that same inflexible constancy that in the defense of their respective faiths (and sometimes in their propagation) rendered them insensible to ridicule, death, or torture. From earliest times on, even learned Moslems referred to the Church of the Holy Sepulchre by the derogatory name *qumama* ("dunghill," in Arabic — a deliberate corruption of *quiyama*, "resurrection"). Mujir al-Din, the chief Moslem historian of medieval Jerusalem, otherwise an eminently sensible man, scorned the Christians of Jerusalem for giving themselves over "in their church of the

---

* Traces of this tendency toward religious one-upmanship survived into this century. In 1970, Louis Kahn, the prominent American architect, was asked to design the restoration of the Hurva. He proposed a new building higher by at least six feet than the most prominent Moslem sanctuary in Jerusalem, the Dome of the Rock. The municipality was more sensitive than the world-famous architect and his sponsors. Mayor Teddy Kollek vetoed the plan on the grounds that the importance of a particular faith need not be measured by the size of a building.

qumama to abominations which make one shudder with horror."
Jews, more delicate — or more vulnerable — referred to the building merely as the church containing the sepulchre of "that man."
During the Crusader conquest of Jerusalem, knights of the Order
of the Templars reduced the prayer niche in al-Aqsa mosque to
a pissoir. Felix Fabri, the fifteenth-century pilgrim quoted earlier,
reported an incident in an inn, adjacent to a mosque, alongside the
highway to Jerusalem. A pilgrim in his company, a German noble-
man, "rose in the night, climbed onto the vaulted roof of the
mosque and defiled it through the hole, which made us laugh much."

In 1860, the open cupola over the tomb of Christ had to be
covered by a protective awning to discourage Moslems on neighboring roofs from throwing in their garbage. In 1967, it was discovered that during the Jordanian occupation of East Jerusalem,
tombstones had been removed from the ancient Jewish cemetery on
Olivet to pave the latrines of a nearby Jordanian army barrack. (At
the same time, Moslems were incensed to discover that an equally
ancient Moslem cemetery had vanished on the Israeli side under a
five-star hotel.)

In Moslem eyes, Christians and Jews falsified their own scriptures
to conceal the prophecies of Mohammed's advent. The muezzins
at al-Aqsa would occasionally pepper their calls to prayer with a
polemical verse from the Koran: "The Lord has not begotten a
son." Christians commonly named Mohammed the firstborn of Satan who falsely claimed to be a prophet. The Jews, of course, were
called the killers of Christ. Until at least 1917 — during the great
ceremony of the Holy Fire, celebrated every Easter at the tomb of
Christ, in the presence of the Greek Orthodox and Armenian patriarchs — the following chant was intoned by ecstatic congregants:

> O Jews! O Jews!
> Your feast is the feast of devils,
> Our feast is the feast of Christ.
> We today are happy,
> And you are sorrowful.
> O the Jews! O the infidels!
> Your feast is the feast of the dead,
> And ours that of Christ.

A series of mutual exclusions barred members of one faith from entering the sacred precincts of another. The custom of excluding infidels was begun by the ancient Jews. Gentiles were barred from the inner Jewish temple. On each of the gates leading into it, an inscription in Latin or Greek proclaimed the so-called law of purity: "No gentile to enter. . . . Anyone caught is answerable to himself for his ensuing death."*

The principle of excluding nonbelievers on the Temple Mount was emulated by the Moslems. Until the middle of the nineteenth century, Jews and Christians were forbidden entry to the sacred Moslem enclosure. A French adventurer caught outside the Dome of the Rock on a Friday morning in 1827 is said to have been hacked to pieces by the mob.

Jews — though not Moslems — were officially barred until 1967 from the Church of the Holy Sepulchre. During the British mandate (1917–1948), suspects were stopped at the door and requested to prove they were not Jewish by crossing themselves devoutly. Pretending to be Christian proved on occasion a highly risky undertaking. In 1922, a young man accused of being Jewish by a Christian Arab taxi driver was about to be lynched inside the church next to the traditional site of Calvary. At the very last moment, after being stabbed in his calf and suffering several blows on his head, he was saved by British policemen.

The Jews of medieval Jerusalem, being powerless, could bar only one another. This happened from time to time for reasons of doctrine and exegesis. In the nineteenth century, Sir Moses Montefiore, the British philanthropist, was excommunicated by the rabbis of Jerusalem for defying the halakic ban on Jews visiting the Temple Mount (he might have defiled the site of the ancient Holy of Holies by his presence).

The Franciscan friar Francesco Suriano, author of *Treatise on the Holy Land,* noted with satisfaction in 1485 that "in Jerusalem where [the Jews] committed the sin for which they are now dispersed

---

* Two such inscriptions from the first century BC, on hard limestone, have been found in Jerusalem. One is on exhibit in Jerusalem today at the Rockefeller Museum. Only after 1967 were all holy places in the city opened indiscriminately to visitors, regardless of their particular faith. (The great mosques on the Temple Mount are accessible to the general public at fixed hours, when no services are held.)

throughout the world, they are by God more punished and afflicted than in any other part of the world." For long periods, Jews were unable to move freely within the Old City itself. An Ottoman firman (imperial edict) of April 29, 1534, on exhibit in the Jerusalem archive of the Franciscan Custodia di Terra Sancta, contains "the order to the Jews of Jerusalem to proclaim on every Sabbath from the pulpit of the synagogue of their nation that none of them is allowed to pass through the piazza of the Holy Sepulchre nor over the terrain of Mount Sion or any other Christian sanctuary."

Three centuries later, the situation was not much changed. On Good Friday in 1864, observed Ermete Pierotti, an Italian architect in the employ of the Turkish pasha of Jerusalem, Jews dared not leave their small quarter west of the Wailing Wall "as the Latins, Greeks and Armenians would insult and otherwise ill-treat them. On some occasions the pasha has been obliged to guard the entrances of their streets with bodies of soldiers and police to protect them from the fanatical Christians, who would have made an attack upon them." According to Pierotti, "all the native population unfortunately still hold the opinion that to injure a Jew is a work well pleasing in the sight of God."

The new class of enlightened western consular officials was not free from the bigotry of the old. James Finn, in Pierotti's days the British consul in Jerusalem, was known for his humanitarian interest in the welfare of Moslems and Jews. As president of the newly formed Jerusalem Literary Society, he defined its purpose as the study of "Mohammedan imposture" and "rabbinical monstrosities." Perhaps faith was not diminished by such statements; organized religion was.

A few decades later, the consolidated animosities began to spill over into nationalism. Eating into the heart of patriotism as well as into religion, they often turned both into rankling spleen and bigotry. As open violence erupted between Moslems and Jews, the dividing line between nationalism and religion was further blurred. "The Moslem clergy in my time [1926–1929]," Arthur Koestler remembered, "used to call on the average twice a year for a holy bloodbath. A peaceful Arab landlord would joke with the family of his Jewish tenant during Ramadan, go to the mosque, listen to the imam, run home and slaughter tenant, wife and children with a kitchen knife. . . . I have never lived at such close quarters with divinity and never farther removed from it."

In the 1920s and 1930s, the mere rumor of a riot would cause the iron shutters in the Old City to roll down noisily. In our own day, Moslem fundamentalists have preached and practiced several jihads (holy wars) against Jews; and Jewish fundamentalists have come to regard Arabs as Amalekites, the people who, in the Bronze Age, Jehovah commanded they make war on and destroy. Jewish fundamentalists cite and re-cite God's promise to Abraham — "Unto thy seed will I give this land" — rarely pausing to reflect that Abraham's seed included Ishmael as well. The fundamentalists are still a minority among modern Jewish Jerusalemites. But the well-known Psalm 137 — "By the rivers of Babylon, there we sat down, yea, we wept, when we remembered Zion" — is not only a song of love and longing, but a savage song of vengeance as well, as in the less frequently cited continuation:

> O daughter of Babylon, who art to be destroyed. . . .
> Happy shall he be, that taketh and dasheth thy
>   little ones against the stones.

A curious similarity evolved over the years between Jewish and Moslem fundamentalists and extremists, as though a mirror had come down between them in the middle of Jerusalem. Amos Oz, the novelist, a native of Jerusalem, was not engaging in mere rhetoric when he said that she is a city where everybody is a kind of messiah, eager to crucify his opponents for their beliefs, ready to be crucified himself for his own.

Most Near Eastern religions, of course, are linked to ethnic groups. Some have always been outright national religions. The Armenian church is fiercely nationalistic. Like the Jewish, it is fired by the myth of a lost homeland to be regained. The Greek Catholic and the Greek Orthodox churches, the Russian Orthodox, the Ruma-nian and the Bulgarian churches, the Egyptian (Coptic) church, the Ethiopian, the Syrian Jacobite and the Lebanese (Maronite) churches — to mention only a few — are national churches. The

Latin church, headed since 1987 by a Palestinian patriarch, is rapidly becoming one. The Anglican church in Jerusalem, established over a century ago for imperial reasons, under a converted German Jew, is today predominantly Arab, under a Palestinian bishop.

The national character of Judaism almost goes without saying. The conjunction of Jewish Passover and Christian Easter in Jerusalem apparently so aroused Moslem apprehensions in the Middle Ages that Saladin, otherwise so tolerant, invented the Moslem feast of Nabi Musa (Prophet Moses) to take place in Jerusalem during the same spring month. In the Jewish tradition, Moses died in Moab and "no man knoweth of his sepulchre unto this day." But according to Moslem lore, Moses disliked his burial place in Moab and rolled himself underground to a tomb on the outskirts of Jericho, down the old Roman road from Jerusalem. Saladin built a shrine on this spot. Under Ottoman rule, a great procession each year wound its way down the mountain to the tomb. The procession would start on Good Friday and was marked by anti-Christian overtones and sometimes by violence, since on that day the Christians would wander up the same road in the opposite direction. In this century, the feast of Nabi Musa took on a nationalistic, anti-Jewish character. As processions of the pious and the ecstatic, together with hordes of the politically turbulent, made their way through Jerusalem on their way to the cenotaph, tempers always ran hot and violence often ensued.

In the 1920s, according to an eyewitness, on a Passover that coincided with Nabi Musa, tensions ran so high "a horse would bolt in the Old City and within five minutes every shop in the bazaar would be closed and armed soldiers would patrol the alleys." Jews and Moslems clashed in bloody riots. In the Jewish quarters of Jerusalem and Hebron, whole families were massacred by the Arab mob. Shops were looted and burned.

Moslem clerics and politicians now claimed that the Wailing Wall was not a Jewish but a Moslem sanctuary. One of their spokesmen told an international commission in 1930 that Jews had no right to worship at the wall except "as a favour granted them by the Moslems. . . . [They may] visit the Wall area but without raising their voices or staging a ceremony there. . . . The Wall is a purely Moslem site and an integral part of the sacred mosque of al Aqsa. Moslems and Christians feel very strongly about this from a political and religious point of view."

By this time, Jewish and Arab public opinion had long removed such issues from the purely religious orbit and had made them political and national problems. When, in 1929, a Jewish boy kicked a football into an Arab garden in the Old City, Moslem fanatics, yelling "Allah akbar!" (God is great), stabbed the innocent child dead. Jews protested this death at a demonstration staged on the occasion of the boy's funeral. Within hours, there was an Arab counterdemonstration. Before long, 133 Jews and 116 Arabs lay dead and 571 (339 Jews and 232 Arabs) wounded.

Politics and religion were henceforth intertwined, in Laocoön complexity, within the history of the city and the Arab-Israel conflict. For the secular on both sides, "history" itself became a kind of faith. The political discourse was suffused with religious rhetoric. Each side insisted that Jerusalem was "more sacred," religiously and politically speaking, to it than to the other. Jews maintained that they had only one Jerusalem. ("Mecca is *their* holy city," ran this argument, "and they have Medina, too. Jerusalem is all ours." Or, "Jerusalem is not once mentioned in the Koran, but over seven hundred times in the Bible!") Arabs claimed that historically the Jewish presence in the city was a passing episode. ("Jerusalem should be handed back to its true children. The Palestinians are the direct descendants of the aboriginal Amorites, Canaanites, and Jebusites!") According to this argument, the ancient Hebrews, under Joshua, had been just another "foreign invasion," like the Babylonians or the British.

No question of current history or politics would any longer be considered apart from some form of religious bias, by opponents whose every move was informed by passionate faith. On the Jewish side, there were at least a few celebrated attempts to resist the growing infusion of national politics with religious bias. (On the Arab side, there were none.) In 1929, during the Jewish-Moslem controversy over the control of the Western Wall area, the Jewish leaders asked Gershom Scholem, the well-known expert on Jewish mysticism, to supply them with kabbalistic texts that might strengthen Jewish religious and historic claims. Scholem refused and for this he was soon attacked in the press as an unpatriotic, if not "self-hating," Jew. Scholem's argument was that the conflict over the Western Wall was political. As such, it should be a matter for political negotiations, not for the mutual brandishing of mystic texts. The political conflict between Arabs and Jews was difficult enough, he argued; there was no reason to make it even more difficult by introducing religious arguments.

Scholem's view would soon be a more or less isolated one, even among Jews. The liturgies of both sides associated the events of 1948 or 1967 with the intentions of heaven or hell, even as the Crusaders and the Saracens had done in 1099 or 1187. In each of the five wars fought between Arabs and Israelis between 1948 and 1982, Moslem clerics have habitually summoned the faithful to jihad, holy war, for the liberation of Jerusalem: "Do not call them dead who fall for Allah — they live forever even if they are insensate!"

When the Jewish quarter in the Old City of Jerusalem fell to the Arabs in 1948, twenty-two of the twenty-seven synagogues there were burned down by the mob and the remaining five were sacked and dismantled by the Jordanian army. In the early 1960s, Christian Arab clerics in East Jerusalem protested the Vatican's intended exoneration of Jews from the guilt of deicide; some warned that this was just another Zionist plot. Jewish clerics, for their part, declared that the Shekinah, the Divine Spirit itself, had marched ahead of the victorious Israeli troops in the taking of Jerusalem in 1967. Secular politicians sounded a similar note. Yitzhak Navon, a future president of the state (and later minister of education), in 1978 published a long patriotic poem about that war. Its essence is a heated plea to God from each of the seven gates of the Old City of Jerusalem. A kitschier application of religion to current politics would be difficult to imagine, especially from a well-known secular Jew. In the poem, the gates "speak." Each gate demands that God order the Israeli armored units advancing on the Old City to break in through it. God is asked to rule "which gate deserves to have the redemption come through it." (God finally decides in favor of the Lions' Gate because, unlike the other gates, it had "belittled itself.")

The late W. H. Auden remembered standing in 1970 with Teddy Kollek, the liberal mayor of Jerusalem, on a terrace overlooking the Old City and the pink, bare, luminous hills beyond. Palestinian terrorists had just exploded a hand grenade at a busy intersection in

downtown Jerusalem, wounding several pedestrians. Orthodox rioters had just clashed with the police in a northern suburb. In an
offhand manner, the mayor remarked that Jerusalem would be a
beautiful place if it were not for the wars, and the orthodox of all
faiths, their squabbles and their riots. He said this, Auden recalled,
"as one might say in London that it would be lovely except for the
weather."

Omar, the Arab conqueror of Jerusalem, had a clear sense of the
dangers inherent in places sacred to more than one faith. As he was
shown through the Holy Sepulchre in 638, he declined an invitation
by the patriarch Sophronius to pray there. "If I had prayed in the
church," he told the clergyman, "it would have been lost to you, for
the Believers would have taken it, saying 'Omar prayed here.' "
Omar's successors were less sagacious, unfortunately, with regard
to the holy places of the Jews. As a result, the pilgrim itineraries of
Moslems and Christians in Jerusalem do not intersect; but those of
Jews and Moslems do.

Next to the great Moslem and Christian shrines in Jerusalem, the
Western Wall, until a few years ago, seemed paltry. There was
nothing spectacular, nothing more than a stone surface completely
unadorned, the remains of an old retaining wall, built by Herod the
Great in 20 BC to support the temple platform in the west (hence
the name). Its full length was invisible. Most of it was hidden by
houses. At the southern end, a short stretch was free. The stones
were huge and beautifully cut. Several rows were still the original
Herodian; the rest were of more recent, Turkish, origin. Next to
the Great Wall of China, this was perhaps the most famous wall in
the world. For centuries, it had also been called Wailing Place of the
Jews. Its legal status was unclear. In the nineteenth century, according to British consul James Finn, the Jewish community had to pay
"300 [pounds?] a year to the effendi whose house adjoins the wall
for permission to pray there." Jews came to the wall to pray and
lament the destruction of their temple. They would kiss the rugged
stones and stick into the crevices bits of paper scribbled with personal prayers or petitions of a more general nature to the Almighty.

During the first two or three decades of this century, the wall area open to Jewish prayer was barely one hundred feet long and ten feet wide. It was a dank alleyway, narrow and short. Gray stone hovels, inhabited by poor Moslem families, came to within ten or twelve feet of the wall itself. The south and north ends were blocked up by other structures. There is no record before the seventeenth century that this narrow alleyway was also sacred to the Moslems. In the seventeenth century, apparently, Moslems began to identify it as the site where Mohammed on his way to heaven had tied up his remarkable horse, al-Buraq. It has been claimed, but not proven, that in the Middle Ages Moslems still venerated the Golden Gate as the site where Mohammed entered the sanctuary. According to this theory, the site of al-Buraq was shifted to the Western Wall only after Jewish rights to worship at the wall were informally recognized by the Ottoman sultans. Be that as it may, much blood has been spilled over the issue in this century.

The first bloody riot erupted in 1919. There were several efforts to restore peace at the wall among the contesting parties. All ended in failure. A succession of more or less judicious British colonial officials dealt with the problem, now siding with the Jews, now with the Moslems. The Jews wanted to sound a shofar, a ram's horn, at the wall, as they do in synagogue during Rosh Hashanah (New Year) services. Moslem clergymen and politicians let it be known that in their view the blowing of a shofar at the wall was a deadly offense to Islam; they could not countenance it even once a year. Their sudden vehemence was, of course, a result of the growing political conflict between Arabs and Jews. The Jews wanted to place a couple of wooden benches by the wall, as they had done for centuries, for old men to sit on while they prayed. The Moslem clergy were absolutely opposed to this, too. They regarded the placing of benches by the wall, even if only for a few hours each week, as a usurpation of inalienable Moslem rights dating back to the days of the prophet and his saintly disciples. Moslem clergymen and politicians claimed the wall was an integral — and sacred — part of the great mosques behind it. Jews might pray there, if they must, but on sufferance only. "Their tears and kisses at the wall do not result from their love for it, as everyone knows, but from their hidden desire to seize control over the sacred mosques of the Haram al-Sharif [Noble Sanctuary]."

The far end of the narrow alley in front of the wall had been a dead end for at least two centuries. In 1920, a new entrance was cut through it by one of the Arab neighbors. The Moslem clergy declared it a public thoroughfare. To further press the point, cattle were driven into the alleyway to harass the worshipers alongside the wall. A muezzin was stationed above to proclaim five times a day the One True God, Compassionate and Merciful.

One morning in 1928, a small, cloth screen, not more than a yard long, was placed in the alleyway by Jewish worshipers, to separate men from women during services, according to Orthodox custom. This scruffy little piece of furniture — according to an eyewitness, "exactly like an ordinary bedroom screen" — marked the opening of a terrible new chapter in the internecine feud between Moslem and Jew. Hundreds died in the riots that ensued. The two sides finally presented their conflicting cases to an international inquiry commission appointed by the League of Nations: a Swedish professor, a Swiss federal judge, and a former Dutch colonial governor. Jewish spokesmen pleaded with the commissioners to recognize their right to worship at the very last of their holy shrines — all others were lost — "one side only of a small part of a wall bordering on the site of their ancient sanctuary . . . and where for two thousand years this people has stood, in the open air, in the heat of summer and in the winter rains, pouring its heart out to God in heaven. And it is denied even this meager right."

Moslem spokesmen argued not less passionately that by canonic law the wall was a Moslem sanctuary; by civil law, it was the absolute property of a Moslem *waqf* (charitable foundation). Moslem rights at the wall were ancient and inalienable. "Moslems will not surrender to any verdict touching upon their faith even if the entire world passes it."

Content and tenor of the arguments presented by the two sides reflected the chasm between them, which the commission's final (mildly pro-Jewish) verdict was unable to bridge. The Moslems rejected it out of hand. The British authorities followed it up with a Solomonic order (issued May 19, 1931) by the King's Most Excellent Majesty in Council. The Moslems declared this new decree a travesty of justice; the Jews labeled it insensitive and humiliating. The Order declared the Western Wall and the pavement in front as unquestionably "Moslem property, . . . seeing that [they] form an integral part of the *Haram al Sharif* area." Jews, however, should have "free access . . . for the purpose of devotion at all times." They may not use a partition, or raise their voices in song. The blowing of a shofar was also forbidden. The Cabinet of the Ark, where the Torah scrolls are kept, had to be portable and removed from the wall area after each Sabbath service. It was no longer permissible to bring the Ark out on weekdays. Its dimensions were defined by law. A high-level government official was to come out periodically to check that it was not in excess of the prescribed 102 by 50 by 30 centimeters. Jews were also allowed "a wash-basin and water container on a stand," both portable, and subject to seasonal inspection by the authorities to ascertain that their measurements were within the rules stipulated by law. All other "appurtenances of worship" were forbidden, especially benches or chairs.

At the same time, the order granted Moslems the right of free passage through the wall area at all times. They were enjoined only from driving cattle through the crowds of worshipers "between 8 A.M. and 3 P.M. on Saturdays and government recognised Jewish holidays." A permanent police post was stationed at the wall.

How futile even this precaution was is evidenced by a contemporary document — the diary kept by Isaac Victor Orenstein, a Jerusalem rabbi in charge of religious observances at the Western Wall. He kept an almost daily record. A few typical entries:

Feb. 9, 1932: Yesterday Arabs beat drums and kettles and disturbed the prayer. . . . British and Arab policemen stood by and did not intervene. A couple of Arab lads walked through the Wall area smoking cigarettes; when a young Jew approached them and told them they were not being fair, a British policeman interfered and told the young man he was causing a disturbance.

Apr. 13, 1933: At 6:30 A.M., Jews who arrived at the Wall for prayer found a heap of human excrement in one corner.

Apr. 14, 1933: The venerable old rabbi Sonnenfeld came in the morning to pray. One of those present pushed up a low stool to enable him to rest awhile. Immediately, the police rushed up and pulled the chair out from under him.

Apr. 2, 1934: Sergeant Wright informed me that the sheik of Abu Madyan [the nearby mosque] has filed charges with the police against me and the caretaker Mr. Mejuchass for having swept the Wall area with brooms and water on the eve of Passover in violation of the law forbidding Jews to clean the Wall area.

Feb. 22, 1936: The [octogenarian] rabbi Moshe Grossman complained that human excrements were thrown on him on his way to the Wall. . . . Later, stones were thrown on us during prayers [from a nearby roof]. The police asked Grossman if he thought the excrement had been thrown deliberately.

Nov. 5, 1935: Sheep were driven past the Wall repeatedly, back and forth, during morning prayers, but since it was not a Sabbath, the police did not intervene.

Dec. 30, 1935: At noon, I found excrement smeared on parts of the Wall. . . . The duty officer asked if I intended to file a complaint. I said I did not know against whom, but that I asked the police to be more alert. . . .

Jan. 23, 1936: The sheik of Abu Madyan has filed charges for finding two nails, where the caretaker hangs the towels on the Wall next to the washbasin. . . . The British corporal questioned me on this. I said we don't need the nails and the sheik can have them if he wishes.

June 4, 1937: I found many bits of paper, of the kind Jews push into crevices in the Wall, burned to ashes on the ground. . . . The policeman on duty claimed he had not seen or heard anything throughout the whole night.

Sept. 1, 1938: Once again, tonight there was no regular guard on duty by the Wall. The British constables told me the reason: the danger of assaults [by rioters] during the night.

Sept. 2, 1938: The expected finally took place last night. While the regular guard was absent during the night, the police post by the Wall was burned down with all its contents. . . . The attackers first fired some 45 shots at the post. Seeing that there was no response, they came down [from the Temple Mount], burned the wooden hut, and took the telephone with them. . . . The [Arab] neighbors claim they have heard nothing and seen nothing. A new telephone was brought. It was screwed on to the Wall proper, which caused much anger among the pious.

Oct. 16, 1938: On my way to the Wall, . . . I was stopped by a police patrol and told they were under orders not to let anyone go to the Wall because of the danger.

Oct. 29, 1938: Arriving at the Wall this morning for the first time — after an intermission of two weeks — I discovered to my sorrow that the Wall was brutally desecrated. Bits of stone were chopped off. The marauders lit a fire and succeeded in blackening the face of the Wall with soot. The congregation was very upset. . . . Accompanied by the British sergeant and constable, I visited the rooms where we store the sacred vessels and discovered they have all been burned and destroyed: Torah scrolls, washbasin, bookshelves, more than two hundred prayerbooks and Psalms. . . .

Nov. 5, 1938: An Arab neighbor, residing in one of the houses facing the Wall, informed me that the desecration was the work of a gang of some two hundred armed men, all of them villagers. There was no way to stop them. Despite the situation, this Sabbath some three hundred visited and prayed at the Wall. . . .

The author of this diary was shot dead by an Arab sniper in 1948.

CHAPTER FOUR

Dangerous City

THERE was still sporadic gunfire in the Old City when, during the war of 1967, the chief chaplain of the Israeli army raced through the via Dolorosa with a Torah scroll in one hand and a shofar in the other. "Don't be rude," he yelled at a young infantry officer who tried to hold him back. The chaplain turned left, ducking gunfire as he ran, and a few minutes later reached the narrow alley in front of the Western Wall. Here, he triumphantly raised the scroll and blew his shofar.

No Israelis had worshiped at the wall for more than nineteen years. Shofars had been outlawed there since 1931. The rare foreign Jew who had reached the area between 1948 and 1967 had been able to do so only by producing a bogus baptismal certificate.

The wall area had been captured by Israeli troops less than an hour before. A dozen or so soldiers were gathered before it, some of them wounded. They welcomed the chaplain with loud cheers. The chaplain blew the shofar again. The harsh wail hung in the hot air, unfurling like a flag. Some of the soldiers wept. All were deeply moved. The scene has been described by several eyewitnesses. There was a smell of gunpowder in the air. The mood was one of exultation. It was not necessarily a religious experience, though for some it must have been that, too. The young soldiers at the Western Wall — and the mass of civilian Israelis who would come soon after — were face to face, many for the first time in their lives, with the most important historic relic of their people.

There was a certain irony in the fact that in a "new" nation, largely secular until this time, the relic was a religious site. But there was no other. The Western Wall was both trophy and myth — what the French call *architecture parlante*. Its capture conveyed a message most people wanted to hear at this time in an unambiguous manner. The wall was a monument in the domain of memory and of faith. At this moment, it symbolized a widespread urge to transform the political into the religious. The victory in the 1967 war — its high point was in Jerusalem, in what was called the liberation of the Western Wall — had come to most Israelis as a surprise. Many seemed to feel something miraculous had been involved. Rabbis spoke of messianic stirrings. Politicians referred to the finger of God. Jerusalem — until 1967, a sleepy little town at the far end of a narrow corridor in the hills — came to personify a new element in the consciousness of the nation. The Western Wall emerged as a national monument as well, a secular shrine, set aside as a sacred space for the self-expression of Israel. The first tendency after its capture was to place it in the care of the National Parks Authority.

Before 1967, Israelis had been a people with too much history and too little geography. After 1967, the opposite became true. The territory of Israel prior to the 1967 war, while rich in Roman, Nabataean, and Crusader ruins, actually had few historical monuments testifying to its Jewish past. The pre-1967 territory of Israel embraced not the historic homeland of the ancient Hebrews, who had been a people of the hills, but rather that of their enemies in the coastal plain, the Philistines, as well as the Negev of the Edomites and the so-called Galilee of the Gentiles. The 1967 war abruptly confronted modern Israelis with the geography of their remote history. Its cradle was not Tel Aviv, an ultramodern city on the sea, but the walled Old City of Jerusalem, where the ancient Jewish temple had stood. In the words of one prominent witness: "We felt we were joining hands with history."

In the weeks following the war, hundreds of thousands streamed to Jerusalem, and to the wall, where for a time it seemed, almost, as though the past was but the backward continuum of the present. For many, it was a dream come true, the ancient Jewish dream to stand at the Wailing Wall as free men. Devout people, who had been unable to worship at the wall for years, kissed and hugged the soldiers who had fought to allow them back. There were also moments when, judging by sights and sounds alone, the scenes at the

Western Wall resembled the rituals in southern Italy following a "miracle." Women ululated. Men sobbed.

The name given to the war suggested six mystic days of creation and rebirth. Israel had won that war against great odds. Her enemies had foolishly provoked it. It had resulted in enormous, unexpected territorial gains. The most emotionally charged gains were in Jerusalem. In the context of that war and of the dread and panic that had preceded it — only twenty-two years had passed since the Nazi holocaust — there was an element of catharsis in the general exultation. There was a foreboding as well.

Amos Oz, the novelist, was serving in the army at that time. He remembered wandering through East Jerusalem one day after the war, in uniform and armed with an automatic rifle, wishing very much to feel like a man who had vanquished his foes and regained the city of his forefathers. He very much wanted to share and be part of the general celebration. "But people are living there. They are at *home* and I am the *intruder*." If only there had not been all those Palestinians. "I saw enmity and resentment, hypocrisy, fear and degradation and new evil being plotted." He felt like a man who had broken into a forbidden place. "A stranger in a foreign city."

This was a minority view in the aftermath of the war. As it fused in some hearts the intransigence of aroused nationalism with the archaisms of religious fundamentalism, so it produced new areas of friction between Israelis and Arabs. The Temple Mount — a great Moslem sanctuary now, but in antiquity the site of the great Jewish temples — was a case in point.

On the Temple Mount, the fusion of nationalism and religion was producing a critical mass. Safety measures to prevent an explosion — with unforeseeable consequences — would henceforth be a major concern for every Israeli government. Friction over the Temple Mount began almost at once. A few hours after it had been taken by Israeli troops, Moshe Dayan, the defense minister, announced: "We have returned to our most sacred sites never to leave them again." But with his keen eye for spots where trouble is best avoided, Dayan immediately ordered the Israeli flag removed from the Dome of the Rock — where it had been hoisted by enthusiastic Israeli soldiers — as an unnecessary and dangerous ostentation. (A photograph of that flag later served Arab and Iranian horror-propaganda: "Jews defile our holiest mosques.")

Dayan did not — or could not — prevent an equally ostentatious military parade in the forecourt of the great mosques. The victorious troops were addressed there by their commander, Colonel Mordechai Gur (a future chief of staff), with the words: "You have been privileged to restore to the people of Israel their capital and their sanctuary." (In his memoirs, Gur described his feelings in the sanctuary, and his reason for choosing *not* to visit the Western Wall on that day, with a certain braggadocio: "I had achieved my aim. The Temple Mount *is* the Western Wall, too. On the Temple Mount, I am in the drawing room. I am not attracted by the exterior walls. Here I feel at home. The farthest frontiers of longing. Temple Mount. Mount Moriah! Abraham and Isaac. The zealots. The Maccabees. Bar Kokhba. Romans and Greeks. All converge in one's thoughts.")

Dayan solemnly promised the Moslem clergy that there would be no tampering with their control over the area. He also reinstated the Arab security men, employed by the Moslem Supreme Council, as guardians within the sacred precincts. He asked only that Jews be permitted to enter as peaceful visitors. The request was granted — not surprisingly, under the circumstances — though with reluctance. "These are Moslem mosques," Dayan later wrote, "and the Moslems are entitled to be autonomous there." He clearly underestimated the passions generated among Jewish nationalist and religious extremists by this policy and his statements about it.

Prominent voices in Israel were soon calling for the eviction of all Moslem "abominations" from the Temple Mount. After all (so the argument ran), the Maccabees, too, in 165 BC, had demolished and thrown out the idols from God's temple, after their victory over the Greeks. Others proposed to construct a Jewish synagogue on the wide platform between the two mosques. The government firmly resisted all such calls.

The government at that time comprised, as it still does today, a secular majority and a minority of religious politicians. The former feared a bloodbath. The latter wished, above all, to conform to the letter of halakah, Jewish religious law. According to Jewish lore, the third temple shall be built only by God after the coming of the messiah. A rabbinic injunction forbids Jews to set foot anywhere on the Temple Mount for fear of a possible desecration of the site of the former Holy of Holies. Though this is often thought to be under the Dome of the Rock, its exact location is not known. Lest someone step on it inadvertently — everyone is considered impure today — the ritual taboo was extended to the entire Temple Mount area.

But the war, which inflamed powerful national passions among the secular, also aroused deep messianic stirrings among the religious. Repossession of the Temple Mount was construed as a sacred duty by a small but vocal minority of fundamentalists. Traditional Jewish religious leaders saw themselves challenged by a new breed of militant radical rabbis who proclaimed that messianic days were near. They were joined by right-wing nationalists, who were attracted to the Temple Mount as a powerful national symbol. Anti-Arab feelings were widespread in the aftermath of the war. A public-opinion poll commissioned by the municipality of Jerusalem disclosed so much Jewish hostility toward Arabs that the results were never released in order not to poison the atmosphere even more.

With the proverbial sword in one hand and the Bible in the other, some of the more zealous in Jerusalem argued that legendary deeds contracted during the Bronze Age were sound legal basis for concrete real-estate claims as good as those made only yesterday in the Jerusalem District Court. One leading Orthodox rabbi bluntly announced that in the war of 1967 Israeli bayonets had established "the Rule of God" throughout the Holy Land. Fervent expectation soon produced spectacular results. Tombs of renowned Hebrew prophets and kings, all said to be absolutely authentic, as well as Saul's own throne and Samson's alleged cave were being discovered almost daily by enthusiastic and inspired amateur archaeologists. The new discoveries also included tombs of relatively minor biblical figures such as Abner, King Saul's chief of staff, and the prophet Nathan. (The "discoveries" were reminiscent of similar finds during the First Crusade — for example, the discovery of the "holy lance" at Antioch and the recognition by Baldwin I of the "cup of the Last Supper" among the booty at Caesarea.) The minister of religious affairs issued an official statement criticizing a well-known ar-

chaeologist, Professor Yigael Yadin, for suggesting in the press that
the medieval tombstones within the great mosque at Hebron were
not those of Abraham, Isaac, Jacob, and their respective spouses
but, more probably, those of a few long-forgotten Arab sheiks.
Some old stones, of whatever origin, became the subject of an
adoration that bordered on fetishism. While reminiscent in many
ways of Catholic practice — the cherishing of bits of the cross, the
handkerchief or footprint of Jesus, the tooth or nail of a saint — this
was a new element in the traditionally abstract character of Jewish
religious worship, at least in the West. In the Levant, there had
always been among Jews a certain amount of tomb and relic worship.

A few hours after East Jerusalem surrendered, Dayan flamboy-
antly ordered army engineers to bulldoze a road through the surrounding hills wide enough to enable "every Jew in the world to
reach the Western Wall." Accommodating the masses at the wall
itself was a more complicated task. In the narrow alley in front of
the Western Wall, there was room for 200 or 250 worshipers at the
most. To make way for the endless stream of people about to
descend on the area, an entire densely populated neighborhood —
including a small mosque — was razed overnight. Its Moslem inhabitants were given three hours to move out. Bulldozers and heavy
road rollers driven by ecstatic civilian volunteers crushed and
packed tight the debris to produce a flat surface. "In two days it was
done, finished, clean," Mayor Kollek boasted in his memoirs. In a
statement characteristic of the mood of the time, he urged
everybody to stop using the century-old term Wall of Tears, or
Wailing Wall. According to Kollek, the time of tears was over.

South of the new plaza by the Western Wall, which was big
enough to hold at least a hundred thousand people, a ramp led up
to the Temple Mount. Large signs, put there by order of the chief
rabbi, reminded Orthodox Jews of the rabbinic rule against entering the sacred precincts. More warnings were posted elsewhere
in the Old City. As time passed, they were ignored more and more
readily by fundamentalists driven by messianic stirrings.

Leading them was one of Dayan's senior officers — soon to be
elected chief rabbi of Israel — the then chief military chaplain,
Major General Shlomo Goren. He believed he was hearing the

footsteps of the messiah and that fate had cast him, Goren, in the role of being his herald. On August 16, 1967 (the 1,897th anniversary of the burning of the temple by the Romans), Goren, in full military garb and followed by a group of fervent disciples, broke through the stunned Moslem guards onto the Temple Mount. Goren claimed he had unraveled the great secret of the ages, enabling him to circumvent the ritual taboo. He did not claim he knew the location of the Holy of Holies, but he thought it was possible to say with assurance where it had *not* been: in the large courtyards between the two mosques. Jews may, even should, set foot there — after due preparation, of course, which included fasting, prayer, and ritual baths. Goren led a prayer service in these forecourts and proclaimed his intention to build a synagogue there. Throwing fresh fuel on the flames of religious discord, Goren argued that the mosques' courtyards were not sacred to Moslems, as they were to Jews. Moslems themselves were admitting to this, he polemicized, by removing their shoes only inside the mosques, never outside, on the surrounding platform.

Panic spread among the Moslems of Jerusalem. Goren was reprimanded by his superiors, but his demonstration lent new weight to an Arab obsession dating from the days of the British mandate, a Moslem preoccupation that was reinforced by Nazi propaganda during World War II: the belief that the Jews were determined to raze the mosques in order to rebuild their temple. The government promised the Moslem clergy that the next time Goren tried to enter the sacred precincts he would be stopped by the police. The panic abated, only to be rekindled a few days later by the minister of religious affairs, the ultra-Orthodox Zerach Warhaftig. The minister declared in an interview that by civil law, the Jews were the "owners" of the Temple Mount and of everything on it. The interviewer wondered how this could possibly be. The minister explained that the Jews had retained a valid title since the days of David, "who had paid the full price for it [fifty shekels of silver] to Araunah the Jebusite, as is recorded in Samuel II, chapter 24, verse 24."

Question: "Haven't a few things happened in the thousands of years since then? Are you saying that the Temple Mount . . . is Jewish property even today?"

Warhaftig: "Yes, [it was] acquired in more than one sense.
Generations have shed blood in order to make the Land of Israel
ours; and the full price was paid [by David] in money as well."

The minister went on to say that while there was no doubt that
Jewish rights on the Temple Mount overrode those of the Moslems, and while the Jews even had a right to raze the mosques there,
they had no intention at the moment of actually doing so. The
implication was that this was so only for the time being, and so it
was understood. The atmosphere has remained poisoned ever since
by the continuing rhetoric of the fervent and by recurrent violence.
The legal battle has remained unresolved. Successive Israeli govern-
ments and courts have thrown the ball back and forth between
them, avoiding a clear-cut decision on this issue.

The 1967 Israeli Law for the Protection of Holy Places was passed
simultaneously with the act of annexation of East Jerusalem. It did
not address itself directly to the question of holy places sacred to
more than one faith. The law guaranteed members of all faiths
freedom of access to *their* holy places. Freedom of access seemed to
imply freedom of worship as well. The courts have since formally
proclaimed the Temple Mount a "Jewish holy place" and have upheld the right of Jews to worship there. But, on the basis of an old
British decree, the courts conveniently sidestepped the main issue
by holding the executive branch responsible for public order at the
holy places. The executive has until now ordered the police to
enable Jews to visit but not to hold prayer services on the Temple
Mount. The situation has left everybody unhappy. Liberals have
protested the absence of a decision in principle. Fundamentalists
have protested the Kafkaesque surrealism of not being able to exercise what is recognized as a "legitimate" right by the highest court
in the land. Islamists and Arabists continue to warn of a possible
Armageddon as a result of tampering with Moslem rights on the
Temple Mount. The Moslem clergy continue to live in fear, knowing that what is "legitimate" might not for very long remain disal-
lowed. They have never recognized Jewish rights at the Western
Wall and are even less inclined to bend on the issue of Jewish rights
to pray on the Temple Mount itself.

This is one of the reasons for the long-standing refusal by the
Moslem clergy to allow archaeological surveys on the Temple

Mount. Aerial photography suggests that there have been extensive physical changes there since 1967. Several pre-Islamic archaeological remains on the Temple Mount seem to have been bulldozed away or buried under lawns. Tunnels leading to ancient Jewish vaults under the Dome of the Rock have been walled up. The Moslem clergy are said to have made great efforts, since 1967, to obliterate all physical traces linking the Temple Mount to its Jewish past. This may be a hopeless undertaking; but it is easy to see the fears that have inspired it.

Prominent Israeli figures have continued to advocate holding Jewish religious observances on the Temple Mount. Among them have been two chief rabbis, Shlomo Goren (1969–1979) and Mordechai Eliahu (1982–). Goren ordered the removal of the signs placed by his predecessor at the entrance to the Temple Mount. Eliahu, shortly before his election as chief rabbi, pronounced him-self in favor of evicting the infidels from the Temple Mount. At the very least, he would establish a synagogue and a yeshiva there. "We see with our own eyes," he explained,

> that foxes roam there and strangers walk upon and desecrate the site of which it has been said that "the stranger that cometh nigh shall be put to death." Our sages of blessed memory ruled that pagans were unclean and forbidden entry to the holy place. There is a sacred duty to prevent this sad state of affairs [from continuing], and let no one fear of what [gentiles] might say.

The fate of the new large plaza in front of the Western Wall is another indication of where things might be heading. After it was cleared and provisionally paved in stone, the Canadian-Israeli ar-chitect Moshe Safdie was invited by the municipality to submit plans for the permanent structuring of the entire site and its im-mediate environs. Safdie and the municipality have submitted at least four proposals since 1970, only to see each rejected by the rabbinate. The rabbinate has even opposed shade trees, preferring the plaza's present rather improvised, provisional look. Meir Yehuda Getz, the rabbi in charge of the Western Wall, explained why: "Safdie's plans were too grandiose. . . . I don't want the Wall to be the Third Temple." It was not that Getz did not want to see the third temple. He wanted it built, he told an interviewer, but in the right place — on the Temple Mount itself. "You will see," he said, "the right moment to build it [there] will come. Perhaps there was such a moment in 1967. We missed it."

Question: "What about the mosques on the Temple Mount?"

Getz: "No worry! They will disappear. . . . The Almighty will destroy them. *We* will lend him a helping hand." Getz, according to the interviewer, gave a knowing smile. Then he added: "The scenario is clear."

Maniacs and cranks have thought so all along. Now and then, someone steps forward to lend God a helping hand. On a hot August day in 1969, at seven o'clock in the morning, flames suddenly shot through al-Aqsa mosque above the Western Wall. A mentally disturbed, twenty-nine-year-old Australian tourist named Denis Michael Rohan had found his way into the locked mosque at this early hour and stuffed a load of kerosine-soaked cotton under a wooden pulpit. After lighting the rags with a match, Rohan calmly walked out, watched by unsuspecting guards (who recognized him later).

Within minutes, the mosque was ablaze. Rohan watched it burn from a distance — laughing (as he claimed later in his confession to the police) and taking pictures with an Instamatic camera. Rohan was a member of a chiliastic Protestant Christian sect. He believed that unless all "abominations" were removed from the Temple Mount, the Second Coming of Christ or that of the Jewish messiah — it was never made clear which — would suffer a tragic delay. His ambition was to end this delay, which he believed was causing sin and unhappiness throughout the world. Rohan believed that the burning of al-Aqsa would usher in the millennium. He saw himself as God's special envoy for that purpose. He wanted the Jewish temple rebuilt, "for sweet Jesus to return and pray in it." He had been roused to his task in Australia, he told the police; it seems he was listening on his shortwave radio to a station called Radio Church of God, and in fact had come to Israel to better hear the transmissions, which emanated from Amman, Jordan.

The fire quickly spread to the dome at the southern end of the mosque and to the heavy old beams under the roof, which came crashing down. Crowds of infuriated Moslems gathered on the Temple Mount, protesting the presumed torching of the mosque by the Jews. Hysterical men and women shouted insults at the firemen, pulled at their tools and overalls, and threw down their ladders. A few tried to snatch away the hoses — which, they feared, were pouring gasoline, not water, on the flames. In the ensuing struggle and confusion, the work of the firemen was considerably delayed. The fire was fully extinguished only five hours later. When the smoke finally cleared, the great damage the blaze had wrought was evident: in addition to an exquisite pulpit, carved in Aleppo in 1187 to celebrate the liberation of Jerusalem from Crusader rule, a good part of the dome and the ceiling had been destroyed.

By this time, Arabs and Moslems all over the world were accusing Israel, and the Jews, of premeditated arson in Islam's third-holiest spot. Incensed crowds from Morocco to Pakistan clamored for jihad. A preacher on Radio Baghdad announced that rivers of blood would not atone for this unspeakable outrage. One of the ulemas in the great mosque of al-Azhar in Cairo called on the faithful to wage uncompromising war against the Jewish enemies of God and human life, "as is evident from their holy book." In Jerusalem, Arab shopkeepers went on strike. Demonstrators filled the streets of the Moslem quarters with cries of "Nasser! Nasser!" and "Death to the Jews." The Moslem Supreme Council in Jerusalem called a press conference and announced that the firemen had been intentionally sluggish; worse still, they alleged, the city had deliberately cut off the water supply to the Temple Mount during the fire.

Official Israeli reaction to the catastrophe was a mixture of apology and fury at its exploitation by the Arabs. In the two years since the 1967 war, Israelis had convinced themselves that the Moslems of Jerusalem were reconciled to Jewish rule. The disappointment of discovering otherwise generated new fears and more anti-Arab prejudice. The mayor of Jerusalem, Teddy Kollek, rushed to the scene and described it as a terrible disaster; he was immediately attacked by right-wing activists for identifying too much with Moslem sensibilities. Prime Minister Golda Meir, shattered by the possible consequences of what had happened, told her cabinet: "We must condemn this outrage." Menachem Begin, one of her ministers (and a future prime minister himself), retorted: "Yes, of course. But not too much." The disaster served the Arab cause so well that at least one Israeli cabinet minister suggested that the mosque had been set on fire by an Arab provocateur.

Rohan was quickly apprehended. He claimed later that he had planned all along to give himself up. He would walk into a police station and say, "Good morning, boys, I burned the mosque. I did it to make Jesus come back to Jerusalem and save the people there." He was eager for all the world to know what he had done, and why. It had been his destiny. He was proud of it. Before setting fire to the mosque, he had wandered around the city drunk with biblical texts and their heavenly revelations. He believed he was chosen to build the Temple of the Lord on the ashes of al-Aqsa. It is facile to say, as many did at the time, that Rohan was "mad." Of course he was mad. The Gnostic doctrine, with its hallowed belief in salvation through the gutters of the world, blurs all distinction between the madman and the fanatic, between faith and frenzy, between fervor and psychosis.

Rohan seemed to enjoy his trial. He remained calm and composed throughout. A young Arab tourist guide who had taken him around Jerusalem on the eve of the fire testified that Rohan had impressed him as a bit of a "fool." He made a popular gesture with his hand to indicate what he meant. "The audience in the court," wrote Professor Shlomo Shoham, a Tel Aviv University criminologist who attended the trial, "burst into laughter in which Rohan also joined. At that moment the barriers between judges and audience, prosecution and defense, sanity and insanity seemed to melt and the gentle smile on Rohan's troubled face reflected the fool in Christ."

Shoham argued that any model of deviance could no longer exclude religious faith and other transcendental factors. "Deviance motivated by religion is not confined to a Rohan, or a Charles Manson mesmerizing his California hippie initiates into a murderous trance, or even a Jean Genet performing a black mass in a desecrated cathedral. The deviant avenues to salvation would appear to be just one logical step further from conventional mysticism." The court found Rohan had acted through an "irresistible impulse" and confined him to a mental hospital. Because of his delusions, it implied, he could not help acting as he did.

The Rohan trial brought back memories of the murder, in 1951, of King Abdullah of Jordan on the same Temple Mount (and in the presence of his grandson, the present king, Hussein). The assassin was a young tailor named Mustapha Shukri Ashu. He was associated with an organization called the Holy Jihad and with a leading Moslem politician of Jerusalem who had spent the war years in Nazi Germany. Ashu was a devout Moslem. On the day before the assassination, he had wandered about Jerusalem as drunk with Koranic lore as Rohan had been with biblical. He shot the king for trying to make peace with the Israeli infidels.

In April 1982, a thirty-eight-year-old American, Alan Harry Goodman, ran amok on the Temple Mount. He shot his way into the Dome of the Rock with an M-16 automatic rifle, killing one man and seriously wounding three others.

Goodman was a so-called penitent, or "born-again Jew." As a volunteer in the Israeli army, he was wearing its uniform. Once inside the Dome, Goodman climbed over a railing and onto the Stone of Foundation — the spot where Abraham is said to have offered up Isaac as a sacrifice — and there he held up his machine gun, much as he had seen Moses portrayed in so many paintings, standing on Mount Sinai flourishing the tablets of the law. Then he quietly surrendered to the police. Goodman claimed that Jerusalem was not liberated as long as its heart — the Temple Mount — was still under alien Moslem control. His aim had been to liberate the mount and become "king of the Jews."

He, too, was a fanatic, who believed that the world was dying, and with it, that death was dying, too, so that he could safely shoot at a crowd of worshipers and kill and set fire to mosques, churches, or synagogues. He believed that he served "eternal peace." His very victims, he claimed, rejoiced in his act. Goodman's reasoning, if it can be called that, was as totally divorced from the environment he assaulted as was that of, say, Kozo Okamoto, the crazed Japanese terrorist who had staged a bloodbath a few years earlier among arriving passengers at the Tel Aviv airport. Okamoto later told his judge that he and his victims would "unite in death" and be reincarnated as stars; their joint illumination, he explained, would shed "eternal peace on earth." Goodman's mind was clouded by similar mystic notions. "I shall be celebrated in heaven," he announced. "The angels will sing my praise."

As Goodman was led away from the scene of his crime, the police had to contend with crowds of vengeful, rock-throwing Moslems who tried to lynch him. Muezzins all over the city called on the faithful to rush to the mosques on the Temple Mount that the Jews were destroying. The ensuing riots lasted the entire day. It was the height of the Easter holiday. Thousands of Jewish and Christian pilgrims thronged the streets of the Old City. Passersby were attacked and tourist buses were stoned. Thirty-two people were injured. Goodman claimed later that he was responding to an overpowering higher voice. He was discovered to have been under mental treatment for paranoid schizophrenia in the United States before his emigration to Israel. It was never made clear how a man so deeply disturbed had been allowed to join the army and had even been given a 97/100 medical profile. The judges rejected Goodman's claim that he had acted, like Rohan, under an "irresistible impulse." They distinguished between an "irresistible" and an "unresisted" impulse, and ruled that Goodman was responsible for his action. He was sentenced to spend the rest of his life in prison.

Since Goodman's trial in 1982, more than twenty religious fanatics have been caught in the act of preparing one or another violent outrage on the Temple Mount. Many more suspects were charged but released for lack of sufficient evidence. Nothing could be proven against Meir Kahane, of the American Jewish Defense League, who was twice placed under preventive arrest (under Israeli emergency regulations designed to combat Palestinian terrorists) for allegedly preparing some spectacular act of violence on the Temple Mount.

Early in 1984, sixteen members of a bizarre Jewish sect of kabbalists and moon worshipers were sentenced to prison sentences for hoarding explosives, ostensibly in order to blow up the mosques on the Temple Mount. At the time, they seemed very much on the fringe. A few months later, twenty-eight young yeshiva students from mainstream rabbinical colleges in Jerusalem were arrested one night at the foot of the Temple Mount with ladders and ropes in their hands. Some were armed. They were charged with trying to break into the ancient tunnels under the Temple Mount that lead into al-Aqsa mosque. Their motives were obscure. They may have planned to barricade themselves inside the mosque in the hope of forcing the government to allow Jewish prayer services there. The attempted break-in occurred a few days before Passover. This led to speculation that the accused may have intended to sacrifice a paschal lamb on an improvised altar (there is said to be an old mystic belief that a lamb sacrificed at Passover on the Temple Mount hastens the coming of the messiah).

The judge who dealt with their case condemned the planned attempt but not its alleged perpetrators, whom he did not take seriously. He allowed them to go free. So what if they were trying to set off the third world war, commented a writer in the *Jerusalem Post*. The possibility of a chain reaction leading to an Armageddon, worldwide or regional, is often mentioned in connection with the conflict over the Temple Mount. Several universities have held simulation games in which the third world war breaks out as a result of an explosion on the Temple Mount. Perhaps this is another instance of Jerusalem hubris. Henry Kissinger, in 1986, said it was highly unlikely that the conflict over the Temple Mount could lead to anything but a regional conflagration.

In any event, the twenty-eight rabbinical students were dismissed as inept amateurs whom the judge refused to take seriously. Less than a year later, however, a conspiracy of totally different dimension was exposed. Twenty-eight members of a fundamentalist, terrorist "Jewish underground organization" were apprehended by the police as they were plotting to blow up Moslem shrines on the Temple Mount. Four were caught red-handed, as they were placing explosive charges under Arab buses. Two more were arrested soon after, on their way from the booby-trapped buses to pray and give thanks at the Western Wall. Twenty-two accomplices were arrested at their homes. The explosive charges had been set to go off under the Arab buses during rush-hour traffic. They would have killed and wounded hundreds of innocent people.

The plotters were not confused kabbalists unfamiliar in the

ways of the world. They were well-known West Bank settlers; several had distinguished service records in the army. A few were public figures. Their pictures had often appeared in the newspapers in connection with new settlement projects, and in the company of visiting government ministers. All were devoutly Orthodox. Most were graduates of prominent religious seminaries. They included ranking officers in the army reserve and a veteran air-force fighter pilot.

The arrests were the result, undoubtedly, of a successful penetration of their ranks by police-intelligence agents. Under interrogation, the arrested men admitted that booby-trapping the buses had not been their first terrorist act. By their own proud confession, three were long-sought-after killers who had shot up the campus of a Palestinian university in 1981, leaving three students dead and half a dozen wounded. Others admitted that in 1981 they had booby-trapped the automobiles of three prominent Palestinian mayors. In the explosions, two of the mayors were badly wounded — their feet were blown off — and an Israeli police officer was blinded. They had acted throughout in the national interest only, the conspirators claimed. The aim had been to avenge — and deter — Palestinian acts of terror against Jews.

The confessions came quickly, almost willingly, in a mood of elation and patriotic self-righteousness. Under interrogation one morning, one of the conspirators confessed that on the eve of the arrests they had been busy preparing for their biggest coup to date: dynamiting the Dome of the Rock on the Temple Mount. They had worked themselves into believing that this particular atrocity would reverberate among the people of Israel, and of the world, as a great "spiritual" event. The reasons they gave in their signed confessions were "religious" as well as "political." They expected the destruction of the Moslem shrine on the Temple Mount would inaugurate an age of "true redemption." It would hasten the coming of the messiah. At the base of this argument was the common stock of Jewish, and later Christian, apocalyptic lore, the dream of Jerusalem as the center of a messianic kingdom. The nation, they insisted, would feel "spiritually reborn"; at the very least, the destruction of the Dome would powerfully enhance "national morale." One of the conspirators claimed he had reached this reassuring conclusion through a photic mystic experience — a sudden flash of light that had changed his entire being, not unlike that which had inspired the prophets.

Once again, the virulent imagination and naïveté of a few demented minds was running wild in the name of "religion" and the "national interest." Unlike Rohan and Goodman, those involved this time were not certified mental cases but respectable officers and gentlemen with a penchant for metaphysical speculation. The leader of the conspiracy was a mechanical engineer with a rare expertise in sophisticated explosive devices. His right hand was an Orthodox yeshiva student, said to be a man of "great learning" (he was also known to advocate revival of ritual sacrifice during the High Holidays). Others in the group — all settlers on the West Bank or the Golan Heights — were a farmer, a wealthy real-estate broker, a public official, and a journalist. All were observant Orthodox Jews. They were convinced that the destruction of the Moslem shrines on the Temple Mount would precipitate the "religious renaissance" of the Jewish people.

They also believed that the "human" act of destruction would be met by a "divine" response — the third temple would come down from heaven miraculously intact. The momentous event of its reappearance on the ancient Temple Mount would have grand moral consequences. Israel would progress from the "vacuum" of "mere existence" and "moral banality" to the stage of "messianic glory." It would rise to be a kingdom of saints. At its center would stand — in the very heart of Jerusalem — the rebuilt temple.

At the time of their arrest, the conspirators had already completed preparations for the planned explosion on the Temple Mount. They had measured and photographed the Dome from all angles. Detailed operational charts had been prepared. The static calculations had been made. They knew where, when, and how the charges must be placed against the seventh-century pillars to cause the great Dome to collapse in an instant. They were found in possession of a great quantity of explosives. Much of it was stolen from army stores. As officers in the army reserve, the conspirators had easy access to army installations. They had been maintaining lookout posts on church towers for months to observe the Moslem shrines at all hours of the day and night.

We know about their plans and so many of their innermost thoughts and beliefs from the detailed confessions they signed, and from *Dear Brothers*, a remarkable book one of the terrorists later wrote in jail. The book contains near-verbatim records of conversations and debates among the conspirators. The author, former journalist Hagai Segal, claims that the conspirators assumed all along that they would be arrested and tried after blowing up the Temple Mount. They were convinced, however, that popular support would be so overwhelming they would be exonerated morally from all formal guilt.

Their sensational trial in the Jerusalem District Court in 1985 was a rallying point for right-wingers and fundamentalists of all shades. The conspirators reveled in the attention they were getting. Constant displays of sympathy were offered them by their many friends and fellow cultists in the West Bank, and, occasionally, by prison and police guards as well. (One prison guard was reprimanded for taking them on an excursion to the beach after a day in court rather than back to the detention center.) Distinguished character witnesses testified that the defendants were misguided idealists. They were visited in jail by the two chief rabbis and by one former army chief of staff. The future prime minister Yitzhak Shamir offered the opinion that they were guilty mostly of "exaggerated love" for the city of Jerusalem and for the land of Israel. In hundreds of synagogues throughout the country, funds were solicited for their defense through an organization sponsored by prominent religious leaders.

Not all the self-confessed terrorists were ready to express regret. When asked whether he had not been worried that blowing up the third-holiest place in Islam might precipitate a bloodbath in Jerusalem, or among Jews in Iran, or at least mobilize great parts of the Moslem world against Israel, one of the conspirators, an ordained rabbi, answered that "they could not hate us more than they already do." A defense lawyer exhorted the judges to remember that they were Jewish judges in a Jerusalem court and not on the bench of the International Court of Justice.

Given the gravity of the charges against them, most of the defendants came away with relatively light sentences. Those who plea-bargained with the prosecution were given prison terms ranging from a few months to a few years. Three found guilty of murder received the mandatory sentence of life imprisonment. No sooner were the sentences handed down than the two chief rabbis formally called upon the president to pardon the convicts. Shamir, by now prime minister under a rotation agreement, joined their appeal. Other politicians, West Bank settlers, and Orthodox rabbis sympathetic to their cause stood vigil day and night for months outside President Chaim Herzog's residence demanding an amnesty. Nearly one million Israelis signed a similar appeal to the president of the state. Of the twenty-eight members of the terrorist underground convicted in 1985, only the three who had been given the mandatory life sentence were still in jail four years later. The remainder had either served out their terms or had their sentences commuted by the president.

The history of violence on the Temple Mount suggested a pattern. The fantasies acted out there had a similar source. Their destructive naïveté was born of common dreams of "vengeance," "chosenness," and "redemption." The plotters were moved by deep beliefs. A few were successfully manipulated by so-called spiritual leaders. Others were manipulators themselves. Some were successfully stopped in the planning stage; others were not. If they were marked, on occasion, by a definite comic-opera flavor, that does not necessarily make them less outrageous or, potentially, less dangerous. All appeared swayed by the rich deposits of malevolent superstitions, of which Jerusalem seems to have an almost inexhaustible supply.

The city attracts the pious as well as the mentally disturbed, the innocent pilgrims as well as the cranks. Jerusalem is often said to have more eccentrics, crackpots, and monomaniacs per square mile than probably any other municipality in the world. Josephus, the first great historian of Jerusalem, early on lamented that the union of the divine and the mortal was disagreeable. The war of 1967, seen by Jewish and Christian fundamentalists as a divinely inspired event linked with the End of Days, lent credence to this observation. It was not only cranks and eccentrics who founded a special institute in the Old City in 1970 to study the ritual to be observed in the rebuilt temple, or who funded a yeshiva to train Jewish priests (cohanim) for actual service there. Its students saw themselves as the vanguard of a movement, the nucleus of a future priestly caste. (There was also a workshop devoted to the manufacture of holy garments, according to specifications found in Leviticus and Ezekiel, to be worn by the future high priest on the Day of Atonement.)

The spinners and weavers may be harmless oddballs. The hundreds of yeshiva students and distinguished rabbis who regularly attend the institute's seminars and public conferences in the Old City are not. These public conferences are devoted to such subjects as "The Third Temple: Its Future Site and Shape," and "The Third Temple: The Sacred Duty to Build It in Our Own Time." The conferences are held under the patronage of the ministries of education and of religious affairs.

The prophet Isaiah insisted — or perhaps warned — that when it comes to rebuilding the temple, the believer "shall not make haste." Those attending the conferences seem to be in a great hurry. They are mostly young people. Many come from government-subsidized religious seminaries on the West Bank and enter the convention hall in the Old City armed with automatic rifles. The atmosphere is a curious amalgam of Wild West and nineteenth-century eastern-European shtetl. The rifles are stowed under the wooden seats; ammunition cartridges lie about on the participants' desks, which are otherwise piled with thick volumes of the Mishnah and the Gemara and other hefty works of rabbinical exegesis. At one such convention in 1985, shortly after the disclosure of the Jewish underground's plot to blow up the Dome of the Rock, the chairman in his opening remarks said that the arrests "proved once again how strong and irresistible are the popular yearnings for the Temple Mount. . . . We do not condone violence, but the intentions [of the plotters] were sacred and pure. . . . We too want to play a role in this irresistible movement. . . . We expect to be led, to lead forward, to the third temple!"

After the opening speech, several well-known rabbinical exegetes delivered learned discourses, which generated questions and lively comments from the audience. The themes discussed were "Opportune Moments for Rebuilding the House of the Lord," "Spirituality and [Animal] Sacrifice," "The Third Temple as a Moral

Value," and "Messianic Signs in our Time." Though the explicit emphasis was on "spirituality" and "messianic signs," the implicit emphasis of most speakers was on the overwhelming power of Israeli arms. In fundamentalist eyes, this is not necessarily a paradox. In Iran, too, fundamentalists are ready to take nourishment from the technological achievements of the "materialistic culture" they condemn in the name of pure spirituality.

When the first round of lectures was finished, a uniformed police officer mounted the rostrum and introduced himself as the man in charge of the local police precinct. He began by wishing "this important assembly success in the great task it has set itself," and went on to sound a warning:

> I see there are many very nice fellows here, but [I see you are] armed. Far be it from me to say that you should not use your guns. . . . Everyone has to be on his guard in these days of PLO terror. . . . Far be it from me to say no. If they shoot at us, we will not run away. . . . But I ask everyone here to think twice before using . . . guns. Remember, they were given you for self-defense only. If someone here thinks of provoking the Arabs, let him first consider the success of this important meeting.

The audience listened tensely to these words. From the street outside came the sound of music and Christian hymns. German pilgrims were passing by, carrying a large wooden cross down the via Dolorosa and singing: "Ich will den Kreuzstab gerne tragen / Er kommt von unserm lieben Herrn [I'll gladly bear the burden of this cross / It comes from our dearest Lord]." During a brief recess, a man in the audience distributed photocopied designs of a mechanical loom he had just imported from the United States to produce robes for priests and Levites out of pure flax.

The keynote address was given by a prominent member of the Knesset, Israel's parliament, an experienced politician representing one of the religious parties. The audience rose to its feet to honor him (he is an ordained rabbi). He mounted the rostrum, followed by an aide carrying an armful of sacred books. The audience followed his every word in rapt attention. "Our reality is inevitably leading us to rebuild the third temple on the Temple Mount," he said, carefully articulating every syllable. "The third temple will stand for ever and ever," he assured the assembly. To prove it, he leafed through the books before him, citing chapter and verse in the Bible, the Talmud, and the sayings of latter-day sages. "The Redemption has already begun. There is no way back! The Almighty, blessed be his name, guides us. There is no way back! Redemption will be complete!" He pushed the books aside and continued to speak passionately, with half-closed eyes. His strong voice filled the hall. The citations flowed effortlessly from his lips, as though fed by computer. He opened his eyes widely and looked around. The audience seemed spellbound. The confidence and enthusiasm he inspired in his listeners seemed also to derive from an almost encyclopedic memory of the sacred texts. His eyes flashed with recognition of the excitement he could see he was generating all around. He was an effective speaker, and it took a few moments before an outsider realized that he was speaking of nothing less than the End of Days. At his feet, the cowboys of the Apocalypse were sitting on their guns. The speaker suggested that the present situation in Jerusalem should be considered as part of a "divine scheme . . . which has put Israel in control of Jerusalem and the Temple Mount in the Six-Day War." The people of Israel, he cried, had been steadily progressing to this day, since the Exodus from Egypt. Because of their sins, the first and second temples were destroyed, but the salvation that was imminent shall be for an eternity. "The Almighty is at present rebuilding Jerusalem, telling us that from now on it will stand for ever and ever. . . . We are all reborn into a new era. The mountain of the house of the Lord shall be established on the top of the mountains and all nations shall flow unto it." He ended by urging everyone to "ready himself." The audience stirred. To the uninvolved outsider, he resembled the rabble-rouser in Chaplin's *Great Dictator,* giving his fiery speech in double-talk. To the initiated, he seemed almost to be praying in tongues.

The growing number of politicians who exploit the Temple Mount for political reasons make it difficult to dismiss such events as harmless eccentricities. A geyser can be capped only before it blows. Some of the money for these eccentricities has come in recent years from evangelical, charismatic, and Pentecostal Christians, too, especially in the United States. Like Orthodox Jews, fundamentalist Christians regard the Bible as free from error. Pentecostals believe in the gifts of Pentecost causing visions and making mortals "speak with other tongues, as the Spirit gave them utterance." In the eyes of the Pentecostals, these visions are true. The men who tried to blow up the Temple Mount were the terrorist fringe of an informal worldwide movement that encompasses fundamentalist Jews and fundamentalist Christians united in a belief that the End of Days is near. To fundamentalist Jews, this means the imminent arrival of the messiah; to evangelical Christians, the Second Coming of Christ — which, many of them believe, will take place immediately after the temple is rebuilt in Jerusalem by the Jews. At this point, the two sides part; for according to evangelical lore, once the Jews have rebuilt their temple, it will be destroyed a third time and all Jews will convert to Christianity.

Disagreement about the ultimate outcome, however, so far has not prevented loose links between the two groups. In 1984, an American evangelist, described as a leading physicist at a California university, flew a number of sorties low over the mosques on the Temple Mount to X-ray its innermost entrails with cesium-beam magnetometers and other sophisticated equipment. He was closely associated with Israeli right-wingers and was looking for the Ark of the Covenant, said to have been buried on the Temple Mount at the time of Nebuchadnezzar. He also was reconnoitering, he said, to acquaint himself with the "strategic" shape of the mount. He believed, as some Evangelists do, that the Final Battle shall take place on the Temple Mount. In that battle, Israel and the Church Militant will triumph. (He flew so low that the police were alerted. Flying over the Temple Mount is forbidden for security reasons.)

There has been a "temple lobby" in the Knesset for years. Major personalities in the evangelical world have been associated with it and with other Israeli militants who campaign for Jewish worship on the Temple Mount. Evangelical Christians have been campaigning for Christian worship on the Temple Mount as well. The temptation of Jesus and the martyrdom of his brother James are said to have taken place in the southeast corner. Over the years, Evangelists, Adventists, Davidists, Charismatic Christians, Southern Baptists, and other Christian denominations in America and Europe have publicly voiced support for rebuilding the Jews' third temple. On their millennial maps, the Israel of the post-Apocalyptic future comprises large parts of Egypt, Syria, Iraq, and Saudi Arabia. In 1985, American "Evangelists for Freedom of Worship on the Temple Mount" took out large advertisements in Israeli papers to protest the arrest of Jewish terrorists. According to these advertisements, Moslem claims to the Temple Mount were "mistaken" and contrary to divine command as enunciated "in the books of the prophets and by Jesus and the apostles."

In the mid-1980s, an entire subculture dedicated to this task flourished in parts of the United States, where in some Protestant churches, in and out of the Bible Belt, there has been an astonishing inrush of Pentecostal fervor. Monthly magazines and pamphlets devoted to this mission, such as *Israel My Glory, Endtime,* and *Vision,* were said to be distributed in numbers that totaled hundreds of thousands of copies. Tours to Jerusalem were advertised and money was solicited to propagate the idea of Jerusalem's temple rebuilt in glory. A senior Jerusalem police officer was so concerned upon receiving a representative collection of these publications, in 1981, that he ordered a special intelligence unit to monitor them on a regular basis. A so-called International Christian Embassy opened spacious offices in Jerusalem in the same year. It claimed to represent hundreds of thousands of evangelical and charismatic Christians all over the world. The "embassy" was headed by a clergyman of the South African Dutch Reformed Church, noted for its support of apartheid in the name of the "divinely ordained" separation of the races. He was quoted in the press as saying that evangelists all over the world were praying "daily for the restoration of Jewish worship on the Temple Mount." The Moslems who occupied it at present were usurpers, according to the clergyman. The site must be returned to the Jews "even if it means Armageddon."

At about the same time, American and European Evangelists began to hold annual conventions in Jerusalem attended by thousands of delegates. The participants are bused directly from the airport to the summit of the Mount of Olives to admire the famous view and be told through a megaphone that they are standing on the very spot where Jesus' feet would stand on Judgment Day. Funds are solicited. Then, all repair to their hotels. The visiting

Evangelists do not, as a rule, enter the Holy Sepulchre (which they consider occupied by Latin or Greek demons) or climb the Temple Mount. But they circle the Old City atop its walls. Once a year, they take over the huge National Convention Center near the Hilton Hotel. To cries of *hallelujah* from the audience, preachers hail the new "strategic era" — the period during which the temple will be rebuilt, and destroyed, and rebuilt again on the mountain of the Lord. But first, a terrible, great war will take place, between the United States and Russia — in Jerusalem. It will bring universal devastation and terror. But the evil king of the north (Russia, the place of the throne of Satan) will be destroyed. God himself will come in power and glory and kill him in a flash and carry out the Last Judgment. There is a Pol Pot logic in this message, as in the apocalyptic rhetoric of fundamentalist Jews: the actual Jerusalem must burn and perish so that the ideal Jerusalem, purged of the evils of the past, may rise from its ashes and its dust.

One wonders how in the common discourse of three great religions Jerusalem ever became the proverbial city of peace. The city was founded by a warrior king. Jehovah was a "Lord of hosts." Christ foretold war and pestilence ("the love of many shall wax cold"); Mohammed was certainly not a peacemaker.

The epithet may have originated in the ancient name of Jerusalem — Salem (after the pagan deity of the city), which is etymologically connected in the Semitic languages with the words for peace (*shalom* in Hebrew, *salaam* in Arabic). Paul's epistle to the Hebrews evokes Melchizedek, the ancient priest-king of Salem, "which is King of peace." And perhaps the epithet was but a prayer, as in the famous, postexilic Psalm 122:

> Pray for the peace of Jerusalem
> They shall deserve quietness that love thee
> Peace be within thy walls
> Calm within thy palaces.

Gotthold Ephraim Lessing, the great German Protestant exponent of the Enlightenment, placed "The Three Rings," his well-known fable of religious tolerance, in, of all places, the capital of the

Crusader kingdom of Jerusalem — perhaps the most fanatic and
cruelly narrow-minded realm of the Middle Ages. Lessing's Jewish
friend and follower Moses Mendelssohn called his own book on
tolerance and religious freedom *Jerusalem*.

Jerusalem's peacemakers often must have felt they were plowing
the sea. Jeremiah was thrown into a dungeon. Jesus was crucified.
Frederick II, who sought a peaceful accommodation between
Christians and Moslems, was excommunicated. Judah Magnes, first
president of the Hebrew University, preached Jewish-Arab compromise; he was ignored by Arabs and vilified by Jews. Folke Bernadotte, the Swedish United Nations mediator, was assassinated on
a Jerusalem street in broad daylight, as was King Abdullah of Jordan. Both were killed while trying to make peace between Arabs
and Jews. One of the suspects arrested at the time in connection
with Bernadotte's murder would be a leading militant, forty years
later, in the movement to rebuild the Jewish temple, and a frequent
speaker at American Evangelist conventions.

While the dominant religions of Jerusalem have alternated, nothing has been more constant than the fanaticism of their militants. In
the past nineteen hundred years alone, the dominant religion was
changed at least eleven times, often at great human cost: by the
Romans in AD 70 and 132, the Byzantines in 335, the Zoroastrians in
614, the Byzantines in 628, the Arabs in 638, the Crusaders in 1099,
the Arabs again in 1187, the British in 1917, the Jordanians in 1948,
and the Israelis in 1967. Few other cities have such a record.

Historical literature abounds with vivid descriptions of the wars
and sieges in the City of Peace. The Crusaders — Gibbon called
them "savage heroes of the cross" — are said to have massacred fifty
thousand Moslems and Jews in Jerusalem alone. Crusader churches
and fortifications are still visible everywhere in the Old City. Their
architecture — it was political architecture, as architecture in
Jerusalem often is — still sets the general tone of the Old City. The
Crusaders built massively, as though their world would last forever.
Somber and grim, dark, in heavy lines and rough decorations, there
is little in Crusader architecture in Jerusalem to suggest the charm
and airy spaciousness of the early Romanesque in Europe, even
though many of the masons were imported from the south of
France. The Crusaders rode into the City of Peace "in blood up to

their knees and bridle reins," exclaiming how just and splendid a judgment this was for the unbelievers. William of Tyre wrote that even more dreadful than to observe the vast number of slaughtered vanquished "was to gaze upon the victors themselves, dripping in blood from head to foot, an ominous sight which brought terror to all who met them."

According to Fulcher of Chartres, half a year after the city had fallen to the Crusaders, it still reeked with the stench of rotting bodies. The Arabs who recaptured the city in 1187 proved more humane than their European opponents. Their rhetoric, however, was almost as violent.* It has hardly changed since then, from the "Let Jerusalem be purified by a bloodbath . . . spill rivers of blood to purify *al Quds*" of the twelfth century, to the theory and occasional practice in the twentieth century of "Slaughter the Jewish infidels!" On the eve of the battle of Jerusalem in 1948, Azzam Pasha, secretary-general of the Arab League, bluntly threatened the Jews with a bloodbath in the manner of Genghis Khan and Tamerlane.

What the Jews call Temple Mount, Moslems call Haram al-Sharif (Noble Sanctuary). The ancients named the sacred precinct Moriah. Walking through it shortly after dawn, you can see the sun rising behind Olivet. The Dome catches the first rays, then the drum lights up in vivid blues and yellows. Long shadows, dark and ghostly, fall on the great platform paved with pink and gray polished stones. At this early hour, it has the aspect and loneliness of a mountain peak. The breeze rustles the cypresses and pines. From afar comes the murmur of the awakening city. The gilded Dome covers the bare piece of raw rock, which has been the sum and meaning of so much exhortation and piety, so much joy and lamentation, and so much violence and bloodshed. The Dome glistens in the sun. The supplicants have not yet arrived. The tourists, nowadays, are allowed in only between 12:00 and 3:00 PM. The chant of Jews praying rises from behind the great supporting wall in the

---

* Saladin's relative mildness was an exception: "The swords of Islam shiver in their sheaths as Allah's knights prepare for the assault. The Dome of the Rock rejoices that the Koran expelled from its premises is about to return."

west. A lonely usher is still asleep in one of the dark doorways leading into al-Aqsa. But on the ramparts in the east and in the south, the guards already walk up and down nervously, carrying walkie-talkies. Up and down they walk, between the watchtowers and the searchlights set up in recent years to keep out intruders during the day and dynamiters and arsonists during the night. No one is taking any chances. According to Moslem lore, the Noble Sanctuary is the spot on earth nearest to paradise, where the righteous are attended by beautiful youths who never grow old and where the one incantation constantly heard is "Salaam! Salaam!"

In the early morning, military jets often slice through the sky like silver knives above the shimmering walls and ramparts. It is odd to think of this cradle of the religions as a forbidding fortress. Its very architecture breathes conflict. The massive walls, the protective towers, suggest siege, rather than pilgrimage. The great sanctuary on the Temple Mount is a fortress within a fortress. So is the Western Wall area nearby, with its cordons of armed guards and special riot police who block every access and search for bombs in every bag and sack. On the rooftops above the wall area, army sharpshooters are forever alert with guns and binoculars, on the lookout for terrorists.

In a nearby narrow alleyway, the memory of a victim recently stabbed to death is commemorated on a rudimentary stone plaque inscribed with Hebrew letters standing for "May God Avenge His Blood." After each such act, municipal workers, in cars marked JERUSALEM CITY OF PEACE in three languages, rush to the scene with rags and brooms. They wash the blood off the flagstones. Life is soon, in the jargon of the newspapers, back to normal. Commerce continues. Tourists, hardly aware that blood was shed here a short time before, throng the souvenir stands. They move in a dream world of their own, donning funny hats and smelling of deodorants and suntan lotion. It is easy to ridicule them. But as you watch the crowds pushing through the narrow bazaars, you feel how right Samuel Johnson was when he said that people are never more innocently occupied than when making or spending money.

The thick human traffic flows through the bazaars, past the commemorative stones, under the bowed arches, down the quaint steps, seemingly unconcerned. The holy sites touch. Some are jammed one on top of the other within the same building — a mosque, a synagogue, a church — all equally bent with age, reliquaries, and tombs. Through a tunnel burrowed out north of the Western Wall after 1967, Orthodox Jews reach a first-century vault, deep under the Moslem quarter, to hold a prayer service. Directly above them, the qadis of the Moslem Supreme Council might be deliberating a fine point of Islamic law. On the ground floor of a rickety building nearby on Mount Zion, Jews venerate the alleged tomb of King David, as they have since at least the fifteenth century. One floor above, in the same building, Christians venerate the Cenacle, the room where, according to Christian lore, the Last Supper took place. To add to the confusion, the building, sacred to both Christians and Jews, is surmounted by a Moslem minaret.

Through the arches, there are glimpses out to the surrounding countryside. Its "fields of tension between conflicting geological and geographic factors, between the desert and the Mediterranean region," writes Leo Picard, a noted geologist, mirror "the history of the city and the spirit of the inhabitants."

One modern writer who captures this precariousness in his work is the poet Yehuda Amichai. "It's sad to be the Mayor of Jerusalem," he says in a celebrated poem. It's terrible. What can he do with her? How can any man be the mayor of such a city? He will build, and build, and build,

> And at night
> The stones of the hills round about
> Will crawl down
> Towards the stone houses.
> Like wolves coming to howl at the dogs
> Who have become men's slaves.

The Arab geographer Muqaddasi, whose very name implies that he was a native of Jerusalem, expressed a similar sentiment ten centuries earlier. "Jerusalem," he wrote, "is a golden basin filled with scorpions."

CHAPTER FIVE

Pilgrim City

A GOLDEN BASIN filled with scorpions — yet, at the same time, so much love and charity; so much trust; so much confidence. Above all, so much hope — articulated daily, all over the city, as it always has been, in ancient and elaborate pageants, in Hebrew, Arabic, Greek, Armenian, French, Latin, Ethiopian, and a dozen other languages. The city is a cradle of hope. The pilgrims, who against hope continue to believe in hope, continue to arrive, as they always have, in times of trouble and in times of peace. Hope is a psychological need, a waking dream. Filled or fooled with hope, the pilgrims bow their foreheads to the ground in the mosques and pound their chests at the Western Wall. They lie prostrate on Calvary and kiss the bare rock as though Christ's body were still there hanging from the cross. In the face of so much continuing piety and so much continuing misery, one is overwhelmed less by the power of faith than by its impotence to live up to its promise. Jerusalem is forever haunted by this failure. But the failure is of such richness it is a kind of victory, desperate and existential.

The psalms bore witness to it very early on. The pilgrims recite them to this day: "*De profundis* — out of the depths have I cried unto thee, O Lord"; "I will lift up mine eyes unto the hills, from whence cometh my help." In their abiding hope, the pilgrims are the absurd, heroic fools in the history of the city. They continue to arrive, more and more every year. The hotels are crowded and occasionally overbooked. Fear and hope were born together. The civil unrest, even the occasional terror, affect the influx of pilgrims only marginally. They come, as they always have, enjoined by

Psalm 48, to "walk about Zion, and go round about her: tell the towers thereof, . . . that ye may tell it to the generation following: . . . Beautiful for situation, the joy of the whole earth, is Mount Zion." The view from the summit of Olivet — today it can be enjoyed comfortably through the bulletproof plate windows of a luxury hotel — is inspiring. It is also sublime. Looking down is often more awe-inspiring than looking up.

Pilgrims have always felt this awe and wonder. God dwelt in Jerusalem; from earliest times, Jews went there to stand before and be seen by him. At first, small barefoot bands would wind their way through the hills to the shrine in Jerusalem. By the third century BC, huge crowds from all over the Mediterranean and the Near East were already gathering in Jerusalem several times a year, in a kind of pan-Hebraic meeting. There was sacred space in Jerusalem and sacred time. Sacred space was the shrine; sacred time was the Sabbath or the feast, during which the pilgrim felt transported mysteriously to become contemporaneous with God. The pilgrim returned home to Greece or Egypt or Mesopotamia, a richer and, presumably, better person. Sacredness was thought to be communicable. It attached itself to those who prayed and honored it "in the place which [God] shall choose."

Pilgrimage was a supreme emotional experience. It inspired awe as well as joy. The famous Psalm 122 was probably a hymn sung by pilgrims as they entered the city gates:

> I was glad when they said unto me,
> Let us go into the house of the Lord.
> Our feet shall stand within thy gates, O Jerusalem.

There were three great pilgrimage festivals every year linked to earlier fertility rites. The first was Passover, perhaps an early pagan spring festival, which became the feast of unleavened bread, the Feast of Liberty, commemorating the Exodus from Egypt. Seven weeks after Passover, the second great pilgrimage took place at Pentecost, or the Feast of Weeks. At Pentecost, Jerusalem celebrated the first harvest of wheat and fruit; later, the feast was endowed with deeper meaning, as a thanksgiving to God for having revealed the Torah to Moses on Mount Sinai. The third pilgrimage was during the Feast of Tabernacles (or Booths). It came in the autumn, the time of the wine harvest and the ripening of olives, pomegranates, and nuts. By the time of Jesus, Tabernacles was the most elaborate of the three pilgrimages. It attracted the largest number of pilgrims and was called simply the Feast, *hagg*. (The same word is used by the Arabs to describe the pilgrimage to Mecca.) The tabernacles were the huts made of palm leaves and branches where the peasants slept to guard their crops from thieves during the harvest; half a century ago, such huts could still be seen on the hills surrounding Jerusalem, and they served the same purpose.

Each of the three great festivals brought hundreds of thousands of pilgrims to Jerusalem. In the first century, according to Josephus, a census was held one Passover and the number of pilgrims counted in the city was 2.7 million. Always anxious to impress his readers with the grandeur of the city the Romans had destroyed, Josephus was probably exaggerating, but not by very much. The Temple Mount was one of the largest artificial structures of its kind — perhaps the largest — in the ancient world. The platform alone could hold some three hundred thousand people. The city was a spectacle of wealth and power. It was also remarkably cosmopolitan:

> And when the day of Pentecost was fully come, . . .
> . . . there were dwelling at Jerusalem Jews, devout men, out of
>   every nation under heaven. . . .
> Parthians, and Medes, and Elamites, and the dwellers in
>   Mesopotamia, and in Judea, and Cappadocia, in Pontus, and Asia,
> Phrygia, and Pamphylia, in Egypt, and in the parts of Libya about
>   Cyrene, and strangers of Rome, Jews and proselytes,
> Cretes and Arabians, we do hear them speak in our tongues the
>   wonderful works of God.

We read a strikingly similar account from a thousand years later of Jerusalem under the Crusaders. "There are Greeks, Bulgarians, Latins, Germans, and Hungarians [in the city]," wrote the German knight John of Würzburg, "Scots, Navarrese, Bretons, English, Franks, Ruthenians, Bohemians, Georgians, Armenians, Jacobites, Syrians, Nestorians, Indians, Capheturici, Maronites and very many others, whom it would take too long to tell." Venice and Constan-

tinople could not have been more cosmopolitan in character than
Jerusalem early in the twelfth century. In the centuries between
Josephus and John, the practice of pilgrimage to Jerusalem had
occasionally been interrupted, but never for very long.

In the Church of the Holy Sepulchre, today, a broad flight of
steps leads down from the ambulatory to an ancient cistern where
Saint Helena, the dowager empress, is said to have found the true
cross and the crown of thorns in AD 327. It is a shrine now, rather
plain, and officially known by the unhappy name Crypt of the
Invention of the Cross. (The name sounds ironic to modern ears
only; the early, now obsolete, meaning of *to invent* was "to discover,
to come upon," from the Latin *invenire*.) The long walls on either
side of the cistern and the stairway leading to the crypt are entirely
covered by thousands of tiny engraved crosses. Countless pilgrims
have stood here in awe and chipped away in the dark to leave neat,
anonymous records of their presence. Today, you can stand here in
the half-dark and marvel at their courage and endurance — for in
their time, travel was always arduous, and often dangerous. (The
very word *travel* came from *travail*, which derived from the Latin
tripalium, a torture instrument consisting of three hooks that rack
the body and tear it apart.) You also wonder whether the pilgrims,
when they finally arrived at their shrines, did not feel a tinge of
disappointment, too. No matter how high-minded they may have
been, they invariably became part of the push and shove of vulgar
commercialism — the very vanities they had traveled so far to evade
— that are a part of every great center of pilgrimage.

In a small cave near the crypt, archaeologists in 1972 uncovered a
delightful little sketch of a sailboat on the wall, and the fragments of
an inscription that seems to read "*Domus Domini Ibimus*" (Let us go
to the House of the Lord). The sailboat is of a kind that plied the
Mediterranean during the fourth century. The inscription alludes to
a well-known psalm. It is the oldest archaeological record of early
Christian pilgrimage to Jerusalem. From the literary record, we
know that pilgrimage was considerable. After the conversion of
Constantine in 313 and the establishment of Christianity as the
official religion of the Roman Empire, Jerusalem experienced an
extraordinary flowering of liturgy and of sacred art. It was the core
of the new Christian faith that streamed out over the entire Roman

world. Drawn to Jerusalem by the news that Helena had discovered the true cross and the site of the holy tomb, the pilgrims arrived to give thanks or simply to walk the earth where Christ had walked. Helena successfully "located" and dug up every spot where each important moment in the life of Jesus in Jerusalem was said to have been enacted. Gibbon said about her that she "united the credulity of age with the warm feelings of a recent conversion" to Christianity. She may be said to have been the most successful archaeologist in all history. Whatever she looked for she found three centuries after the event and promptly identified (not surprisingly, since she did so by imperial fiat): the tomb, Golgotha, the true cross, the instruments of the passion, the cave of the nativity, the site of the ascension of Christ. (In Evelyn Waugh's romance of Saint Helena, the exact locations are revealed to her in a dream by the Wandering Jew, who speaks in the Yiddish accents of a hustler in the London East End.)

Helena's example authorized the zeal and piety of successive waves of pilgrims. The pilgrims adopted her locations and invented new ones. They came from every land. It was an early form of ideological tourism. The earliest known Christian pilgrims came from different social classes: a bishop, an empress, a rich Roman widow, a civil servant, a peasant, a man from Bordeaux, a Spanish lady, and a great many nuns and monks, who retired in the caves that can still be seen today in the hills surrounding the city. Countless others came after them. They produced a new kind of literature: the itineraries of the devout. It continues to this day — jumbling together myths and facts, devotional reflection and personal adventures, descriptions of buildings, meals, and prices with pious admonishments, prayers, and observations.

The earliest extant travelogue is by a man from Bordeaux who went to Jerusalem in the spring of 333. Curiously enough, he did not go by boat; Roman galleys were known to make the journey from the south of France to the eastern shore of the Mediterranean in less than three weeks. The so-called Pilgrim of Bordeaux took the land route, which was longer but perhaps less harzardous. It was maintained by the Roman imperial post, with perfectly kept roads paved with large, smooth stones to a width of twenty feet, and convenient inns and staging posts. The Pilgrim of Bordeaux must have been a man of means. His average speed was twenty-five miles per day. (More than fifteen centuries later, in 1876, the forty-mile trip from Jaffa to Jerusalem still took at least two days, according to Baedeker's guide.) Who was this man? We do not even know his name. He must have been privileged or he would not have used the imperial post. He may have been a converted or, possibly, a secret Jew. In Jerusalem, his first visit was not to the holy tomb, "miraculously" discovered only a few years earlier, but to the former Jewish Temple Mount, where, he tells us, there is "a pierced stone [*lapis pertusus*] to which the Jews come every year and anoint. They mourn and rend their garments and then depart."

Through the eyes of the Pilgrim of Bordeaux, we are able to "see" the abandoned Temple Mount for the first time after its destruction in AD 70 (and for the last, until the arrival of the Moslems in 638). His lean, dry text portrays a ghostly countryside. Other than the Jews who wail on the Temple Mount, there are no people anywhere, only sites and buildings. Of these, he says only that they are "beautiful."

He lists the names of all the imperial post-stations he has passed and the distances between them. His account reads almost as a guidebook — as though he knew that many more pilgrims would come after him. In the following centuries, hundreds of thousands, in fact, did. Saint Jerome wrote that they came from as far as Britain in the west and India in the east. They jostled to pray at the bare rock of Calvary and touch the spot — it is still pointed out today — said to be the center of the universe and where God took the clay to fashion Adam. They marveled at the relics, splinters of rag, wood, and metal, teeth and old bones. There were the nails, the lance, the bottle of vinegar said to have been instruments of the passion, the crown of thorns, the ring of Solomon, and the horn from which the kings of Israel were said to have been anointed.

But first and foremost, there was the true cross. After the miracle of the "invention" of the true cross, there had been the miracle of its "multiplication." The cross was cut to little pieces to gratify the enormous demand. But it was said by its guardians to possess the happy faculty of renewing itself and thus proved an inexhaustible source of souvenirs (and revenue). No matter how many pieces were chopped off, it continued to vegetate and remained entire and unimpaired. Nevertheless, the cross had to be guarded day and night against pilgrims who, as they kissed it, bit off little pieces and hid them in their mouths. Tons of fragments of the true cross reached Europe from Jerusalem throughout the Middle Ages, as did the reputed teeth of Saint Matthew, Veronica's handkerchief, and no less than five heads of Saint John (they were on display at Amiens, Soissons, Nemours, and Rome). In the nineteenth century, it was said that enough pieces of the true cross were still around to build a battleship. The holy sites had to be completely dressed in marble or the pilgrims would have taken them home.

A large population of hermits lived in caves and tombs in the hills around Jerusalem. The incessant tumult of worldly business and of pleasure in the city roused their ire. The early church fathers denounced the uses or abuses of pilgrimage. Less than fifty years after the Pilgrim of Bordeaux, Gregory of Nyssa condemned the "extreme licentiousness" of the pilgrims he had seen in Jerusalem. Saint Augustine, among others, warned them to "wander with the heart, not the feet." The advice was not heeded. Similar warnings would be reiterated throughout the Middle Ages. They had as little effect among the Latins as among the orthodox adherents of the Eastern churches. In the first half of the twelfth century, the Russian monk Cyril asked the archbishop of Novgorod how he should respond to the enormous demand for permits to go on pilgrimage to Jerusalem. The archbishop's advice was unequivocal: no permits should be given. It was not followed for very long.

To go on pilgrimage to Jerusalem was considered a means of gaining remission for sin. Pilgrimage was a form of criminal punishment — and atonement — for offenders. Some penitents undertook it voluntarily. Others were condemned to it. Still others led lives of utmost asceticism, begging their way from Ireland or Normandy to Jerusalem, wearing hair shirts and chains.

There was also fabulous ostentation, as when Sigurd, the king of Norway, a twenty-year-old lad who spared "no expense where his honor is concerned," came on pilgrimage and rode into Jerusalem on a road lined with precious silks against the dust ("the nearer to the city the more valuable"). Sigurd feasted on gold plates with the patriarch, who gave him a splinter of the holy cross. Charlemagne, from all we know, never left Europe but was able to make pilgrimage vicariously. An entire stained-glass window in the ambulatory of the Chartres cathedral depicts the legend of his magnificent entry to Jerusalem.

Most pilgrims, however, were extremely austere. Some walked all the way and vowed to change or wash their clothes only in Jerusalem. As many as five hundred were often jammed below deck on boats only a hundred feet long. The discomfort and stench must have been terrible. Most pilgrims exhausted their resources, whatever they may have been, long before they reached the city. In the eleventh century, scarcely one in a thousand was able to provide for himself. Wretched, helpless, a prey to all the hardships of travel, local wars, heat, cold, piracy, sickness, hunger, and thirst, the perseverance of so many testified to the fantastic power of their obsession.

Things improved slightly after the founding of the Order of the Knights Templar — the first great tourist agency in history — which was charged with, among other tasks, the transport of pilgrims to Jerusalem and their protection along the way. Pilgrims could now travel in well-protected groups of up to a thousand men and women. The flow of pilgrims was not interrupted by the fall of the Crusader kingdom of Jerusalem in 1187. Marco Polo was among those who visited Jerusalem after it fell back to the Moslems. He was on his way to China and stopped only to take some oil from the lamp that burned above the holy tomb (it was a present for Kublai Khan in Peking, who was interested in western religion). In 1219, Saint Francis of Assisi came; his pilgrimage was to have considerable spiritual and artistic repercussions in Europe. Little is known about other pilgrims in his time. Jacques de Vitry, the thirteenth-century historian, deplored the large number among the pilgrims of "parricides, perjurers, adulterers, traitors, pirates, whoremongers, drunkards, minstrels, dice players, mimes and actors, apostate monks [and] nuns that are common harlots." Pilgrims sometimes turned even the Holy Sepulchre into "a complete brothel"; according to an old superstition, children begotten in the church would be of good fortune.

An old Arab saying, cited approvingly by many travelers (from Jacques de Vitry to Flaubert), admonished the wise to protect

themselves "from anyone traveling to Jerusalem." Others cited a
Turkish proverb: if your friend makes the pilgrimage once, distrust
him; if twice — cut him dead. What would they have said of
Chaucer's Wife of Bath, who had made the pilgrimage to Jerusalem
thrice, in addition to visiting the shrines of Cologne, Canterbury,
and Santiago de Compostela? She may have inspired the unknown
author of the proverb

> He that on pilgrimage goeth ever
> Becometh holy late or never.

In the fourteenth and fifteenth centuries, pilgrimages to Jerusalem became ever larger and more numerous. Piety was now often
allied with other promptings — curiosity, love of adventure, business. Even the Crusaders had often pretended they were simply
"armed pilgrims." All fell under the spell of Jerusalem. Site and
story melted in the minds to create a collective practice.

Less ostentatious and fewer in numbers, Jewish pilgrimage, too,
continued throughout the Middle Ages. Christians entered the city
singing hymns; Jews rent their garments in mourning. In the early
days of Byzantine rule, Jewish pilgrims were allowed in only once a
year to mount the former temple platform — it was now a garbage
dump — and wail over the ashes. Saint Jerome's vivid description of
this annual ritual is a classic example of early Christian anti-
Semitism. He scorns the "faithless people who killed the Son of
God himself" and who now groan in their misery. He virtually
revels in schadenfreude, mocking the "mob of wretches," the "pit-
eous crowd, that comes together, woebegone women and old men
weighed down with rags and years, all of them showing forth in
their clothes and in their bodies the wrath of God. . . . At the price
of their tears," he says, they try to buy back "the city they once sold
for the blood of Christ."

The annual ritual seems to have been discontinued after a while.
There is no record of it later than the fourth century. In the fifth,
Jews were allowed, after paying a tax, to view their "desolate house
of splendour" from a distance. After the Moslem conquest, they
were permitted once more to enter the city proper. It was once

customary to dismiss Jewish life in Jerusalem during the first centuries of Moslem rule (638–1099) as practically nonexistent. The discovery last century of the genizah — a hoard of early medieval Jewish manuscripts, letters, and deeds — in the attic of an ancient Cairo synagogue, forced a thorough reevaluation of this view.

The find brought to light documents that revealed a permanent Jewish settlement in Jerusalem during much of this period and a steady movement of Jewish pilgrims to the city. A ninth-century Italian rabbi named Ahima'az, much like Chaucer's Wife of Bath several hundred years later, made the pilgrimage three times. Another well-to-do pilgrim endowed a synagogue to serve a permanent local community. Jewish pilgrims of an apocalyptic frame of mind reappeared in the ninth century. The Jerusalem that obsessed them was still the same: an earthly destination to be reached, and an icon, the image of a prodigious hope. The sacred rock now being a Moslem shrine, their chief place of prayer was the summit of Olivet with its familiar view over the city. The hill was the scene of ecstatic Jewish rites and pageants. The documents found in the Cairo genizah refer to a tenth-century mystical sect in Jerusalem called Mourners of Zion. Its members apparently were in the habit of climbing the Mount of Olives three times a day — morning, evening, and noon — to pray for deliverance. Jewish pilgrims came not only to pray but to remain and live. They seem to have formed a sizable community by the end of the tenth century. Muqaddasi grumbled in 985 that everywhere in Jerusalem the Jews (and Christians) had the upper hand. The Crusaders' massacre of the local Jews interrupted the Jewish presence in the city, of course, but not for long. As a spiritual (and perhaps political) model, the Crusades soon caused another upsurge of Jewish pilgrimage. Sixty years after the massacres, Benjamin of Tudela passed through Jerusalem and reported two hundred Jews dwelling under the Tower of David.

In the century following the Moslem reconquest of the city, more Jewish pilgrims arrived than at any time since the destruction of Jerusalem by the Romans in AD 70. Pilgrimage was now actively encouraged by the rabbis. Husbands were legally permitted to divorce wives who refused to come with them to Jerusalem, and vice versa. Moses ben Nahman (Nahmanides), a luminary of thirteenth-century Judaism who settled in Jerusalem in 1267, anticipated the nineteenth-century Zionists by expounding not on the End of Days but on mining and farming in the Holy Land, on the growing of wheat and the raising of cattle, and on the building of houses and synagogues in Jerusalem. Remnants of a synagogue he founded survived in the Old City until 1948. His attitude was hardly widespread among Jews of his time. But it would be remembered, and would later figure importantly in the Zionist catechism. A few Jewish pilgrims changed their names upon their return to Europe or Mesopotamia and were hence known as Yerushalmi (Jerusalemite).

From the twelfth-century Spanish-Jewish poet Ibn Ezra and his dirge — "How much longer shall there be weeping in Zion and mourning in Jerusalem? / O have mercy upon Zion and rebuild her walls!" — to the "messiahs" and Gnostics that shook Judaism in the seventeenth and eighteenth centuries, Jerusalem remained the symbol of an unconquerable hope. Jerusalem — or the disembodied idea of it — remained a compulsion, a ruling passion that gripped Jewish mystics everywhere. The kabbalists were possessed by it. In Jerusalem, they expected to celebrate an occult Sabbath of their history. As city and as symbol, Jerusalem was at the core of their identity as individuals and as a people. Christians and Moslems had other sanctuaries, too — Canterbury, Assisi, Compostela, Mecca, and Medina. Jews had only Jerusalem.

The travelogues become especially fascinating during the Renaissance. Superficially, the approach is still medieval in both Christianity and Judaism. Jews expressed it in the ancient prayer, repeated every morning, "I believe with all my heart in the coming of the messiah and even if he be delayed, nevertheless I shall wait for him every day." The Christian ideal was life led as a pilgrimage — as Chaucer put it in the last of the Canterbury tales:

> Jhesu, for this grace with me send
> To shewe you the wey, in this viage
> Of thilke parfit gloriouse pilgrimage
> That highte Jerusalem celestial.*

* May Jesus, in his grace, send me the wit to show you the way on this most perfect, glorious pilgrimage to the celestial Jerusalem.

Relics and souvenirs of the city could be found all over Europe. Not all pilgrims were as acquisitive as William Wey of Exeter College, Oxford, was in 1458 — otherwise little, if anything, would have remained. Wey left a list of his acquisitions, which included

> a stone of Mownt Calvery
> a stone of the sepulkyr
> a stone of the hill of Tabor
> a stone of the pylar that our Lord was stowryched to
> a stone of the place where the cros was hid and founde
> also a stone of the holy cave of Betlehem

The fifteenth and sixteenth centuries inaugurated a new age of discovery and invention. Curiosity now often took the place of contemplation, even among the pious. It was thought odd, to say the least, that as many as fourteen foreskins of Christ were on view in various European churches in Poitiers, Coulombs, Chavraux, Hildesheim, Le Puy-en-Velay, Antwerp, and Rome. Calvin cynically recorded the large number of phials ostensibly filled with the virgin's milk and observed that even if she had been a cow she could not have produced such an enormous quantity. Sir Thomas More, the friend of Erasmus, charged that most pilgrims came not for devotion but for good company, babble, and drink. Questions may have always been asked but were never recorded.

A new kind of worldliness informs many of the itineraries. Before he settled permanently in Jerusalem in 1487, the Italian-Jewish pilgrim Obadiah di Bertinoro must have had a firsthand experience of Italian city-state politics at the height of the Renaissance. He sounds like a man contemplating a coup as he writes that in Jerusalem "an intelligent man, versed in political science, might easily raise himself to be chief of the Jews as well as of the Arabs, for among all the inhabitants there is not a wise and sensible man who knows how to deal affably with his fellow-man; all are ignorant misanthropes intent only on gain." He died in Jerusalem, still out of power, twenty years later.

Felix Fabri, the Dominican friar who made pilgrimage to Jerusalem twice, in 1480 and 1483, was disillusioned almost to the point of disbelief upon realizing that the Valley of Jehoshaphat, where the Last Judgment supposedly shall take place, was so nar-

row. It would hardly be big enough for one nation, he surmised
("the Swabians who are now actually alive could barely find standing room in it"), let alone those not yet born and those already
among the dead. Such remarks would have been unthinkable half a
century earlier. Fabri's account is directed to a lay audience. He
endeavors to satisfy his readers' worldly interests, their love of adventure and curiosity regarding strange and distant races. Fabri is
the first true reporter among the authors of pilgrim books. He has a
good eye and ear. We follow him, as he follows the other pilgrims
through the Fish Gate — the present Jaffa Gate — singing Te
Deums in a low, subdued voice, that they may not offend their
Moslem escorts. But once inside the Holy Sepulchre, Fabri is intrigued more than impressed by their frantic excitement. The men
"groan, sigh and sob. The women shriek as though in labor. . . .
Those weepings and sobbings arise for the most part from the fact
that when one pilgrim weeps another cannot refrain from tears."
Fabri is also conscious of their boredom, once the novelty has worn
off. He finds the continuous walking from place to place in the heat
and dust exceedingly toilsome. He hates the graffiti the pilgrims
leave behind on the walls and even on the slab of stone that covers
the tomb of Christ. He hints at a doubt about the authenticity of
the tomb itself. This, too, would have been inconceivable a short
time before in a pilgrim's book written by a monk.

Fabri echoes the new European cliché image of the East as a
domain of opulence and sensuality. Jerusalem, though a backwater,
seemed a part of it. He was intrigued by the institution of polygamy
among the Moslems and, though he only hints at it, by their sup-
posed sexual prowess. Fabri favorably contrasted the beauty and
cleanliness of the mosques, notably the Dome of the Rock — seen,
of course, only from afar — with the unspeakable sanitary conditions in the dome of Saint Peter's in Rome. (This, at the very time
[1480–1483] Botticelli, Ghirlandajo, Perugino, and Signorelli were
painting the frescoes of the walls of the Sistine Chapel!) He was
blind to the fact that the worshipers in those mosques were also
pilgrims like himself — devout, pious, and believing, as he did, that
by going on pilgrimage they became contemporaneous with God
(*their* God). Moslems too had the idea that by the very act of
pilgrimage, they were reinstating the original condition of man.

Since the Moslem counter-Crusade under Saladin, three hundred years earlier, Jerusalem had been closely linked in Moslem minds with Mecca. Thousands of Moslem pilgrims would stop in Jerusalem on their way to or from Mecca. Special rewards were offered to those who made pilgrimage to both cities in the same year. Moslem pilgrims to Jerusalem were also men and women from Syria and the neighboring regions who, for one reason or another, could not go to Mecca and made pilgrimage to Jerusalem instead.

The idea of the sanctity of Jerusalem had originally been incorporated in Islam from the Judeo-Christian heritage. During the Crusades, the city came to be linked in Islam with the idea of holy war (jihad). The many hadiths extolling the virtues of Jerusalem were a form of war propaganda and appealed to faith as well as to the more mundane sense of the practical. Praying at the holy shrines of Jerusalem was recommended as an especially efficacious way to absolve Moslem pilgrims of sin. In Jerusalem, the pilgrim was said to become "as innocent as on the day of his birth." Small acts of piety by a pilgrim in Jerusalem were said to weigh heavier than elsewhere: "A loaf of bread in alms [given in Jerusalem] is tantamount to giving the weight in gold of all the mountains upon earth."

It is difficult to say how effective such practical appeals were. They may not have been necessary in the first place. Well before the arrival of the Crusaders, the eleventh-century Persian traveler Nasir-i-Khusrau reported that up to twenty thousand Moslem pilgrims were in Jerusalem during the first days of the pilgrimage month. It is likely there were no fewer afterward. Moslem pilgrims certainly outnumbered all other ones in the city, Christian or Jewish. Moslems came from at least as far. The world of Islam extended from Spain to India and beyond. Donning white ihrams, the traditional garments otherwise worn only at Mecca, and with the right shoulder exposed even in the bitter cold and snow of a Jerusalem winter, the pilgrims circled the holy rock under the golden dome, much as they circled the famous Kaaba at Mecca. They then followed a fixed route as indicated by their leaders or in their guidebooks, from one sacred spot on the Temple Mount to another (Burhan al-Din' in his *Book of the Souls that arise to visit the Holy Walls of Jerusalem,* a fourteenth-century guidebook, listed several dozen).

What little record there is of contacts between Moslem and Christian pilgrims points mostly to their mutual disdain. They regarded each other as idolators. The Moslems had revived on the former Temple Mount the ancient Jewish concept of an impersonal deity worshiped in an abstract space. They were shocked by the Christian pilgrims' idea of incarnation and by their attachment to pictures and individuals. Shown a picture of Mary with the Christ child in her lap and told that this was God as a little baby, one Moslem pilgrim, cited by Usama ibn-Munquid, sharply retorted: "Allah is well beyond what infidels say about him." The tendency by some Moslems to endorse Jewish or Christian eschatological traditions aroused the anger of Moslem purists. "It is said that the dead will be resurrected and gathered together in Jerusalem," one wrote. "But this is only an invention of the men of Syria. Allah will resurrect the dead wherever he pleases."

In the more rationalist atmosphere of the eighteenth century, pilgrims' accounts of Jerusalem were sometimes mocked and for the first time distrusted. "I have never been to Judea, thank God!" Voltaire boasted, "and I never will go there." Even in Russia, one distinguished pilgrim was admonished by the czar's foreign minister to "write back only the truth, with *no parables*." The nineteenth century inaugurated a great age of literary tourism to Jerusalem. Her name alone was still one of the most evocative in the language. The first great literary pilgrim, in October 1806, was that quintessential romantic and *réactionnaire*, François René de Chateaubriand. Outside of France, he is remembered today mostly for the Porterhouse steak invented by his chef Montmireil; in his time, he was famous as a leader of the romantic school, as Napoléon's minister to Rome, and as secretary of foreign affairs under Louis XVIII.

He was not a man of very deep beliefs. "I went out to look for images, that's all," he wrote. Perhaps his only true, deeply felt attachment was to his girlfriend, Madame Récamier; we remember her reclining gracefully on her sofa in David's famous painting. Chateaubriand's convictions were hollow but came wrapped in a rich epigrammatic style, and his influence in French literature and politics was immense. André Maurois claimed that as a romantic

Chateaubriand was the original of which Byron was so often the copy. The French statesman's *Itinéraire de Paris à Jérusalem,* published in 1811 after an equally famous literary tour of the American wilderness, was a huge success. Twelve editions appeared within three years of publication.

For Chateaubriand, Bonaparte was the last Crusader, and he himself, a noble Latin pilgrim — the last of a dying race. His vehement text combined the chivalrous spirit of the eleventh century with the bigotry of the nineteenth. Chateaubriand rebelled against the influence of the rationalist philosophers of the eighteenth century who had presented the Crusades in an odious light. He argued that the wars of the Crusades had been fought not merely to deliver Christ's tomb from alien hands but to decide the infinitely more important question of who should have the upper hand in this world — "the enemies of civilization, systematically favoring ignorance, despotism and slavery" (Islam, that is) or the cult of which Catholic France was a principal representative, the cult that in modern times had "resurrected the genius of antiquity and abolished base servitude."

Chateaubriand passed through Greece on his way to Jerusalem and returned through Egypt and Tunis. He would not travel cheaply, uncomfortably, or at his own expense. The wife of Czar Alexander I paid his expenses, which amounted to forty thousand francs. She expected his book would counteract the evil spirit of the French revolutionaries. Chateaubriand's magnificent travel coach was loaded with furs, guns, and bullets for any contingency. He stayed only four days in Jerusalem, but claimed he did not need more since he had read two hundred modern books on the Holy Land as well as all the "rabbinical compilations" and ancient sources he could find. He believed in fleeting visits and explained that in most cases he needed only one look either to confirm or to correct the preconceived impression he had brought with him.

In this spirit, he esteemed himself as Napoléon's counterpart in the intellectual world. "I speak eternally of myself," he confessed — so much so that Stendhal, no self-negator himself, attributed Chateaubriand's failure as an artist to his "stinking egotism." And yet, egoists often write excellent travel books. They take us not only on an exterior voyage to see interesting sites and meet strange people but on an interior voyage as well, into the author's heart, and into our own.

Chateaubriand could be courageous, too: he was the only man in Napoléon's service to resign in protest against the assassination of the Duc d'Enghien. He was also the most conspicuous figure in French literature during the empire. His most intimate acts were recorded by, among others, his barber Adolphe, his secretary Danilo, and his valet Julien, who left us his own obsequious version of their pilgrimage in a book also entitled *Itinéraire de Paris à Jérusalem* ("by Julien, domestique de M. de Chateaubriand").

He was ethnocentric in the distinctive manner of the French, who ascribe their moods to the century itself and the world as a whole. The Armenian patriarch of Jerusalem pleased Chateaubriand with the assurance that all of Asia waited anxiously for the arrival of the French: a single French soldier was enough to suscitate general uprisings everywhere. The high point of Chateaubriand's stay in Jerusalem was his induction as a knight of the Order of the Holy Sepulchre. His craving for the medieval was answered by this ancient honor. It was conferred on him (against payment of an important donation) by the Franciscan guardians. The ceremony took place behind locked doors in the Latin chapel to keep it secret from the Turkish guards outside. Chateaubriand was fitted with the spurs, and the officiating priest struck him three times on his shoulders with the "sword of Godfrey of Bouillon" preserved in the Franciscan treasury. The friars knelt around him in a circle. Chateaubriand was deeply moved. "I am French, as was Godfrey of Bouillon. The touch of his ancient sword instilled me with new love for the glory and honor of France." He carefully preserved the shirt he wore during the ceremony "as a relic." Many years later, his widow presented one sleeve of this shirt to the university library of Geneva "with a guarantee of its authenticity."

Chateaubriand was one of the last to see and describe the Holy Sepulchre before the great fire of 1808. It impressed him as a citadel of piety and Christian charity. The city itself he scrutinized with barely suppressed rage. It was unspeakably miserable and misgoverned by the tyrannical Turks. The streets were unpaved, dark under their vaultings and deserted, like the scattered remains of a "great cemetery in a desert."

In the middle of this "extraordinary desolation," Chateaubriand paused to contemplate "two even more extraordinary things": the Christian friars (presumably the Franciscan guardians of the holy tomb) and the Jews. Both found in their religion the fortitude that enabled them to overcome their horror and their misery among the ruins of Jerusalem. The bitter fate of the friars under the Turks recalled that of the French "under the Reign of Terror." The friars, he claimed, deprived themselves of the last resources of life to ransom their suppliants.* Pillaged by the Turks in the morning, they were back in the evening to pray at the foot of Calvary. Nothing could compel them to abandon the holy tomb,

> neither plunder nor mistreatment nor threat of death. Night and day they chant their hymns. . . . What prevents the armed oppressor from pursuing his prey and overthrowing such feeble ramparts? The charity of the monks.

The Jews of Jerusalem were equally extraordinary; they were

> a petty tribe, scorned and hated. They live apart from the other inhabitants of this city. They bow their heads without complaint; they endure every kind of insult and do not demand justice. . . . If their heads be required they present them at the cemetery. What they did five thousand years ago they still do today. Seventeen times they have witnessed the destruction of Jerusalem, yet nothing can discourage them, nothing can prevent them from hopefully turning their faces to Zion. One must see them in Jerusalem, in their own country, daily expecting a king who will deliver them.

Chateaubriand was touched by such a plight. And yet it served only to emphasize his prejudice. He castigated the Jews' "deplorable blindness." They were "ragged, crouched on the dusthill of Zion, picking at the fleas that devoured them." What were they waiting for? What was there to expect of them? Nothing. There was a new chosen people now: the French.

Twenty-five years after Chateaubriand, another great romantic litterateur arrived in Jerusalem — one who saw her in an entirely

---

* Dr. Edward Clarke, an Englishman who visited Jerusalem five years before (1801), drew a different picture of the holy friars. He said they lived in great comfort and were "the most corpulent he had ever seen issue from the warmest cloisters of Spain or Italy."

different light. Benjamin Disraeli came in search of inspiration by what he called the Asiatic mystery. His notions were eccentric and, like Chateaubriand's, often bordered on camp. Disraeli, too, was a conservative sentimentally enamored of the medieval style. But he believed that the collapse of the Crusader kingdom, on which so much money, courage, and glowing faith had been wasted, had been inevitable. "Jerusalem will always belong either to Israel or to Ismael." Perhaps it would belong to both, for the Arabs, he concluded, were simply "Jews on horseback."

Disraeli rode into Jerusalem on a sunny day in February 1831, swaddled in extravagant Turkish robes and wearing a belt full of pistols and daggers, red slippers, and a red cap. He was twenty-six years old, a young dandy of adventurous temperament, already famous, or notorious, in London for a daring roman à clef, *Vivian Grey,* in which the leading figures of English society, under thinly disguised names, engaged in lively plots and witty dialogues.

Baptized into the Anglican church at the age of thirteen, Disraeli was fascinated by the romance of his Jewish roots and by Jewish history. He was the inventor of the political novel in the English language (Stendhal, in *Le rouge et le noir,* had just pioneered it in French). He came to Jerusalem in search of material for a new political novel, based on the story of David Alroy, a legendary Jewish figure of the twelfth century who had risen against the caliphate of Baghdad to reestablish a Jewish kingdom in Jerusalem. The protagonists of Disraeli's novels often echoed his pet political views. In *Alroy,* they seemed clearly autobiographical. Buckle and Monypenny, Disraeli's biographers, claimed that Alroy represented his "ideal ambition." In the novel, an old Jewish sage tells Alroy: "You ask me what I wish: my answer is a national existence which we have not . . . my answer is the Promised Land . . . my answer is Jerusalem."

Disraeli's grand tour had taken him first to Constantinople, where he had had an audience with the sultan and had reposed "on voluptuous Ottomans, smoked superb pipes, and daily indulged in the luxury of a bath which required half a dozen attendants for its perfection." There were few, if any, such luxuries in Jerusalem. And yet, the few days the young dandy spent there in the winter of 1831 were among the most thrilling and memorable of his life. "I was

thunderstruck," he wrote his sister in a rapture of nostalgia. For
Disraeli, Jerusalem was a hall of ancient fame and glory; within its
walls, he felt he was touching his very roots among the people from
which he was derived by blood and name. "I saw before me apparently a gorgeous city. . . . Except Athens, I never saw anything more
essentially striking. Athens and Jerusalem in their glory must have
been the finest representation of the beautiful and the sublime." As
for its landscape, "nothing can be conceived more wild and terrible
and barren than the surrounding scenery [but] rich woods and
sparkling cultivation would be misplaced."

The February weather was mild. Every night, Disraeli dined out
under the stars on the flat roof of his hostelry in the Armenian
compound, eating spiced oriental food "which would have de-
lighted my father." Every morning, he gazed out on "Yehova's lost
capital." He felt rejuvenated. It was as though during the night
angels had stood watch on the surrounding hilltops, so sweet the air
was, and so still the earth. Every day heightened his exotic imagination and reconfirmed his mystical belief in the heritage of the Jews
— the oldest, purest aristocracy, the most privileged of all living
peoples. In 1831, non-Moslems were still banned from the Moslem
shrines on the site of the former Jewish temple. Disraeli had the
daring to seek entry into the Dome of the Rock but was quickly
surrounded by a crowd of "turbaned fanatics" and escaped with
difficulty.

Many passages in his later books — some eloquent, some expressed in overly flowery prose, and some in embarrassing racial
platitudes — testify to the permanent impression of the city upon
the mind of the young author. The impression was personal, devoid
of all politics. Disraeli was not and would not in the future be a
Jewish nationalist. He was interested in the Jewish past, not the
Jewish future. He took no notice of several prominent Englishmen,
before and during his prime ministry, who proposed the establishment under British protection of a Jewish commonwealth in Palestine with Jerusalem as its capital. Nor did he eye Jerusalem as a
likely object of British colonial ambitions, though as prime minister
he exerted himself to secure Cyprus and the Suez Canal for the
British Empire. Disraeli felt a nostalgic pride in his Jewish roots.
They meant little or nothing to him in the present. He was a

modern Jew at least in the sense that he was in conflict with his
Jewishness. Queen Victoria asked him what his religion was.
"Madame," he responded, "I am the blank page between the Old
and the New Testaments." And yet, like so many Jews, Disraeli felt
the pull of Jerusalem in his bones. He broadcast it in his novels.
Though he was unconnected with the restoration of Israel, he
helped to prepare the ground for it. As Barbara Tuchman has written, "it would be as absurd to leave him out of the story as to leave
the ghost out of Hamlet."

Alphonse de Lamartine was another romantic, poet, statesman, and
man of letters who made Jerusalem a testing ground for his various
ideological and religious obsessions. He claimed to travel with the
heart and soul rather than with the eyes and mind. His heart lay in
the Middle Ages, as did Chateaubriand's; his soul yearned for the
restoration of the Bourbons and the Jews. When, in 1832, one year
after Disraeli's visit to Jerusalem, he took leave of French politics
to tour the Levant, he did so primarily because as an aristocrat
he resented the bourgeois revolution of 1830 and refused to serve
under it.

He believed he was living in an age of decadence and disintegra-
tion and moaned over the *maladie du siècle*. The timing of his visit to
Jerusalem was inadvertently perfect, since it coincided with the
worst outbreak of the plague in two hundred years. Lamartine took
this as an omen. He traveled with an escort of fierce-looking Beduins, "twenty-six horses and bandboxes full of small, frequently
kissed dogs." To protect himself against the plague, he rubbed
himself with oil and garlic — a medicine he himself invented, as "it
was well known that in Constantinople oil merchants were least
affected by the disease." He was, nevertheless, warned that he could
enter the city only at the risk of his life. After some hesitation, he
reconciled himself to riding around the city walls several times on
horseback. It was a bleak day in November. The heavens above
reflected the gloom on earth. In the cemeteries outside the city,
women were moaning over the dead. Many fresh tombs covered
the brittle, dried-out sand, which was "like a heap of ashes fallen
down from the city." There were no birds, no trees — only a few

figs and olives on the ashen soil. "We saw nothing, we heard nothing; no one came out of the city, no one entered; the same desolation, the same silence . . . as we should have expected before the entombed gates of Pompeii or Herculaneum. A complete eternal silence reigns." Later in the day, four funeral processions came out of the Damascus Gate, slowly winding their way alongside the walls. Jerusalem, Lamartine decided, was the "tomb of a whole people."

Nikolai Gogol, the Russian writer, came on pilgrimage because he suffered from writer's block and was going to pieces, unable to complete the second part of *Dead Souls*. He was at work on its third version; the first two, he had burned. The great humanist was sinking into deep mysticism, convinced that God was deliberately depriving him of his creative faculty because of his sins. In this mood Gogol arrived in Jerusalem. He believed he still had a great spiritual mission to perform in Russia, but "until I have been to Jerusalem I shall be incapable of saying anything comforting to anyone."

He was frantically in search of a religious experience. When this was denied him, he broke down completely. He was in addition aghast at the dirt, indifference, and disorder in the Holy Sepulchre. He tried to pray, but there was too much confusion in the basilica. The liturgy sped so quickly "that the most winged prayers could not have flown after it. Before I had time to pull my wits together it was over." He left the church in a state of total shock, as though there had been some terrible misunderstanding. He was repelled by the gaudy decor and the glossy marble. Like so many pilgrims before and after, he reflected how much more moving the crypt would have been had it been left a naked rock, starkly bare, a hole gaping in the dark. To Count Tolstoy, he wrote, "Not only were my prayers unable to rise up to heaven, I could not even tear them loose from my breast."

Gogol was equally discouraged by the monotonous hills in the environs. He likened them to gray waves of the sea in a gale. No doubt they had been very fertile and picturesque in the time of Jesus when every Jew sat under his vine and under his fig tree, Gogol reflected; but now the landscape was merely depressing. There were only a few olive trees straggling up the slopes — trees that were dusty and gray like the rocks themselves. They said nothing to him. Perhaps Russia was the Promised Land, after all. He keenly felt his insensitivity. He felt dry and hard like a block of wood. "I have never been so little content with the state of my heart as in Jerusalem and afterward." Gogol sailed back wondering why God did not destroy such a wretch as he. He fell into melancholy after his return, and came even more under the influence of fanatic mystics. They convinced him that his art was sinful. He struggled on with the third version of his book. In 1852, he destroyed it, and shortly afterward died.

With the arrival of Gustave Flaubert, a different age dawned (or perhaps the spirit of the eighteenth century was rekindled). Flaubert was the first great literary iconoclast to communicate his true feelings about the earthly Jerusalem. He rode into Jerusalem in 1850 with the idea of *Madame Bovary* beginning to take shape in his mind. What made him come? He could not have hoped for spiritual discoveries at this time and place. Madame Bovary was already supplanting in his heart his girlfriend Louise Colet. Was he running away from her? Or from the provincial boredom of his mother's house at Rouen? What was he looking for? He was a little too self-conscious at first. "We enter through the Jaffa Gate and I let a fart escape as I cross the threshold very involuntarily." Next, self-consciousness gave way to debunking. "I was even annoyed at bottom by this Voltaireanism of my anus."

Everywhere Flaubert went in Jerusalem, he sought out the macabre. His first visit was to the slaughterhouse in a paved square entirely covered with coagulated blood. He felt throughout that he was stepping on human bones, while all around him, weird and musty, the old religions were "rotting in the sun." The light — in August — seemed to him as on a day in winter, it was so hard and white. He was spellbound by the spectral sight of ruins, which he found "diabolically grand." Everything else was *rotten* — "the dead dogs in the street, the religions in the churches (great idea). The Polish Jew in his fur cap walks silently by his falling wall, in whose shade, smoking, the inert Turkish soldier counts his beads. The Armenians curse the Greeks, the Greeks detest the Latins who excommunicate the Copts."

Disillusioned even before he came, Flaubert noted the complete absence of all the "expected sensations," whatever they were. He was neither moved religiously nor stimulated as an artist. He was not even able to drum up a little "hatred for the priests, which at least would have been something. . . . This morning, in the Holy Sepulchre, a dog would have been more moved than I. Whose fault is it, merciful God? Theirs, yours or mine? Theirs, I believe, next mine but especially *yours!* How false everything is! What lies! All is whitewashed, veneered, polished; calculated for propaganda and the exploitation of the customer." Inside the basilica, the bad taste reached "monumental proportions," and Flaubert could not decide whether it was more sad than grotesque or more grotesque than sad that a full-length portrait of Louis Philippe adorned the Latin chapel.

In the evening, he and his travel companion, the journalist and photographer Maxime Du Camp, repaired for rounds of hashish or opium in the French consulate.* The consul was Paul Emile Botta, a famous naturalist, physician, and archaeologist. Flaubert and Du Camp could not have found a more kindred spirit. Botta cultivated an atmosphere of fin de siècle even before the century was half over. He was "a human ruin, in the city of ruins, who believed in nothing and hated everything, except the dead," Du Camp wrote. He was at the same time delightful company, hospitable as an Arab chieftain, lean, passionate, and a great music-lover. As a Protestant, he was inclined to favor the reestablishment of the Inquisition exclusively against Catholic dignitaries. When the debate got overly heated, Botta "reached for his cello, played a melody by Schubert and became calm as Saul by the harp of David." Flaubert came away more embittered by Jerusalem than before. He was also suffering from the first symptoms of syphilis — contracted earlier on his trip, in Beirut, during a homosexual adventure with a young Maronite.

* Jerusalem attracted photographers before most European capitals. Within a few weeks after the first successful photographic process was made public in 1839 at a meeting of the French Academy of Sciences, "pioneers of the new art were already at work in Jerusalem."

In the first half of the nineteenth century, European pilgrims still felt that in Jerusalem they were stepping back into the Middle Ages. The roads to the city were unsafe. The gates were locked at night. By midcentury, public amenities in Jerusalem began to improve. Turkish rule, or misrule, was still as arbitrary and erratic as before. But Jewish and other European immigrants were beginning to change the face of the city. The opening of the Suez Canal in 1869 directed the growing flow of tourists to Jerusalem, which until then had attracted only the very pious, the rich, or the very eccentric. Like navigators, pilgrims still carefully recorded the exact hour they first saw the city from a distance and the hour they saw her last, on their way back to the Mediterranean coast. There were faster and more comfortable boats awaiting them there. In 1869, Thomas Cook, a Baptist lay preacher, launched his Eastern Tours and personally led the first party of middle-class English tourists to Jerusalem. The travelers camped outside the walls and were served English tea and crumpets on tables laid with silver and starched linen as they contemplated the view from their carpeted tents.

Travel to Jerusalem was becoming easier and safer than at any time since the fall of the Roman Empire. New steamers made the journey from Naples to Port Said in five or six days. Jerusalem was not yet free of certain barbaric sights. Criminals were still executed publicly by sword outside the Jaffa Gate. In 1867, according to an eyewitness, the first blow of the executioner, a novice, swerved and the unfortunate victim yelled, "You are hurting me." Blow after blow struck him wildly until at the sixteenth cut he still was not yet dead. The executioner then turned his victim around and proceeded to saw through his neck as though he were killing a sheep.

Close to a million European pilgrims and tourists visited Jerusalem during the nineteenth century. This resulted in an avalanche of books and travelogues about Jerusalem and the Holy Land. In England alone, the number of pious Holy Land travel books published between 1840 and 1880 was estimated at sixteen hundred. Many were written in a tone of breathless excitement. Jerusalem was described as a dream city in a countryside that teemed with improbable biblical figures: Bath-shebas as queenly as Renaissance Madonnas, and handsome young Davids and Jonathans tending the sheep. There were woodcuts and hand-colored lithographs portraying picturesque Arabs reclining on broken columns in Jerusalem among stately palms and Rembrandtesque old rabbis facing the Wall of Tears. None portrayed the prevailing poverty and dirt, or the idolatry of the relic and souvenir industry. The Jordan River, rarely wider than thirty feet, was seen as a Delphic, mighty, rolling stream.

Among the arrivals was Herman Melville. Like so many others, he was torn between the will to believe and the tendency to doubt — a malaise he had already worked into *Moby-Dick* as a major emotional theme. Melville spent hours outside the basilica, in the little niche, visiting with the Turkish guards whose job it was to prevent members of different Christian sects from stabbing one another.

Yet another visitor was Edward Lear, landscape painter and poet, author of the famous nonsense rhyme

> There was an Old Man of the East
> Who gave all of his children a feast
> But they all ate so much
> and their conduct was such
> That it killed the Old Man of the East.

Lear had been commissioned by the Prince of Wales to make a painting of Jerusalem. He produced the picture of a mystical, serene, exquisitely beautiful city. Privately, in a letter to Lady Waldgrave, he called Jerusalem "that vile place, the foulest and odiousest on earth."

And there was Mark Twain, of course, who came in 1867 to laugh and mock, and, in *The Innocents Abroad,* to denounce the illustrators and devout authors of books on Jerusalem, many of them Protestant parsons. They "could no more write dispassionately and impartially about it than they could about their own wives and children," he observed. Twain believed that irreverence was a champion of liberty and its best defense. He walked through the city and saw not the Jerusalem of the devotional guidebooks, whose authors had entered her with weeping eyes, but a monotonous "pauper village, . . . knobby with countless little domes as a prison door is with bolt-heads." Twain raged against the Bible, which he knew so well ("some good morals and a thousand lies"), and against Jerusalem, which he did not want to know ("the abode of ignorant, depraved, superstitious, dirty, lousy, thieving [Arab] vagabonds." There will not be a Second Coming, Twain warned: Christ had been in Jerusalem once; he will not deign to come again.

The city exercised a fatal spell upon her beholders, skeptics or devout; it clouded their visions to fit an inner image.

The spell was nowhere more powerful than among the great mass of poor Russian peasants who began to come on pilgrimage during the second half of the nineteenth century. As a mass movement, its roots were half religious and half political. Pilgrimage to Jerusalem had been frowned upon until then by the Russian church. The mass movement of Russian pilgrims to Jerusalem started only in 1847, with the active encouragement, for imperial reasons, of the Russian government.

Up to twenty thousand Russian pilgrims, in a state of high excitation, would congregate in Jerusalem at Easter time alone. Their piety, if not poverty, demanded that they arrive on foot. They came singly or in twos and threes, from the most forlorn and distant points in the czarist empire. Many walked from the far interior or the upper Ural. Some crossed the Black Sea in December — a thousand of them packed together on the shelterless decks of Black Sea steamers no bigger than riverboats. Others were led like cattle, on foot, across Turkey and Syria, offering no complaints, only endless murmurs of "Glory be to thee, O God! Glory to thee!" Many perished along the way. Most brought their provisions with them: piles of black bread, not in loaves but in waste ends and saved-up crusts, often gone moldy, which they would spread out in the sun to dry and make edible again.

They came ashore at Jaffa, kissing the ground, crossing themselves profusely, singing hymns, while tears of emotion flowed from their eyes. They would call one another *brat* (brother), *atets* (father), or *dyed* (grandfather), according to what their relative ages were. They walked everywhere, bathed in every sacred pool, approached every sacred site on hands and knees. Emerging from the waters of the Jordan, into which they dipped clad in white shrouds of the kind used for burials, they would look like the awakened dead on the day of the Last Judgment.

They did not expect a miracle. They expected to return home as changed men and women; many, perhaps, did. Everywhere they went, they sang hymns — and were pursued by money changers, hawkers of cheap souvenirs, and beggars. However poor they were, they still spared a kopeck or two for alms. Many observers noted their tenderness and constant good cheer. In 1884, a new twelve-thousand-pound bell, cast in Russia, was pulled from Jaffa to Jerusalem and to the top of the Mount of Olives by Russian pilgrims, mostly women, who chanted all the way. The road to Jerusalem was still unpaved. The transport took weeks. The women changed places every few minutes, the rested taking the places of the tired. The Russian government built an entire compound in Jerusalem where the pilgrims were freely housed and fed cabbage soup and kasha (boiled buckwheat). The Russian consulate and the local offices of the Imperial Russian Palestine Society were on the same premises. So were a few "superior" apartments, for "pilgrims of a higher class." The proximity of wealth and wretchedness in the Russian compound, like living and dead bodies chained together, reflected the situation of the czarist empire as a whole.

What made the Russian peasants come? Stephen Graham, a young English writer who traveled with them from Russia disguised as a pilgrim from the Don area, did not pretend to know the full answer to this question. It was sometimes a vow made during illness to save the dying or expiate a sin. There was also something older, more basic, Graham wrote, "a force much deeper than their power of articulation." Like Tolstoy, he assumed that in the world of the poor muzhik there was a new road, leading to a "new Jerusalem."

Royalty now also came, in ever-increasing numbers. For their pleasure, Cook & Son imported gilded furniture and European chefs and set up little tent cities outside the city walls. Crown Prince Rudolf of Austria and his party arrived in 1881 in nine carriages with 145 horses and mules attended by "28 servants, 5 cooks, 2 of which were *maitres chefs de cuisine*." The Austrian prince and his party were housed in

25 tents of the first class, two of which [were] lined with rich silk of tricolor green, red and yellow, to represent the Austrian flag, 2 dining tents, 1 reception tent for H.H., 1 sleeping and 1 dressing tent for H.H., with toilet set, mirror, jugs, basins of first China porcelain, each furnished with finest Persian carpets, 2 elegant silk velvet sofas and 6 upholstered armchairs as well as 30 chairs called *pliantes à la mode de Paris* and 30 camp stools, chandeliers, Chinese flower vases, 3 different sets for coffee (Chinese, Turkish and one Sèvres porcelain), nargilehs, chibouks and cigarettes *à volontée* and a costly musical box that plays twelve tunes.

We owe knowledge of these details to Alexander Howard, Cook's agent in Jaffa, who wrote a little brochure in 1888 "to convey to those who have travelled through Palestine an idea of the difficulties met and overcome." The meals he served included French oysters and barrels of Russian caviar. There was no refrigeration in the great heat but there were no upset royal stomachs either or Howard would not have been made a Chevalier of the Gold Cross of Merit of the Imperial Austrian Order of Francis Joseph, and soon after, by the future Victor Emmanuel III, a Knight of the Order of the Crown of Italy.

Prince Edward, the future king of England, also came, and had himself tattooed on the chest by a tattoo artist in the Old City, before being entertained by the Turkish pasha with sixty-two dishes, including dessert. Ten years afterward, his son, the future King George, was tattooed "by the same man who tattooed Papa" — but unlike Papa, George insisted on having his tattoo on the nose (it was carefully removed by surgery shortly before his coronation). The German kaiser, Wilhelm II, came in 1898. He was driven up to the Mount of Olives via a new road built especially for his visit. He ordered the car stopped at one bend so that he might lecture his Turkish hosts that the curve was far too sharp and narrow to allow a cannon to pass through. Kings, dukes, princes, American millionaires, and a host of other eccentrics, rich and poor — monomaniacs, oddballs, and cranks — poured into Jerusalem after Wilhelm. For cranks especially, the city became a magnet at the turn of the century, and it remains one today.

As a gathering place of three separate creeds that contained the still wider disparities of sect and sect, nation and nation, Jerusalem's attraction for eccentrics and cranks was hardly surprising. There was a psychic affinity between the frenzies. A similar thread ran through the self-tortured asceticism of the early Christian era, the fanaticism of Moslem dervishes, and of the self-proclaimed Jewish messiahs of Jerusalem in the late Middle Ages. The affinity is recognizable today among holy-war mongers of Islam and Jewish fanatics who expect to generate a so-called spiritual renaissance by throwing the Jews into the sea or dynamiting a mosque. "It is a recognised fact that a large proportion of insanity takes the form of religious mania," the author of a popular guide to life in Jerusalem pontificated — apparently with good reason — in 1904. At the turn of the century, Jerusalem attracted several of the more striking eccentricities of Christianity in America and in northern Europe. Every year, several visitors or tourists claimed they were reincarnated Isaiahs or that they had been sent out by Christ to announce his imminent second coming.

There were some who claimed to be the prophets Nathan or Elijah. Others came to live a biblical verse, disastrously, to the letter — "a fire shall come forth," for example, or "if thy right eye offend thee, pluck it out, . . . for it is profitable for thee that one of thy members should perish, and not that thy whole body should be cast into hell." Still others traveled to Jerusalem because they had calculated the exact day and hour of the Advent. When the time passed with no distinguishing features, they collapsed, or threw their clothes off in the Holy Sepulchre, or tried to commit suicide on the summit of Olivet. The English lady who settled on Mount Scopus in constant readiness to welcome the Lord's return with a cup of tea was harmless; the man who jumped off a church tower because he had been assured by Ezekiel in a dream that he would fly straight away to heaven was not. A Dutch countess spent a fortune building a huge, mysterious building on Mamilla Street (today Agron) because she felt a responsibility to house the "hundred and forty and four thousand . . . children of Israel" spoken of in Rev. 7:4. The empty skeleton of the building was still standing seventy years later when it was pulled down to make way for a luxury hotel.

For months on end in 1883, a solitary Englishman, of brick-red complexion, with a measuring rod and a Bible under his arm, could be seen wandering about the outskirts of Jerusalem, explaining in a low, soft voice that he knew not only the true spot of the crucifixion (the place called Calvary was "false," he pointed out) but also the exact position of the Garden of Eden. He continued his search until a cable arrived calling him back to duty to fight another fanatic, the mahdi in Sudan. The Englishman was General Charles George Gordon and he died not long afterward in the battle of Khartoum. There were also Lydites, Millerites, Tishbites, and other obscure sects whose members would faint of excitement during their various manifestations; and men who fasted seven days on the top of Olivet and expected the mountain to cleave in two before them. In 1928, Arthur Koestler struck up an acquaintanceship with a self-proclaimed prophet who lived in the burial shafts known as the Tombs of the Judges. According to Koestler, the seer claimed he had already predicted every event that had happened in his, the seer's, lifetime and that 1928 would be the year of the Last Judgment. (In 1953, he communicated once again with Koestler, this time from his sanctuary outside Los Angeles.)

Doctors once spoke of a form of hysteria that attacked pilgrims only. It was called "Jerusalem squabble poison," or *fièvre Jerusalem-miene*. The phenomenon is rampant today, too. The pilgrims come and make the rounds, dazed with wonder and sun. Some expect the quiet of a church or a museum and are shocked to find a bustling city — a city in tension and even war. Every year, there are pilgrims for whom this is too much, and they collapse. Local psychiatrists now speak of a Jerusalem syndrome. A hundred-odd pilgrims and tourists are treated each year at Kfar Shaul Hospital, the government mental-health center serving the Jerusalem area, for breakdowns related to this syndrome, which involves messianic fantasies and delusions of being Mary Magdalene, John the Baptist, or other biblical characters. They are mostly Americans and almost all are Protestant. Many have a strong grounding in the Bible. In Jerusalem, they suddenly take off their clothes or shout prophecies on street corners, only to revert to normal after a few days' treatment.

The director of Kfar Shaul — fittingly enough, his surname is Bar-El, which means "Son of God" — was quoted a few years ago in the newspapers as saying that the Jerusalem syndrome was a malaise specific to this city and probably caused by the difference between the image and the reality of Jerusalem. The difference precipitates in those affected a mystical experience tantamount to a deep shock. "They are disappointed and frustrated, and their reaction is to try and lift their spirits by losing control. They do things they wouldn't do elsewhere." Patients are usually placed in a closed ward and given sedatives and intensive treatment to bring them back to reality. Once recovered, according to Dr. Bar-El, they often say that their collapse was not traumatic or unpleasant but a "good experience." Their pilgrimage, they say, has been worthwhile.

CHAPTER SIX

View from the Ramparts

Edward Gibbon, often dubious of a higher motive, wrote that Jerusalem derived her reputation "from the number and importance of her memorable sieges." We know of at least fifty major sieges, sacks, captures, and destructions during the past thirty centuries (three in this century alone). Sieges are the most ancient form of total war. During sieges, civilians are more vulnerable than soldiers. They are the first to die and the last to eat. Soldiers are fed better and they fight from behind high walls and other well-protected positions.

In Jerusalem, soldiers have usually fared almost as badly as civilians. Her high walls have demonstrated over the ages their limited defensive value. They remind us that in the Western mind Jerusalem has also been — and for many, still is — a metaphor for destruction and the vengeance of an offended God. She is the city where believers have killed unbelievers to give life to faith.

Josephus's description of besieged Jerusalem in AD 70 is often quoted: the houses stacked with unburied corpses, the streets teeming with starving children and old men. Josephus's tale reads like a history of the siege of Leningrad, where more civilians died of starvation alone than were killed by the atom bomb in Hiroshima and Nagasaki. Within a few months of the Roman siege of Jerusalem, according to Josephus, seven hundred thousand people perished. The mass of dead bodies was so great that the living no longer cared to bury them. Titus, the Roman commander, called God to witness — such cant is common in the history of war — "that this was not his doing."

We get an idea of what total war meant in the ancient world from the text of the so-called Israel stela (preserved in the Cairo Museum), which bears Merneptah's victory hymn of 1230 BC:

> Plundered is Canaan
> Carried is Ashkelon
> Israel is laid waste.

In the same vein is an inscription by Sargon, the Assyrian general. Sargon was the conqueror of Samaria, in the hills north of Jerusalem, a century before the first total destruction of Jerusalem herself. In his inscription, he presents himself as the man who "despoiled Ashdod, . . . caught the Greeks [on their islands] like fish, [and] exterminated Kasku." He then boasts: "I smashed like a flood storm the country of Hamath, I destroyed the sixteen districts of Damascus [making them look] like hills of [ruined cities over which] the flood [had swept]."

Sennacherib's famous tablet commemorating his total destruction of Babylon a few decades later (the Bible records similar feats of his in the vicinity of Jerusalem) has a similar ring: "The city and its houses, from its foundation to its top I destroyed, I devastated, I burned with fire. The wall and the outer wall, temples and gods, towers of brick and earth as many as there were, I razed. . . . I made its destruction more complete than by a flood."

The act of destruction, as well as its moral justification, anticipated the nuclear age. In *The City in History,* Lewis Mumford said that Sennacherib lacked only our efficiency, our missiles and bombs, and our massive hypocrisy in disguising our motives even from ourselves.

The Bible is filled with equally vivid images of slaughter and devastation. Destructiveness is the rule, not the exception in the Bible. In Judges, we read that Abimelech took a city and, as a matter of course, "slew the people that was therein, and beat down the city, and sowed it with salt." The strongest metaphors of ruin focus on Jerusalem. In 2 Kings, we read of the burning of every house in the city by an army that "broke down the walls of Jerusalem round about," and of forces that wipe Jerusalem "as a man wipeth a dish, wiping it, and turning it upside down." In

Jeremiah, "no man dwelleth therein," and the carcasses of men fall
"as dung upon the open field."

Devastation is the subject of an entire book. In dirgeful, elegiac
rhythms — like the sound of doom — the anonymous author of
Lamentations broods over the scenes of famine, carnage, and destruction in Jerusalem after her fall to the Babylonians in 586 BC. As
an eyewitness, he offers dramatic glimpses. His shock is unrelieved
by hope. God himself is "as an enemy."

> How lone she sits
> The city big with people
> Is widowed.
> Famed of nations
> Queen of countries
> And now enslaved.

An enormous bas-relief from the royal palace of Nineveh, today in
the British Museum,* enables us to visualize one of the great sieges
mentioned in the Bible. It depicts the sack of Lakhish, a Judean
fortress southwest of Jerusalem. The sack of Jerusalem cannot have
been much different. The bas-relief covers an entire wall and is
remarkably well preserved. Its three well-articulated parts picture
the main stages of the battle and its aftermath. Viewing it, we seem
to occupy a ringside seat overlooking the battlefield — some five
hundred feet from the southwest corner of the city — on a spot
where Sennacherib might have stood supervising the advance of his
troops.

We see one of the great siege trains employed to attack and
level entire cities. It advances on Lakhish from the northwest. We
observe her double walls and towers, very much like those of
Jerusalem. Within the walls, in the background, we see a great
palace. The site is teeming with people. A great human mass surges
forward and backward. The defenders man the battlements and
shoot at the assailants with bows and slings. We see Sennacherib's
archers and stone throwers scaling one of these battlements under a

---

* A copy is on display in the Israel Museum, Jerusalem.

shower of burning torches and arrows. The moat is littered with corpses. The assailants are led by men in war helmets who are armed with spears and great shields. Others heap mounds of earth and timber against the city wall to form a great ramp. They are steadily moving up their ladders, battering rams, and their wheeled war machines (not unlike modern armored cars or tanks).

The battle over, we see Sennacherib sitting on a throne outside his field camp. A procession of captives is led before him. Other prisoners — perhaps their leaders — are being put to torture or executed by decapitation and impalement. The legend reads: "Sennacherib, king of the world, king of Assyria, sat on his throne and the spoil from Lakisu [Lakhish] passed in review before him."

Behind the king, we see forlorn women and old men — the surviving civilian population of Lakhish — with bundles on their backs, wandering off into exile or slavery through a familiar landscape of vines, olive trees, and figs.

Sennacherib was as thorough at Lakhish as he had been at Babylon. The city was almost completely dismantled. The site of Lakhish, according to the archaeological evidence, remained uninhabited for almost a century. Lakhish was one of the great cities of the plain. On level ground, each rampart and each house had to be knocked down separately. It was simpler, relatively speaking, to devastate a hill city like Jerusalem. Her structural fragility is apparent even today to anyone walking around the walls of the present Old City. The city rested on an artificial substructure of terraces and retaining walls. Each was buttressed by the fill of the next-lower terrace, all the way down the steep slopes. The stability of the whole system ultimately depended on the walls downhill that supported Jerusalem at the base. Once these lowest walls were breached, the fill behind them, supporting the terraces, collapsed. This in turn made the upper terraces come down too. Within a few years, rain and erosion would spread the destruction far up the remaining built-up area. The resultant cascades have come to light in several archaeological excavations.

> The Lord was as an enemy: he hath swallowed up . . . all her palaces: he hath destroyed his strong holds, . . . he hath abhorred his sanctuary, . . . he hath not withdrawn his hand from destroying: . . . he

made the rampart and the wall to lament; they languished together.
Her gates are sunk into the ground; he hath destroyed and broken
her bars: . . . the mountain of Zion . . . is desolate, the foxes walk
upon it.

Great lost cities, of course, are common archetypes in most cultures.
Flaubert, in *Salammbô,* saw the fall of Carthage as emblematic of
civilization as a whole. Tolstoy used the burning of Moscow in *War
and Peace* as a "sign": above the swarm and scramble of catastrophe,
there emerge, as in a jeremiad, eternal laws that govern the universe.
The catastrophes of cities often appear as mythic events — and
nowhere more so than in Jerusalem after the fall of 586 BC and,
again, in AD 70. Both were seen as awesome events fraught with
metaphysical meaning. Jerusalem has since been so enmeshed in its
own myth that it has often been hard to separate myth from reality.

   In recounting the fall of a great city — be it Jerusalem or, for that
matter, Babylon or Hiroshima — it is easy to lose perspective and
fall into rhetoric. The account of the actual fall often becomes a
repetitive tale of uniform calamity: siege, fire, rape, famine, devastation, spoilage, slaughter, the sale and occasional ransoming of captives. Such catastrophes have often been seen as heralds of greater
things — the advent of a new way of life, and the defeat of an
outdated one. The sense of loss — or the theology of the fall —
depends on the moral climate of the time. It is not always commen-
surate with the actual extent of destruction. The religious fantasies
of early Reformation Europe had much in common with those of
first-century Jerusalem. Hence, the fall of Constantinople to the
Moslems in 1453 and the sack of Rome seventy-four years later by
the troops of Charles V (many of them Lutherans) were seen as
apocalyptic events, heavy with cosmic consequences, even though
both cities had been subjected to far worse catastrophes in the past.
The physical and social results were quite limited. Rome and Constantinople did not shrink into complete obscurity as did Jerusalem
after her fall. Constantinople experienced a great flowering under
the Ottoman sultans. Within two years of the sack of Rome, the
carnival was celebrated with great pomp; within six, Michelangelo
was back at work in the Sistine Chapel, painting the Last Judgment

on the end wall — an attempt, perhaps, to atone for the sack or externalize a bad dream.

The Jewish theology of the fall of AD 70 was even more alive with superstitious obsessions and supernatural expectations. In the final days of the Roman siege of Jerusalem, when the Temple Mount was already in enemy hands and burning, the Jewish garrison holding out in the Upper City continued to post daily sentinels on the rooftops to scan the near mountaintops for the coming of the messiah: he was expected to descend momentarily from one of the surrounding hilltops. The collective fears of the besieged Jews made the denouement appear as more than just another military defeat. Not only they were defeated, God himself was. Not only they were driven into exile, God himself was in exile. It was a theological and existential calamity. A later age might have called it Kafkaesque or spoken dejectedly of the "death of God." The whole world was out of joint. The destruction symbolized it.

A new Hebrew word was coined to describe the cataclysm — *khurban* — an abstract noun, never before or after used in this sense, to denote a state of transcendental ruination. Time did not soften the sense of loss. The city followed the exiles like a ghost. Wherever they went, they looked back to her. Her ruins continued to rise into view. There was no new land for them anywhere. She became their disemboweled Capital of Memory. Nothing like this ever happened to another vanquished people. It is vain to speculate today whether this happened by design or through accident or a whim. The consequences were considerable and are still evident. The loss and destruction of Jerusalem was enshrined in learned books of speculation written long after the event. Surmise and exegesis attested to the continuing power of the obsession. Centuries after the destruction, the Talmud still saw fit to describe and enunciate the daily ritual in Jerusalem's temple as though it were still taking place. For centuries, the same prayers were said in her memory. The same dirges were read. Interpretation was piled on interpretation in an endless attempt to come to terms with what seemed a preternatural eclipse.

The Christian theology of the city's fall was equally rife with unearthly calculation, and with some occult spite. The church fathers saw the devastation of the city as just punishment for her rejection of Christ. Whatever Christ himself may have intended, her ruin was seen as the literal fulfillment of his prophecy. It was thought remarkable that the flames of war had consumed the temple of Jerusalem and the capitol of Rome at almost the same time. (The capitol was burned on December 19 in AD 69, during the civil war between Vitellius and Vespasian; the temple was burned the following year, on August 10.)

To emphasize his conviction that the destruction of Jerusalem was the outstanding event of his military career, Titus built a triumphal arch in Rome that still stands today at the south end of the Forum on the via Sacra. A relief inside the arch displays the looted instruments of Jewish worship: the seven-armed candelabra, the silver trumpets, the table of the shewbread. Titus had deposited these pieces in the Temple of Peace. They must have been especially noteworthy among all the glories of Rome, since they were still preserved and remembered four centuries later, after the sack of Rome by the Vandals, when they were transferred to Carthage.*

It says something about collective fantasies that, eighteen centuries after Jerusalem's devastation by the Romans, the French orientalist and historian Ernest Renan still defined the event as an *"immense bonheur."* Had the city been spared, Renan feared, not Christianity but Judaism might have conquered the world. Within a few months, Moses Hess, one of the early ideologists of modern Zionism, published his seminal *Rome and Jerusalem,* in which he urged all Jews to reassemble in Jerusalem and enact "the Sabbath of their history," as the Italians were then doing "on the ruins of ancient Rome." Faith is proverbially blind. Hess ignored the presence of Arabs in Jerusalem, both Moslems and Christians. They disappeared before his eyes as in their own *Arabian Nights.*

The accumulation of so many counterpart memories — a rich debris of conflicting meanings, promises, and desires — makes

* Nineteen centuries later, the arch of Titus, or what remains of it, figured in a bizarre plot of "historical vindication": Jewish soldiers from Palestine serving in the British expeditionary forces in Italy in 1944 made preparations to blow it up. The plot was uncovered before damage was done and the affair was hushed up by sympathetic officers.

Jerusalem into a city of reflecting mirrors. Each tier in the ancient walls that still surround the historic core stands for one — or more — of the conflicting frenzies. The present walls were built between 1537 and 1541 under the Ottoman sultan Suleiman the Magnificent, who announced himself in this fashion:

> I, who am Sultan of the Sultans of East and West, fortunate lord of the domains of the Romans, Persians, and Arabs, Hero of creation, Neriman of the earth and time, Padishah and Sultan of the Mediterranean and the Black Sea, the extolled Kaaba and Medina the illustrious, and of Jerusalem the noble . . .

There follows a long list of kingdoms and lands; Baghdad in the east, Hungary and Algeria in the far west; Yemen in the south, Ctesiphon and Azerbaijan in the north. Jerusalem was one of the least important outposts of the sultan's realm; his impact upon the architecture of the city was nevertheless considerable. Suleiman was the most serious threat to Christendom since the rise of Islam. His advance into central Europe stopped only at the gates of Vienna. He might have changed the course of European history had the torrential rains not prevented him from bringing up the bulk of his heavy artillery. In the middle of his European campaign, he ordered his architects to rebuild the walls of Jerusalem. The new walls are generally thought to have been designed by his military architect, the great Sinan, who built, among many great monuments, the Suleimaniye mosque in Istanbul. There is no mistaking Sinan's originality and distinctiveness. His architecture constitutes one of the major Ottoman contributions to culture.

The new Jerusalem walls followed more or less the same lines as those built by the Crusaders on earlier foundations left behind by the Arabs, the Byzantines, the Romans, and the Jews. The Crusader walls had been dismantled in 1219 — an early form of "scorched-earth" tactics — by the Ayyubid sultan Malik al-Muazzam Isa, Saladin's nephew, to discourage a Crusader reoccupation of the city. For three centuries, under the Mamluk sultans of Egypt, Jerusalem was an open, unwalled city — a place of retirement, or of stylish banishment, for members of the Egyptian military hierarchy. Their stately townhouses, the elegant design of their minarets and convents, their richly endowed religious colleges, their fine colonnades and public fountains, contrast oddly, but not unpleasantly, with their reputation as a caste of ruthless militarists (former slaves) selected and bred as one bred dogs, hawks, or horses.

The Mamluks built no fortifications in Jerusalem but nevertheless left a physical stamp upon the secular city, an architectural legacy more graceful than that of most other Moslem regimes before or since. Many of their civil buildings still stand and, though dilapidated, compare with the best in Cairo. They are vaulted and entirely built of stone; no bricks were used, nor wood for roofs.

In the last quarter of the fifteenth century, two Jewish travelers reported that Jerusalem was an unwalled city, yet with a population, apparently, of 10,000 Moslem and 250 Jewish households. This is how the Ottomans found her in 1516, after an unusually brief battle.

> Our Lord the great Sultan and brilliant governor, Sultan of the strangers, Arabs and Persians, has commanded the construction of this blessed wall. . . . Suleiman the son of Salim Khan, may Allah preserve his reign and his kingdom.

Thus reads a sixteenth-century inscription over the Damascus Gate, the largest and most fanciful of the gates set in the Ottoman walls. It is not entirely clear why the Ottomans decided to rebuild the walls after three centuries with none. The improved security under Suleiman did not warrant new walls. Perhaps they were built as a decoration, for aesthetic reasons, or as a monument to the sultan's glory. The sawtooth rim and narrow firing slots were already made obsolete at the time of building by the invention of firearms. Two Ottoman tombstones (each neatly capped by a stone fez) inside the Jaffa Gate commemorate the memory — or the shame — of two native craftsmen employed in the construction. They are said to have been executed for those same transgressions often imputed to public contractors.

The lower visible tiers — Roman or Herodian — are notable for their distinctive masonry: layer upon layer of huge, beautifully cut stones, each with smooth margins, three or four feet high and up to ten feet long. The more recent layers, of Byzantine, Arab, Crusader, and Ottoman origin, look small and shabby in comparison.

Restoration of the walls was begun in 1919 by the British, thanks to the indefatigable governor Ronald Storrs; but all work was suspended, after Storrs's departure, owing to lack of funds, civil unrest, or both. Restoration work was resumed by the Israeli municipality after 1967. A promenade was built on the rim. It is now possible to walk on the rampart, in reasonable comfort, around most of the city. The only section closed to the general public, for reasons of public safety, is in the east, where the wall runs alongside the ancient temple platform.

The view from the promenade, almost everywhere, is dramatic and — if seen imaginatively, through the past — full of suggestion for the curious walker. It evokes more effectively than any other site in Jerusalem "the number and importance of her memorable sieges." You soon realize how small the historic city was; and how vulnerable to attack, especially in the north. In the north, the ground is flat and does not fall off into deep ravines. You understand why most conquerors, from Nebuchadnezzar to Dayan, chose to attack from that direction.

A fast walker will circumnavigate the entire city on her ramparts in less than two hours. The total length of the trip is only 2.5 miles. From the ramparts in the southeast, across the ravines, there are sweeping distant views. One is over the desert, in the direction of Jericho — one of the oldest known urban habitations in the world; in Jericho, men built citadels of war long before they domesticated certain animals and plants or learned to forge arrowheads of stone or bronze.

Another dramatic view is up the Valley of Hinnom, where sheep graze on the municipal lawns and the scene is pastoral and peaceful — unless black-clad ultra-Orthodox Jews or Palestinian youths in checkered kaffiyehs happen to be rioting, and the valley resounds with shouts that archaeologists are violating the sanctity of ancient bones or with PLO slogans calling for an end to the Israeli occupation: "Down with the oppressors!"; "Arab Jerusalem!"; "In spirit and in blood, we'll free you, Falastin!"

Farther up the valley, hugging the steep slopes alongside the present walls, were the legendary Salem of Abraham's days and the old Jebusite city wall, which David and his *giborim* (literally, "bravados") took in roughly 1000 BC; no traces of Salem have yet been found. There are glimpses of the original City of David (now outside the walls) among the tumbles and cascades of stones, some of which are still blackened from the fires of 586 BC; and of its royal pool, nestling in the shade of fig trees and tall date palms. There are remains of a sixty-century-BC tower, under which Babylonian and Israelite arrowheads were found, as were bullae, ancient Hebrew seals, with the name of a royal scribe known from the Book of Kings written on one. Such finds give the ancient texts a concrete basis, a real location.

From the ramparts, you see the tourists, like so many ants, in the distance, lining up to visit the elaborate, ancient underground waterworks and tunnels. The tunnels under the wall were completed, we are told in Jeremiah, on the eve of the arrival of Sennacherib's forces, in time to safeguard the city a regular supply of water from her only spring. The spring was sealed and its water channeled underground into the city. The brook of Siloam no longer ran down through the open ground, for, as Hezekiah said, "Why should the kings of Assyria come, and find much water?" (They did not.)

The water still runs through the astounding tunnel carved by Hezekiah's men through the soft rock under the date palms and fig trees. It is 1,680 feet long, nearly a third of a mile. Two crews made their way toward each other from opposite ends, 200 feet under the ground — a daring scheme in view of the technical possibilities of 701 BC. The two teams advanced by trial and error (as can be seen in several abandoned parts). They made contact by means of sound and eventually joined up with each other. A Hebrew inscription (now in Istanbul), one of the oldest in existence, was discovered inside the tunnel in 1880. It describes the event in spare, dramatic terms, as in a pre-Homeric poem:

> The tunnel . . . this is the story of its cutting. When yet [the hewers were lifting] the pick, each toward his fellow and when yet there were still three cubits to be bored, the voice of a man calling to his fellow was heard, for there was a resonance coming from both north and south. . . . And when the tunnel was driven through, the quarrymen struck, one against the other, pick against pick, and the water flowed from the spring.

Down by this same pool, in 444 BC, Nehemiah surveyed the

ruined city after his return from the Babylonian exile, as recounted in his chronicle. Jerusalem lay in waste, consumed with fire, a ghost city. It was "large and great: but the people were few therein, and the houses were not builded." Three days after his arrival, Nehemiah arose in the night and left the ruined city through the Gate of the Valley, telling no one "what my God had put in my heart to do at Jerusalem. . . . And I . . . viewed the walls of Jerusalem, which were broken down, and the gates thereof were consumed with fire." Nehemiah draws a lively picture of the city he saw and describes an itinerary so eminently realistic that archaeologists have tended to accept it as a "factual record in a historical document."

"I went on to the gate of the fountain, and to the king's pool," Nehemiah relates, "but [because of the rubble] there was no place for the beast that was under me to pass." From a vantage point on the rampart, you can all but make out the circuitous route Nehemiah took. The path by the brook was blocked by rubble. Nehemiah was forced to turn around and return by the way he came. He had resolved to rebuild the city from her ruins. His book is an autobiography unique in the ancient world. Its subject is not the common one, of the devastation of a city and a people, but rather one of rebuilding. Nehemiah recruited builders from among the burghers and the country people. "Come," he told them, "and let us build up the wall of Jerusalem, that we be no more a reproach." The work was shared by all classes — tradesmen and priests, nobles and peasants from the near countryside. An efficient gang system was found. Defined lengths of wall and specific gates were assigned to trade or professional corporations among the householders and those who came in from the nearby towns. All worked with their hands, and because of threats, they built, as people often do in these parts, "with the sword in one hand and the trowel in the other."

Work was quickly done in the ancient world. The rebuilding of the destroyed walls, Nehemiah tells us, took only fifty-two days. On the eve of the next complete devastation of the city, Josephus informs us, Roman soldiers and slaves achieved the extraordinary feat of completing the circumvolution wall in a mere three days. It was six or seven miles long and completely enclosed the besieged city.

To be effective, it must have been at least six feet high and (since it was made of loose stones, without mortar) at least two feet wide at the base. We know that it *was* effective. The famine within the entrapped city soon consumed entire families. The besieged fought each other for a handful of flour. According to Josephus, men were hung up by the most sensitive parts of their bodies and pointed sticks driven into their flesh to make them confess where they might have hidden a morsel of bread. Tacitus claimed that six hundred thousand people were trapped in the surrounded city. Many were pilgrims, driven to Jerusalem by habit or blind faith in the middle of a war and allowed through by the shrewd Titus to increase the number of useless mouths to be fed in the besieged city.

Walking on the ramparts on a summer evening, you are tempted to visualize the Roman troops massed in the golden shadows on the slopes of Scopus, or on the other side, across the Valley of Hinnom, behind their circumvolution wall. It passed right under the present King David Hotel, through the lawns, next to the present swimming pool. The entire surrounding landscape was denuded of trees. The Romans had felled them to build their huge siege machines.

From the ramparts, you can visualize Josephus himself, the future historian, a few months after his defection to the Romans. Josephus is one of the most fascinating characters in the history of treason. You imagine him marching around the besieged city, at a safe distance from its walls, sweating in the heat, crying, imploring, exhorting his compatriots in the trapped city to surrender. He tells them to save themselves and spare their families, their country, and their holy temple. He spells out the advantages of collaborating with Rome. The beleaguered Jews merely throw insults and stones at him from the wall. "O miserable people!" he cries. The tears are running down his cheeks. "How can you be so unmindful!" The rest of the world has bowed to Roman rule; only they are still foolishly defying it. How can they be so unrealistic! Roman power is invincible, he yells. Roman civilization is great. Yes, even "God is now settled in Italy!" God, too, has fled out of his sanctuary of Jerusalem; he now "stands on the side of those against whom you fight."

Those who took his advice and escaped the city were nevertheless crucified by their Roman captors within view of the walls: "Their multitude was so great that room was wanting for the crosses, and crosses were wanting for the bodies." The countryside must have reeked from the stench of dead bodies nailed to wooden crosses. The Roman field camp was north of the city at the so-called Camp of the Assyrians, where Sennacherib had bivouacked 771 years before. In a changing Jerusalem, nothing is as permanent as geography.

On a winter day on the wall, the fog sweeping over the rooftops blots out the New City, the television antennas, and the parked cars, leaving the historic core shorn of all modern accoutrements. Very briefly, the view is what it must have been in Isaiah's or Josephus's days, timeless — "your heaven as iron and your earth as brass." We know these flat roofs of stone from Isaiah's "What aileth thee now, that thou art wholly gone up to the housetops?" The compact little houses, which crowd in close on somber, narrow lanes, climb steeply. In a moment, the narrow lanes that Josephus often wrote about in the first century sparkle again with a glassy beauty as the sun breaks out through the clouds and hits the wet stones.

In the soft light, there is a good view now from the ramparts into the Upper City, on Mount Zion, where the last of the Jewish zealots held out for another month after the rest of the city had fallen to the Romans. The rich and the priestly families lived in the Upper City, where they looked down, as high priests often do, on the Mountain of God, which gave them their livelihood. The Upper City was separated from the burning temple by a great bridge, across which, Josephus says, the Romans harangued and harassed them. The past nineteen hundred years have wrought additional havoc on this hill. Of the temple below it and its courts, only the vast platform has remained. Yet it is still possible to identify many prominent points mentioned in Josephus, including the bridge. They conjure up in the mind's eye the vanished splendor of the city and the last bloody scenes of her overthrow. It is clear why the Upper City held out to the very end. The Romans were unable to take it by storm after they had taken the temple platform below. They were forced to raise additional banks against it. Wood had to be hewn and brought in from afar; there were no trees left in the environs to a distance of a hundred furlongs (twelve and a half miles). Fierce house-to-house fighting was followed by close man-to-man combat in underground passages, and by another great fire. The slaughter, claimed Josephus — and perhaps he was not exaggerating by much — "made the whole city run down with blood to such a degree indeed that the fire of many of the houses was quenched with these men's blood."

Of the destruction of AD 70, several dramatic sights have been unearthed in recent years by two leading archaeologists, the Britisher Kathleen Kenyon and the Israeli Nahman Avigad. In some ruins, churned up by the winter rains outside the present walls, Kenyon found human bones, including three smashed skulls, "a reminder of the slaughter described by Josephus which filled the streets with blood." The dating of these skulls was facilitated by a purse, found among the bones, filled with coins minted a few months before the destruction of the city. The site excavated by Kenyon was never inhabited again. The remains she found lay immediately under the topsoil, with nothing Byzantine, Arab, or Crusader in between.

Inside the Upper City, Avigad has uncovered the remains of several priestly palaces. Each is covered in soot. Here again, the date of the fire was suggested by coins minted in AD 69, as well as by household utensils and other identifiable objects found in the ashes. But it was a family seal found in the debris that gave the excavator that rare and exhilarating feeling that he was in touch with specific human beings. The inscription on the seal suggested that one of the burned mansions belonged to the rich Kathros, a high priest much hated for his rapacity and corruption, and remembered in a well-known Talmudic skit on the priestly oligarchy:

Woe is me from the House of Baytos, woe is me from their sticks,
Woe is me from the House of Hannin, woe is me from their
    whispers.
Woe is me from the House of Ismael, woe is me from their fists,
Woe is me from the House of Kathros, woe is me from their
    poisoned pens.
All are high priests and their sons are tax collectors, their sons-
    in-law are cashiers and their servants beat the people with whips.

The ruins were still smoking when the survivors began to spin the theology of the disaster. They refused to believe that God had given them up. He could be weary or old, or simply in exile, as they were. But he would come back one day. There would be a Return. Until that day, they would be a people of sorrows. On the anniversary of the destruction, they would fast. They would sit on low stools and cover their heads in ashes. For centuries, they would speculate on the meaning of the event.

Some of these speculations — transmitted orally at first — were collected in the fifth century and codified in the midrash (the rabbinical commentary) on the Book of Lamentations. The end of the physical city made the survivors redouble their speculations on the spiritual. In the process, the tradition of exegesis acquired a sacredness of its own.

Lamentations was the great elegy on the first destruction of Jerusalem in 586 BC. In the midrash on Lamentations, every word, every phrase in the original text was applied to the later tragedy, thus presaging similar preoccupations and perplexities that would manifest themselves down through the centuries. The first sentence in Lamentations reads: "How lone she sits, the city big with people, is widowed." The key word here, according to the exegetes, was the first: *How* (*Eykha*).

In Hebrew, as in many other languages, *eykha* (pronounced "ayhaa") has a distinctly woeful, onomatopoeic sound. *Eykha* sounds like a howl. "How *could* you!" *Eykha*, not Lamentations, is the Hebrew name of this book. But the midrash on Lamentations is not just obsessive anguish, self-pity, or lament. There is wit in it, and the freewheeling philosophy of a fascinating and complex society of scholars — rabbinical Sherlock Holmses in search of a new religious philosophy. They inhabit a unique republic of letters where the religious drama is no longer enacted in a physical setting, as in the destroyed temple, but in the mind. God is everywhere. Men are called upon to contemplate his glory by concentrating on the study of the sacred books. For this purpose, any study room, any little synagogue in the world will do. Jerusalem is still the code word that releases glorious visions of a messianic age. The exegetes do not, at this stage, take such daydreams too literally. The memory of the lost city is still alive; the messiah, however, is no longer necessarily the heavenly figure of apocalyptic thought. As the centuries pass, the emphasis is on the here and now, on man and on reason. Chaim Raphael, a modern student of the midrash on Lamentations, has suggested that its authors were unconscious precursors of nineteenth-century liberalism. When the walls of Jerusalem fell, a higher form of religion rose from the debris. The ghosts of the old remained.

From the Ottoman citadel, with its imposing Herodian towers, which the Romans left standing as a monument to the valor of their arms, the walls of the Old City run in a straight line alongside the ravine to the crest of Zion. Here, as in the north, the walls have been more vulnerable because of the shape of the terrain. Thus, they encapsule more of the city's history. The foundations were probably built or rebuilt by Nehemiah's men in 445 BC. Antiochus IV (his Greek title, Epiphanes, meant "God Made Manifest") stormed that wall in 168 BC, in order to destroy the national superstition, we are told by Tacitus. Eighty thousand were slaughtered and as many sold into slavery. The temple was looted. The success of Antiochus, however, was short-lived. Soon afterward, the Maccabean rebellion broke out and Jerusalem was restored to an older faith. The Hasmonaean foundations survived the destructions of AD 70. They can be seen today at ground level covered by remains of a great Byzantine construction.

Few Byzantine things can be seen nowadays from the promenade on the walls. We have a fairly good general idea of how the Byzantine city looked, however, thanks to a sixth-century bird's-eye view of Jerusalem, the so-called mosaic of Medeba, found last century under the transept of a church in Transjordan. It shows two monumental colonnaded streets running north-south through the city, with great basilicas at either end. In the north stood a tall column with, perhaps, the emperor Hadrian's statue on top. Monumental remains of the two streets and of the basilicas — the Anastasis and the Nea — have been uncovered in the extensive excavations in the Old City, especially after 1967.

The Byzantine city was sacked in 614 by the Persians under

Khosrow II. As Zoroastrians, the Persians regarded as abomination everything Christian. They were helped by the Jews of the countryside, who rejoiced at this opportunity to get back at their Christian tormentors. The most beautiful churches were burned. The accumulated splendor of three hundred years was lost. The most moderate accounting put the number of slaughtered at 33,877. A monk named Sophronius recorded the catastrophe in an ode, which included an inventory of all the destroyed edifices. The Arabs arrived twenty-four years later and took the city without a battle. Like most conquerors of Jerusalem, they, too, claimed that God had been victorious. The Arabs restored the walls — and the Crusaders laid siege to them in 1099.

As usual, the city was invested by the Crusaders from the north and from the southwest, where the terrain favors an assault unhampered by steep slopes. The siege was mounted early in June and ended with the fall of Jerusalem in mid-July. As you stand on the wall on a hot summer day, it is tempting to visualize the European assailants below, dressed in heavy suits of armor designed for cooler climes, under a sun burning above like the eye of an enemy. Once again, the countryside was almost denuded of trees. There was almost no shade. The Crusaders had to bring in the wood for their scaling ladders, and other siege machines from the Mediterranean coast and from another faraway spot in Samaria (Torquato Tasso's "enchanted forest").

Standing on the rampart of the Jaffa Gate, as the traffic roars on the road below, you think of the Crusaders' astounding opening move: thirteen hundred knights, twelve thousand foot-soldiers, and perhaps twice as many pilgrims — all barefoot — wind their way around the entire city in a solemn procession. First, the bishops and priests; then the princes and knights, singing hymns. The Arabs are gathered on the walls, mocking them. The mockery only moves and inspires the host. The final assault comes a week later, reportedly on a Friday, the day and hour of the Passion. Under showers of stones and liquid fire, the Crusaders finally scale the walls. The terrible massacre follows. "It was this blood-thirsty proof of Christian fanaticism that recreated the fanaticism of Islam," Steven Runciman, a historian of the Crusades, has written. "When, later, wiser Latins in the East sought to find some basis on which Christian and

Moslem could work together, the memory of the massacre stood always in their way."*

Like other conquerors of the city, the Crusaders wished not only to occupy but to possess. Their great building enterprises were carefully recorded. Crusader Jerusalem is so well known from the chronicles of travelers and historians that the city can be mapped today almost in its entirety. We are able to visualize her streets and squares and churches better than those of most medieval cities. Today's Old City still mirrors the city of the Crusaders. The main streets coincide in many places with those of the Crusaders. Their functions are sometimes the same. Two beautifully vaulted covered streets called, in Crusader days, Greengrocers Street and Rue du Malcuisinat (Street of Bad Cooking) are still as they were and still deserve these names, though by now they have new ones. Melchior de Vogüé, the nineteenth-century French archaeologist, was so taken by the coincidence of modern and Crusader town plans that he asserted the thirteenth-century chronicles could safely be used as guidebooks to the present city. Another French archaeologist, Félicien de Saulcy, assumed a spiritual affinity between Jerusalem and Paris. The drama of Jerusalem, he suggested, was not only national but even more revolutionary, since the French Revolution, in its main stages, had "retraced" those of the insurrection of Jerusalem against the Romans.

Walking north on the wall from the southwest corner, toward David's Citadel and the Jaffa Gate, you reach the great breach cut in the city wall in 1898 to allow the German kaiser's train to drive through. General Allenby, the British conqueror of Jerusalem, entered by the same route in 1917 but dismounted his horse at the breach and humbly walked through on foot — a gesture that was widely remarked on at the time.† Throughout the long and difficult campaign, the general daily read his Bible and G. A. Smith's

* Gibbon's devastating judgment on the ancient Hebrews was remarkably similar: "The conquest of the land of Canaan was accompanied with so many wonderful and with so many bloody circumstances that the victorious Jews were left in a state of irreconcilable hostility with all their neighbours." (This sounds almost like a critique of modern Israel, which has often felt secure only at the price of making her neighbors feel insecure.)

† He was following cabled orders from the British war office: "Strongly suggest dismounting at gate. German emperor rode in and the saying went round 'a better man than he walked.' Advantages of contrast will be obvious."

Historical Geography of the Holy Land. He was able in the end to take the city without firing a single shot. "It has never fallen so tamely before," T. E. Lawrence ("Lawrence of Arabia"), who marched into Jerusalem with Allenby, wrote his mother, adding rashly: "These modern wars of large armies and long-range weapons are quite unfitted for the historic battlefield." Before fifty years passed, he would be proved twice wrong.

Climbing onto the wall again after the breach and walking farther north, you discover small gardens inside the Old City and good views over the stone roofs and towers, despite a forest of television antennas. A plaque on the rampart bears the words "Jordanian Post." It denotes its function between 1948 and 1967, when this part of the wall was a military zone, on the edge of a narrow strip of no-man's-land between Israeli and Jordanian-held Jerusalem. Jordanian snipers sometimes used this spot to shoot at Israelis passing through the deserted border area. There were also lighter moments during those years of intermittent warfare, as when a nun, on the Israeli side of the line, coughed her dentures out a window into no-man's-land and a temporary cease-fire was negotiated under United Nations auspices. A brace of blue-helmeted UN truce supervisors, brandishing white flags, combed the debris-covered terrain where few persons had ventured for years and fewer still had come back alive. The false teeth were successfully retrieved. Nowadays, this section of the ramparts is a popular tourist attraction. The former no-man's-land has become a busy traffic artery. The Franciscan fathers sometimes complain that tourists wandering on the wall peer into their bedroom windows — which brings to mind the chorus in *Oedipus Rex:* "Walls are nothing when no life moves in the empty passageways."

Below the walls, underfoot almost everywhere, are the tombs. The city is ringed by a great necropolis. South, east, and west of the city walls, old and new cemeteries present themselves as in a single tableau: tombstones of all kinds, caves, crypts, vaults, catacombs, mastabas, rock monuments, churchyards, and burial grounds of all races and faiths. In Jerusalem, tradition long ago gave the vote to remote ancestors, establishing a kind of democracy of the dead. As

Rimbaud said of baroque Rome, death seems to have been born here. The most enduring monuments in Jerusalem are tombs and cenotaphs. They seem to be among the oldest in the Near East. In summer, when the heat hangs heavily over the twisted spurs of hardened dust, children climb over the scattered tombstones and sense the slow fire inside. It is amazing how much trouble people who treated life so casually took with death and with their tombs — kings as well as paupers.

The author of the Book of Nehemiah called Jerusalem "the city of my fathers' sepulchres." The oldest Jewish sepulchres are cut into the rock, in deep, sunken courts. As usual in the East, the fear of grave robbers gave birth to elaborate devices to keep them out. Some tombs still have a heavy round stone rolled back from their mouths, revealing dark, cavernous chambers with finely chiseled walls inside, and holes (*kokhim*) for the disposal of bones. A fifth- or sixth-century Jewish epitaph, perhaps that of Shebna, the king's steward whose hewn-rock sepulchre is mentioned in Isa. 22:15, reads: "No silver and gold here . . . cursed be the man who . . . opens this." A first-century anklebone with a nail driven through it and thus suggestive of a crucifixion by the Romans has also been found — the only one anywhere found so far. The city's museums are filled with coffins and elaborately decorated bone-pots and urns. The connection between religion and death, or the fear of death, is well known. There was a widespread Jewish cult of tombs. The rabbis were opposed to it and yet their own tombs eventually became objects of veneration. Later on, a belief grew that dying and being buried in Jerusalem was a shortcut to paradise. "Men from all parts of the world" come to Jerusalem to die, the Persian traveler Nasir-i-Khusrau reported in 1047. Jews and Moslems believed that if they died in Jerusalem their flesh would not rot. At the End of Days, when they are finally summoned by their maker to free them of all memory, they would be spared the ordeal and discomfort of rolling to Jerusalem under the ground.

There are tombs of all ages, beginning in the eighth century BC, and a few noteworthy gaps: no tombs from the time of the Persian conquest, even though hundreds of thousands were massacred then (Zoroastrian religion forbade defiling the pure earth with unclean corpses), and only one grave of a Crusader. There must have been

thousands of Crusader tombs, including many monumental sepulchres. But tombs have habitually played a part in the struggles over
Jerusalem. Their destruction has often marked the transition from
one faith or sect to another. The Greeks waited till 1810 to dismantle
two royal Crusader tombs, which Chateaubriand had seen still extant four years earlier. Tombs describe conflicting domains of memory in the city. Of approximately seventy thousand Jewish graves on
the Mount of Olives and its slopes, some fifty thousand were destroyed or defaced during the nineteen years of Jordanian rule between 1948 and 1967.

Moslem sepulchres of some importance were built conspicuously
on the surrounding hilltops. Henry Maundrell, a seventeenth-
century English traveler, observed (perhaps sardonically) that "you
will find among the Turks far more dead saints than living ones." In
the more recent cemeteries, Moslem tombstones are twin-posted
like "husband and wife facing each other across the breakfast table."
A memorial to the Arab dead in the Six-Day War, erected in 1967
with the encouragement of the liberal Israeli mayor Teddy Kollek,
nearly proved to be Kollek's political undoing. Where in London is
there a memorial to the German dead? the critics cried. Kollek's
answer was that London was not a German city as well, as Jerusalem is partly Arab.

In a Protestant cemetery that occupies the side of Mount Zion,
several Hebrew tombstones commemorate the extremely meager
results of great efforts by English missionaries last century to convert the Jews. Opposite the northeast corner of the Old City, on
top of Mount Scopus, there is a British military cemetery for the
casualties of World War I. Its boisterous tone is quite inappropriate
to the horrors of that war fought in the crusading and salvationist
style of the imperialist heyday.

Further in the west, an entire mountain is covered by new Jewish
cemeteries. It is known as Mount Herzl. In 1949, forty-five years
after his death, the remains of Theodor Herzl, founder of modern
Zionism, were flown to Israel from Vienna and buried here under a
square block of black marble. The national movement Herzl helped
found and that he hoped would lead to the reestablishment of a
Jewish state in peace with its Arab neighbors has not yet reached its
goal. The north slope of Mount Herzl is a military cemetery, a

reminder of the heavy toll exacted by five Arab-Israeli wars since 1948 and of the many skirmishes in between.

The south slope is occupied by a monumental tomb of another sort, entirely symbolic, awesome, called Yad Vashem (literally, "Memory and Name"). It honors the memory of the six million exterminated Jews of Europe, who Herzl, sensing the approaching catastrophe, vainly tried to rescue.

As a ritual site in the civil or political religion of Israel, Yad Vashem is second only to the Western Wall. It bears witness to the fact that Israel is founded on new ashes as much as on its biblical past. Yad Vashem does not face the city but instead looks toward the sea, the direction from which those who were slaughtered by the Nazis might have come. Its architecture of pain is the most powerful where it is understated. In the austere Memorial Hall, the names of the main annihilation camps are inscribed in the floor. Stunned visitors of all nationalities stare at them at all hours of the day: Majdanek, Sobibor, Buchenwald, Theresienstadt, Bergen-Belsen, Mauthausen, Dachau, Treblinka, Auschwitz. An eternal flame rises from a kind of vault in the ground where ashes found in one of the death camps have been buried. Cantors intone the ancient Hebrew prayer for the dead, a rapt, intense lament, which by its primitive strength might have been composed only yesterday.

As a "sacred space," Yad Vashem fulfills a political and religious function in Israeli public life similar to that of the Tomb of the Unknown Soldier in other countries. As a monument, it triggers awe. Foreign heads of state and ambassadors come here to lay wreaths. In the austere Memorial Hall, they solemnize their recognition of the new state and legitimize its raison d'être. President Sadat of Egypt visited Yad Vashem in 1977 and wrote in the visitor book: "May God guide our steps toward peace. Let us end all suffering for mankind."

In the Jewish tradition, catastrophe is theologically linked with redemption. Death and rebirth are juxtaposed. This gives Yad Vashem its peculiar political twist. The historian Saul Friedlander has written about Yad Vashem: "Redemption here loses its explicit religious connotation and becomes rebirth, in secular but no less mythic and meta-historical terms." Yad Vashem symbolizes the negative pole of the positive energy that went into the building of the Jewish state during the past hundred years. This was made clear during the 1953 Knesset debate over establishing an annual day to commemorate the annihilation of European Jewry. Mordechai Nurok, who headed the subcommittee in charge, said: "We have seen a graveyard in front of us, a graveyard for six million of our brothers and sisters. Maybe because of their blood, shed like water, have we been privileged to have our state."

CHAPTER SEVEN

God and Man
in Jerusalem Today

Urban space in Jerusalem is sharply divided in seemingly immovable rigor. Invisible lines cut the historic core into rough quadrangles, not unlike nation-states in the Balkans: the Moslem quarter, the Jewish quarter, the Christian and the Armenian quarters. Moving from one Old City quarter to the next is like crossing into an alien land.

Each has its own religion, its own distinctive tongue or tongues. Each comes with its own peculiar alphabet. Within each quarter, there are divisions and subdivisions anchored in time-honored historic rights. The principal languages are Hebrew, Arabic, and Armenian. Greek, French, Yiddish, English, Assyrian-Syriac, Russian, and Ethiopian are also spoken. Thirty religious denominations, worshiping in at least fifteen national languages and seven different alphabets, squeeze into a few acres of densely built-up land. They touch upon one another but are worlds apart, and the air, almost everywhere, is thick with animosities.

It is entirely in character that only non-Moslems refer to the existence of a "Moslem quarter" within the Old City walls. Moslems never call it by that name. To them, the entire city is Moslem, as it is Jewish in the eyes of the Jews; "quarters" are fit for minorities only. Nor is there any affinity between the historic minorities. The cultural diversity between the quarters seems greater than that between, say, England and Spain.

In the New City, spatial divisions are less obvious than in the Old. The differences are likely to be as staggering. National and religious groups live separately from one another within complex but clearly defined ethnic or sectarian frontiers. There are walls within walls, enclaves within enclaves, ghettos within ghettos. The two main national and religious groups — the Israelis and the Palestinians — live completely apart from one another. But the contrast between two all-Jewish neighborhoods such as Ramot (inhabited mostly by secular, or nonobservant, Jews) and nearby Mea Shearim (settled by ultra-Orthodox Jewish fundamentalists who do not "recognize" the State of Israel and refuse to serve in its army or pay taxes) is on the whole even more dramatic than the contrast between Israeli and Palestinian neighborhoods. The difference is not only in weltanschauung but in dress, daily language, and architecture as well. Tensions and disagreements can be almost as sharply felt as those between the warring Israeli and Palestinian nationalities.

Palestinians and Israelis uphold their national languages with equal fervor. But among the latter are sixth- and seventh-generation Jewish Jerusalemites who consider the use of the Hebrew language for secular purposes blasphemous. They will converse only in Yiddish, a medieval German vernacular spoken until World War II by millions of Polish and Russian Jews, whose forebears, in the Middle Ages, developed it in the Rhineland.

Jerusalem is a city of three Sabbaths. On Sunday, the ceaseless toll of church bells rolls over the stone-tiled rooftops, and processions wind through the narrow alleys of the Old City. Friday is the Moslem day of rest. At the amplified call of the muezzin, thousands march through the same alleys to attend services on the Temple Mount. In summer, prayers are held outside the two mosques on the mount, at the southern end of the great stone platform. Saturday is the Jewish Sabbath. Sirens herald its beginning shortly before sunset on Friday afternoon and all Jewish commercial life ceases. The synagogues — there are more than one thousand in the Jewish parts of the city — fill. The pace and atmosphere of the Sabbath in Jerusalem is of a quality entirely its own. The empty streets echo with the sound of singing prayers. Several neighborhoods are closed entirely to automobile traffic, and elsewhere cars are diverted away from the main synagogues during hours of prayer. There is no public transportation. (Arab buses passing through Jewish quarters are not allowed to stop for passengers.) There are no newspapers; theaters, cinemas, and most restaurants and cafés are shut.

The adherents of one faith are not always aware of the holidays of the others. One diligent researcher — needless to say, an agnostic — a few years ago compiled a comprehensive list of the holidays observed by all the various religious denominations active in Jerusalem. He discovered there were many more holidays than days in the year. The High Holidays of the Jews and of the Moslems, however, are difficult to overlook. On their most important holidays, the secular city turns into a ritual city. Its visual outlines are molded almost exclusively on faith. On Yom Kippur, traffic is banned throughout the entire Jewish part of the city. An eerie, beautiful silence hangs over the deserted streets. With no traffic, only human voices and footsteps are heard, as in Venice. Men in prayer shawls walk through the streets on their way to and from the crowded synagogues. During Ramadan, most inhabitants of the Moslem city fast every day, from sunrise to sunset, for an entire month. In the late afternoons, the mosques are overcrowded; soon afterward, the streets of the Moslem neighborhoods empty as the faithful rush home for the *iftar,* the breaking of the fast.

Even on ordinary workdays, religion is never wholly absent, especially in the early morning hours. In other large cities, the first to rise in the dark are sanitation workers and bus drivers and newspaper deliverers; in Jerusalem, it is the devout. The muezzins are first, and the faithful answer their summons, in the half-dark, each on his little prayer rug at home. Outside, pious Jews hurry through the vacant streets for early morning services at the Western Wall or in one of the *stiebls* (prayer rooms) of neighborhood synagogues. At the Western Wall and in the Church of the Holy Sepulchre, prayers continue through the entire night. Shortly before midnight, Greek brothers go around the Holy Sepulchre with clappers to awaken their clergy, whose offices begin first. Armenian matins follow, at 1:00 AM. After that, Egyptian Copts intone a hymn in the language of the pharaohs.

National, linguistic, and sectarian differences abound. Moslem sects include Sunnites, Shiites, Sufis, Beduins, and Gypsies. Most Moslems nowadays wear western dress, but the young often display their Palestinian nationality by demonstratively wearing checkered

kaffiyehs. Some of the Christian religious orders can also be distinguished by their national dress. Armenian, Greek, Coptic, Syrian,
and Ethiopian monks wear different habits. White Russian brothers
(under a patriarch-in-exile presently living in New York) still dress
in the same style as Red Russian brothers controlled from Moscow
but are not on speaking terms with them. Most Benedictines are
French; the Franciscan order has traditionally been predominantly
Italian.

Israeli Jerusalemites are a hybrid people. A more or less homog-
enous Jewish community has existed in Jerusalem since the early
Middle Ages, but the great influx of Jews into the city began in the
middle of the nineteenth century. Jews have since flocked here from
all corners of the earth. They have brought with them their distinctive habits, cultures, languages, and traditions. Statisticians list over
eighty countries of origin. Two-thirds are nowadays thought to be
natives of the city, but many still worship in "ethnic" synagogues
according to the country of their origin two or more generations
ago. There are several Ashkenazic and several Sephardic prayer
rites. Certain synagogues serve Polish congregants; others follow
only the German, Lithuanian, Hungarian, or so-called Anglo-
Saxon rites of their members. Among the Sephardic, certain
synagogues are dedicated to (and sometimes named after) the
different rites of Italy, Kurdistan, and Morocco, as well as of Istanbul, Cairo, San'a (Yemen), Tangier, Salonika, Sarajevo, and Sofia.
Some Ashkenazic rabbis still dress like Polish noblemen of the eighteenth century, in black coats, black or white leggings, and — on
holidays — majestic fur hats, all transplanted to the heat and white
light of Jerusalem from the grim landscape of remote northern-
European Sabbaths. These distinctive costumes of the ultra-
Orthodox are also a result of seventeenth-century Ottoman law in
Jerusalem: each millet, or "nation," was required to wear its own
costume "in order to make the difference clear to see."

Within the Hasidic and other sects, there are further differentia-
tions of dress. Some wear only black silk caftans, belted at the waist
like dressing gowns; others wear only gray, or white, or striped
ones. Some tuck the cuffs of their black trousers into white or gray
socks; others do not. Some don wide-brimmed black hats like Ro-

man cardinals'; others wear silk yarmulkes under black homburgs; still others wear only knitted skullcaps made of pure wool.

The transitions from one community or sect to another are sudden and unannounced. They assault you, so to speak, xenophobically. Between two bus stops, you can pass from one national or religious experience (or resentment) to another. The two bus stops seem centuries apart, even though they remain within the territory of a single religious or national group. You arrive at a different historic time. Suddenly, there is another sensibility, another past, another present.

The time zones overlap, as in those historic paintings in Italy and France where personalities who lived centuries apart (Dante and Virgil, for example, or Charlemagne and Napoléon) are seen conversing side by side in the present. In the Old City, the crowds mingle on terms of reciprocal antipathy. Few other people, save perhaps the Irish, live so intimately together, yet each with his distant, mutually antagonistic past.

There is a touch of *Arabian Nights* here and there: turbaned men, veiled ladies, green tiles, mysteriously blocked gates; and American-style steel-and-glass office buildings tower over domed medieval stone rooftops. The Eastern churches are resplendent in their colorful rites. The bishops sweep down the aisles like royalty, their robes hung with glittering emeralds; preceding them are their kavasses, fierce-looking attendants, splendidly arrayed in gold and blue, who announce their masters' arrival by knocking silver-topped maces against the stone pavement. At the same time, in the bazaars, packs of Israeli youngsters in jeans and T-shirts (and often armed with automatic rifles) press noisily through the maze, past sullen-eyed Palestinians and old Orthodox Jews in tailcoats and fur hats. The latter gather in small groups. Their pallid faces are ringed with wild-looking beards and baroque earlocks. Some look moth-eaten, as though they have just spent the night on the shelf of a public library. Close by are the Moslem ulemas in turbaned fezzes that show they have made the hajj, the pilgrimage to Mecca. Greek and Armenian priests, bearded and robed, with towers of black silk upon their heads and thick, long shafts of hair bound ponytail-fashion behind their necks, wander in and out of the crowd.

The bazaars buzz in a dozen languages. The traditional routes for visitors cater to the patriotic and to the devout. Jews visit the Old City to worship at the Western Wall and to recall through the tiniest archaeological remains the thrilling distinctiveness of a wonderful and affecting history. From David to Dayan: the rise, the fall, and the recent restoration of their ancient capital. Christians come to follow the presumed route of Jesus from cradle to grave. Moslems come to touch the stone under the golden Dome where Mohammed is said to have risen to heaven. There are many moving sights and some incongruous ones: ardent pilgrims lying prostrate at the Stone of Unction, or crying at the Western Wall; state-of-the-art loudspeakers on venerable minarets, linked to one another through computers, alerting the Moslem flocks; a television dish antenna sitting atop an abode of monks sworn to long periods of penitence through abstinence from talk.

There is in Jerusalem the publicly endowed Institute for Halakic Technology, where ingenious gadgets are designed to reconcile the needs of modern life with ancient Talmudic precepts. These devices might include elevators, telephones, or teakettles for use on the Sabbath without fear of violating the Mosaic decalogue.* And nearly half a century since it was established to pacify the city, there still exists in Jerusalem a United Nations High Command, with a large staff of officers and secretaries, charged with "observing" and possibly upholding the 1949 truce between Arabs and Israelis. Isolated behind high barbed-wire fences, it still officiates from its quarters in the British high commissioners' former palace, perched on a wooded hill in the south, with perhaps the best view from any residence in the city. "The mediators, the peacemakers, the compromisers, the pacifiers," Yehuda Amichai has written,

---

* Profanations of the Lord's day are avoided through complicated, still controversial interpretations of the sacred texts and hairsplitting distinctions between primary and secondary causality. Only primary, or direct, causality (such as the actual turning of an electric switch) is thought to constitute a violation of the Sabbath. In the "Sabbath telephone," an automated delayed-action device establishes a *secondary* causality said to absolve the user from direct responsibility. The Sabbath elevator is more straightforward: the user need not touch a button; the elevator goes up and down at regular intervals and stops on every floor.

Live in the white house
And receive their nourishment from far away
Through twisting channels, through dark veins, like a foetus.
And their secretaries are lipsticked and laughing
. . . the trees whose shadow shades them have their roots
   in disputed territory.

There is a feeling in Jerusalem, sometimes, of stepping, like Alice, through a looking glass. In 1982, the president, the prime minister, and the entire Israeli cabinet flew by helicopter to a remote spot below Jerusalem in the Judean desert, to attend an elaborate state funeral accorded, at the prime minister's orders, to a handful of human bones nearly two thousand years old. The bones, otherwise unidentified, had been dug up by archaeologists in a nearby cave twenty years earlier. They were — or perhaps were not — the remains of Jewish zealots who participated in the disastrous Bar Kokhba uprising against the Romans in the years 132 to 135. The prime minister assumed they were; in an impassioned funeral oration, he addressed his "glorious brothers" who through the millennia had endowed their people with honor and immortality. Then, to the beat of martial music, accompanied by the drums and guns of a military guard of honor, the bone fragments, encased in a flag-draped coffin, were carried to a common grave on the shoulders of six brigadier generals. Afterward, the official party helicoptered back to Jerusalem to another ceremony in honor of the second-century national heroes.

It is unlikely that the memory of Boadicea, the first-century queen of the Britons who, like Bar Kokhba, staged a disastrous uprising against the Romans, could generate similar ceremonies, let alone passions, in today's England. But in Jerusalem, the second-century uprising of Bar Kokhba against the Romans is liable to be evoked, polemically, as an event of almost contemporary relevance. Intellectuals will shuffle and reshuffle Solomons and Bar Kokhbas, Saladins and Isaiahs, like cards in a pack. One reason, probably, is that Jerusalem is the capital city of a young country — a country at war since its establishment in 1948 — whose citizens, still unsure of themselves, are searching for evocative symbols. Another reason may be the use of the Hebrew language. Hebrew today is basically the same language of three thousand years ago. It brings on a singular sense of continuity; the remotest past is never as remote here as it might be in Cairo or Rome, where the national languages have changed. In Jerusalem, even a twelve-year-old visiting the local museum knows how to read a first-century inscription and without too much difficulty understands the Dead Sea Scrolls or the text of a message by Bar Kokhba himself to one of his lieutenants. "The Israeli-born population," writes Jonathan Frankel, a Hebrew University historian, "grows up with a kind of historical amnesia ensuring that events that took place two or three thousand years ago are grasped more vividly than anything from the intervening period until the present."

There is often a feeling in Jerusalem of being inside a time machine. Men see the past, present, and future, like William Blake, existing all at once. On the roof of the Holy Sepulchre, Ethiopian monks, pounding on African drums, celebrate and recelebrate the marriage of Solomon to the queen of Sheba, a union they believe they sprang from directly. The so-called Holy Fire (first recorded in the ninth century) still descends "miraculously" from heaven onto the tomb of Christ every Easter, in a barbaric ceremony that is part Greek-Dionysiac, part Christian, part Zoroastrian fire worship. A stroll in the environs of the Old City heightens the time-machine effect. On Mount Scopus, you wander through the new campus of the Hebrew University, with its ultramodern facilities and computers that are linked by satellite with similar institutions all over the globe. Scopus stands 2,736 feet above sea level. In winter, it is freezing cold, and the university, like the rest of the city, can be buried under snow. But it is only a short ride from the university on Scopus down to Jericho, 820 feet below sea level — one of the lowest spots on earth — where there is eternal summer among the bougainvillea, palms, flowering mangoes, and flame trees. Like the ancient Hebrews in the Middle Bronze Age, migrant Beduin still cross from the wild Ghor to pitch their tents under the palms alongside some ancient canal. The ride down, from the university atop the freezing summit of Scopus to the Beduin encampment basking in the warmth outside Jericho, takes only twenty minutes.

On one short, winter afternoon, you have free pick of the climate —
plus, the century of your choice.

There are many Jerusalems, of course: the Jerusalem of the Moslems and the Jerusalem of the Christians and that of the Jews; the
Jerusalem of the old-timers and the Jerusalem of the new Jewish
immigrants who have recently "come on aliya" (literally, who have
"ascended" — a description akin in feeling to "taking the cross").
There is the Jerusalem of the freethinkers, whose bastion is the
university; the synthetic Jerusalem of the movies; the Jerusalem of
the missionaries. There is the Jerusalem of the wild-eyed fanatics,
forever impatient with that which is only human, pitiless in their
judgment on man's effort to compromise; the city has a three-
thousand-year-old reputation of both following and disowning
them.

There is the Jerusalem of the shopkeepers, the tourists, and the
pilgrims, and of the foreign diplomats who drive up from Tel Aviv
for an hour's stay to confer at the Foreign Ministry. Politicians and
lobbyists fill the hotels every week for two or three days in order to
attend sessions of the Knesset and then leave as soon as they can.
There is the Jerusalem of the political exiles, George Seferis's

> Jerusalem, ungoverned city
> Jerusalem, city of the refugee.

And there is the Jerusalem of the eccentrics, the "god-intoxi-
cated," who roam her streets barefoot in summer to proclaim their
direct line to heaven. Some dress in flowing white robes and carry
placards with biblical quotations and dire warnings. Jeremiah was
among the first to call for restraints on every madman in Jerusalem
who "maketh himself a prophet." Yet who is to tell the difference in
Jerusalem between the prophet and the madman? A few years ago a
"prophetess" dressed in fantastic robes marched up and down Zion
Square in downtown Jerusalem announcing that she had a daily
link to God. She occasionally sold amulets and talismans. One day,
the poet Dennis Silk bought God's telephone number from her for
half a pound. It was a Jerusalem number, of course. The next time
Silk saw her, he told her the number never responded. To which she
replied sympathetically: "Well, isn't it just like God not to answer
his telephone."

There is the Jerusalem of the foreign "consuls general" — obsolete institutions left over from the days of the defunct British mandatory government. They still adhere to a UN General Assembly resolution of 1947 under which Jerusalem was to be internationalized as a corpus separatum. They do not recognize, and in turn are ignored by, the government (although they do pay homage to the mayor elected by the same people). They retain the self-importance, though not the power, of the European consuls in Jerusalem during the last century. (In the nineteenth century, an Italian consul who felt slighted by a minor street incident successfully demanded formal redress in the form of a twenty-one-gun salute.)

And, in addition, there is the Jerusalem of the modern poets. All somehow echo Gogol's disillusionment: Yehuda Amichai's "only city on earth where the vote has been given to the dead"; Chester Kallman's Jerusalem in "Dome of the Rock" (written a year after Wystan Auden's death) —

> I do not give a damn for their questionable yen
> To worship something somewhere and I pray . . . dear
>   Wystan, pray for me!

Other poets equate love with possession, praying with Saul Tchernichowsky, one of the classicists of modern Hebrew poetry, that Jerusalem cease "being sacred to three orthodox faiths" and belong to "her people only [secular Jews], not to foreigners, my love." (This, even at the cost of her "obliteration" — a kind of suicidal pact between the city and her lovers; poetic license is rarely driven so far.)

In the southeast corner of the Old City, it is only a few steps from the teeming Arab bazaar to the restored Jewish quarter. The original population of pious Jews was sent across the lines of the divided city in 1948; the quarter was looted and burned by the mob and later dynamited by the Jordanian army.

When the Israelis took it back in 1967, they discovered that during the two intervening decades of Arab rule, the Jordanians had wiped out just about every trace of a Jewish presence in the Old City, where Jews had constituted a majority since before the middle of the last century. The major synagogues had been razed. The

Western Wall had been renamed for al-Buraq. All street signs with
Hebrew letters had been plastered over.

The massive Israeli reconstruction work in the Jewish quarter
that began in 1967 was a defiant assertion of presence even more
than a restoration of what had been lost. The new Jewish quarter
is considerably larger than the old. It was built by a public-
development company on ground partly expropriated from Arab
owners. Only Jews have been allowed to purchase homes in the
rebuilt area. When a former Moslem resident of the area challenged
this restriction as discriminatory, in 1974, the ban was upheld by the
supreme court. In dismissing the suit, which one of the judges
described as cantankerous, the court cited overriding political and
historic reasons. There had always been a distinctive Jewish quarter
in the Old City, the court argued, and there were good reasons that
there be a distinctly Jewish quarter there once again. At this writing, non-Jews are still legally barred from acquiring or renting
property in the Jewish quarter.

Before 1948, the quarter had been settled mostly by indigent
pious Jews who lived crowded together in crumbling habitations
with little regard for sanitation and comfort. ("I do not know that I
ever received a deeper impression of the fallen condition of Zion,"
W. H. Bartlett, an English engraver, wrote in 1852 after a visit to the
Jewish quarter of Jerusalem.) Few of the original Jewish families
expelled in 1948 returned after 1967. Most could hardly have afforded the new prices in the restored, "gentrified" quarter. The
present population numbers some five hundred families and a few
hundred yeshiva students — altogether, about four thousand Jews.
They are mostly middle-class professionals and practicing Orthodox
Jews. Many are immigrants from the United States and born-again
Jews attending one of several religious seminaries.

Determined that their world will last forever, the Israelis have
built massively in Jerusalem since 1967: huge housing estates that
look like gigantic fortresses, great synagogues, high office buildings, hotels, and university halls, like hilltop lines of Maginot.
Everything is massive. The restored Jewish quarter in the Old City
is no exception. In an introverted, walled-in, defensive setting, it is
harsh and stony, with surprisingly few green spaces; its new, colos-
sal synagogues and religious seminaries tyrannize through sheer

scale. The private homes in the new quarter have been built in more humane proportions, of gaunt clean stone, in a postmodern, eclectic, neoromantic style, highlighted by arched passageways, domed ceilings, flat stone roofs, vaulted windows, and a number of Italianate squares and enclosed courts. The narrow alleys and cozy little courts form a pedestrian zone permanently closed to vehicular traffic. Four of the intimate old Sephardic synagogues, looted and burned in 1948 — the eldest dated back to 1600 — have been restored as well, some with furniture that survived the destruction of Jewish temples in Italy during World War II. The fine open space of Batei Machseh Square is marked by a huge Ionic column, possibly from the Herodian temple. On the far wall, next to which young children play ball and old men rest on benches in the shade, is an engraved inscription from Zechariah:

> Thus saith the Lord of Hosts; There shall yet old men and old
> women dwell in the streets of Jerusalem, and every man with his
> staff in his hand for very age.
> And the streets of the city shall be full of boys and girls playing.

In the years just after its restoration, the Jewish quarter still attracted many nonobservant Israeli residents. Most of them have since left, overwhelmed by the increasingly ultra-Orthodox atmosphere, or eased out by subtle social pressure. In the heart of the Jewish quarter, the remains of a twelfth-century church were excavated in the early 1970s. Initial attempts to label the partially restored site with a plaque mentioning the church's name (Saint Mary of the Germans) were foiled by local vandals; the present sign outside the site refers merely to an "archaeological garden."

Residents of the Jewish quarter have few, if any, contacts with residents of the nearby Moslem quarters. They avoid walking through the Arab streets. Early proposals to establish joint clinics or community centers met with active opposition from both sides. Today, the quarter is an enclave within the larger enclave of the Arab city, much as it was in the Middle Ages.

Mea Shearim, in the heart of the New City, is another enclave within an enclave. Founded in 1874, it was one of the first urban settlements outside the Old City walls, in what was then almost complete wilderness (hence the wall that still surrounds much of it today, and the four iron gates, which are no longer locked at night). The founders were five local Jewish public figures who sought to escape the discomfort and congestion of the Old City. They were citizens of five countries — one English, one German, one Austrian, one Russian, and one Turk; the uncertain circumstances under Ottoman rule made it advisable to enjoy the protection of as many foreign powers as possible. The original charter, drafted by the five and subscribed to by the heads of 114 prospective families, stipulated the establishment of a planned and well-disciplined community. It allowed the removal by majority vote, but with full compensation, of any householder who "causes intrigue, disorder and quarrel, God-forbid." The founders called the new community Mea Shearim (literally, "Hundredfold"), an invocation of fruitfulness and plenty, as in Gen. 26:12 — "Then Isaac sowed in that land, and received in the same year an hundredfold: and the Lord blessed him."

Today's Mea Shearim is a living museum of life-styles that existed for centuries among ultra-Orthodox Jews in the ghettos and shtetls of eastern Europe. Its energies are turned almost exclusively upon itself. Dressed still in the somber, confining clothes of an eighteenth-century northern-European ghetto, the residents of Mea Shearim inhabit the austere, long-vanished world of Marc Chagall's canvases and Shalom Aleichem's bittersweet tales. Mea Shearim is one of its last strongholds. Nowhere can the ultra-Orthodox live out their customs more fully and more securely than here. It is a medieval world of poverty and unbroken faith — and of fanatical intolerance of other worlds of thought or ways of life.

Here they live in their Zauberberg, outside of time and place, keeping company with a horde of abstractions, all in their own image. Here, as Johan Huizinga wrote in a celebrated line of *The Waning of the Middle Ages,* daily experience still has in the mind of the ultra-Orthodox "the directness and absoluteness of the pleasure and pain of child-life." Every feature of daily life — food, hygiene, worship, dress, work, learning, repose — is prescribed and expressed in solemn forms that raise them to the dignity of a ritual. There is very little privacy; life in Mea Shearim (as Huizinga wrote of life in the Middle Ages) is of a "proud or cruel publicity." Life in Mea Shearim is intense, more public and more ceremonious than elsewhere. Change is conceived as evil. The ultra-Orthodox possess nothing certain except the past. They are disinterested in the new, and resentful of the modern, largely secular State of Israel beyond their semiwalled neighborhood. The most extreme among them regard the secular Israeli state as a scandal, an outrage, an abomination in violation of holy scripture, while the more moderate merely consider it flawed from a theological point of view, premature, and in the hands of sinners and impostors.

Both groups consider themselves "exiles," even though resident in the holy city; they bear this "cross" (for want of a better word) in the land of the freethinking Jews. In their world of thought, galuth (exile) is a metaphysical term. God himself is in exile until the arrival of the messiah. Galuth is a psychological state as well; the ultra-Orthodox of Mea Shearim regard the secular Israeli government as a government of goyim (gentiles).

There are shades of difference between the most extreme and the more moderate wings in ultra-Orthodox Mea Shearim. The most extreme may refuse to pay Israeli taxes or to speak the official language (though they know it well). In their eyes, Hebrew is the sacred tongue, the language of prayer and learning; it must not be debased by everyday, profane use. The ultra-Orthodox will not vote. Some of their leaders have gone so far as to say that the extermination of six million Jews by the Nazis was divine punishment for the Zionists' efforts to create a secular state. The young men will not serve in the Israeli army. Unlike ultra-Orthodox Jews anywhere else in the world, those of Mea Shearim are likely to refrain from including the host country (Israel) and its people in their prayers. In Cairo, Brussels, or New York, they would readily intone at least once a year a special prayer for the well-being of Egypt, Belgium, or the USA. But in Mea Shearim, it is of doctrinal importance to them that they do not.

The more moderate will converse in Hebrew and even vote in the national elections. Their elected deputies will support any government in return for generous treasury subsidies for their yeshivas, and for exempting their young from military service. This is not necessarily hypocritical. Seen through their eyes, but for the yeshivas, which teach the Torah to the young, the world would no longer exist.

During the first three decades after the establishment of Israel, the ultra-Orthodox parties, though very small, were adroit in exploiting frequent deadlocks in the Knesset between the secular right and the secular left wing of Israeli politics. Their interests, at most times, remained strictly sectarian — for example, the aforementioned public financing for ultra-Orthodox religious institutions and securing exemption from military service for their young. They were "neutral" — amenable, that is — on other issues in the fields of security or foreign affairs. In recent years, however, they have moved toward the far right of Israeli politics, opposing territorial concessions to the Arabs and consistently supporting the hard-line expansionist, "messianic" line.

All ultra-Orthodox in Mea Shearim anathematize the regular Israeli Orthodox establishment, headed by the chief rabbinate. They consider its ritual baths "unclean," its slaughterhouses insufficiently kosher, its chief rabbis flawed and their rulings deviant. They boycott its rabbinical courts, its burial societies, and its inspectorate of kosher slaughterhouses; they have their own rabbinical courts, their own ritual baths, their own burial societies, slaughterhouses, and inspectorates of kashruth.

On Israel's national holidays, some of the ultra-ultras, known as Neturei Karta (Guardians of the City), don sackcloth and hoist black flags. Mea Shearim is the stronghold of Neturei Karta. During the Arab siege of Jerusalem in 1948, Mea Shearim was only a few hundred feet from the Jordanian-Israeli front line. Leaders of Neturei Karta made preparations to go over to the Arab side in the belief that life under Moslem rule would be preferable to life under a godless Jewish government. They were prevented from hoisting white flags only by threats of summary execution.

Nearly all of today's residents of Mea Shearim and adjacent quarters are ultra- or ultra-ultra-Orthodox. Many are *talmidei hakhamim* — disciples of the learned and wise — engaged full-time in study and worship. Reading themselves blind in dark, dank rooms, they rely on charity for support while their wives raise their large families and earn what they can between pregnancies (seven or eight children are common). Sect members attend one of several yeshivas of ancient renown; here, over the centuries, the words have been pounded so fine they have long ago fallen to dust. Again and again, one line of sacred text is interpreted in the light of another. Again and again, the studious speculate upon the meaning of a single passage. In quick succession, one exegesis follows another. Young and old scholars pronounce them triumphantly: like Pythagoras, they hear the music of the spheres made by the planets turning in their orbits. Not more than fifty years ago (according to Gershom Scholem, writing in *Major Trends in Jewish Mysticism*), there were thirty or forty "masters of mystical prayer" practicing in Mea Shearim following years of spiritual training.

The streets of Mea Shearim are mean and narrow, filled with peddlars and beggars, quacks, idlers, and feeble old folk; there are many little shops and a small vegetable-and-meat market. Scruffy, airless little houses crowd onto small plots littered with refuse. The population density is one of the highest in the city. A third of the residents of Mea Shearim live more than three to a room. Great notices everywhere issue warnings about proper attire for women: "Jewish daughters, the holy Torah obligates you to dress modestly at all times, with long sleeves and closed necklines"; "Dear Jew! Keep your wife and daughters away from the abyss of corruption — mini dresses are the epitome of moral deprivation." Other placards denounce the display of "graven images" in the galleries of the Israel Museum, protest the opening of a swimming pool allowing mixed swimming for men and women, or solemnly ban the watching of television, "this unmitigated abomination, which causes so much disorder and suffering throughout the world. . . . Cursed is the man who rents a flat or shop to anyone possessing this destructive instrument. It is strictly outlawed by authority of the learned and saintly rabbis."

The world of Mea Shearim, with its ultras and ultra-ultras, has grown considerably in recent decades and now spills over into the neighboring quarters of Geulah and Makor Baruch. If not for the occasional plane or helicopter in the air, under a summer sky as white as zinc, you might think you were in one of the dismal ghettos of Poland or Lithuania in the latter part of the nineteenth century. Yiddish is spoken by almost everyone — and among recent newcomers from America, an amalgam of English and Yiddish.

("Er is meshugge, he calls from New York every day un sugt er kumt. Ober er kumt nisht. No, not on your life.") It is, however, a mistake to believe that most people in Mea Shearim are new immigrants. At least half of them are second- and third-generation natives. Modern Israelis, whether secular or observant, walk through these streets confused by the double illusion of strangeness and familiarity. They are attracted by a notion of encountering their own roots and at the same time they are repelled, for it was against this sunless, sedentary way of life that the Zionists revolted early in this century in the hope of creating a "new Jew." When they gaze now at these bearded men, with their alarmingly pallid faces — the "skin tone a breath away from the morgue" — at their ringlets and strange clothes, so unsuited to the climate, and at their tired-looking wives, modern Jews are torn by conflicting feelings. At one moment, they recognize a ghetto past overcome long ago (the Zionist leader Chaim Weizmann once defined that bygone life as a fossil, "the disembodied ghost of a race without a body"); and at another, they see their own grandfathers and grandmothers, who went up as smoke through the chimneys of Auschwitz and Treblinka.

"Because of Hitler you have no right to oppose this kind of Judaism," the novelist Amos Oz wrote in 1982. One must not admire their vitality, either, Oz felt, for it threatened one's own. He was watching the ultras and ultra-ultras take over his native Makor Baruch, the Jerusalem quarter adjacent to Mea Shearim. The walls in Oz's old neighborhood were now covered with graffiti that protested the devilish machinations of the "Hitlerite Zionists" and of the "Nazi municipality of Jerusalem." Here, Hitler and the messiah dominate the walls and confound the souls of men, Oz wrote. Propelled by a mystic faith in the arrival of a messiah, "they overwhelm us and threaten to repossess what was taken from them."

There are at least fifty synagogues in Mea Shearim alone (plus more than a hundred others in the immediate environs of the quarter) and almost as many Torah schools and yeshivas. Most are simple and unadorned. Some are little more than a single, stark room, directly off the street, filled with benches and books. Others are hidden away in attics and cellar rooms. A few are more recent, vaguely modernistic structures with classrooms and dormitories accommodating many hundreds of rabbinical students. (On Friday afternoons, shortly before the beginning of the Sabbath, the janitor turns a switch to disconnect the yeshiva from the national power grid, because the network is presumably run by Jews violating the day of rest. He turns another switch to activate the yeshiva's own automatically run emergency electric generators.)

Many of these synagogues and yeshivas are affiliated with particular rabbinical sects and Hasidic movements. Hasidic sects are ruled — almost feudally — by hereditary dynasties. For the most part, membership, too, is passed from father to son. The ruler of a Hasidic sect, who is known as the *admor* (an acronym for "our master, teacher, and rabbi"), is chosen not only for his learning and piety but for his kinship, through birth or marriage, with the family of the founder. Dynastic marriages between members of two ruling Hasidic families, or "courts," are not uncommon. Heads of Hasidic sects are often charismatic figures endowed with great administrative skills. The disciples pay homage to them at regular intervals — some as often as once a week, during the so-called *tisch,* the ceremony of the third (evening) meal of the Sabbath. During *tisch,* the *admor* expounds his Hasidic Torah at his table. The disciples turn to him for advice on mundane affairs, too, big and small. No business deal is concluded, no doctor chosen, no voyage taken, no betrothal arranged without consulting the rabbi.

Hasidic sects originated in Poland and Russia in the eighteenth century (a time of mystic revivalism among the Christian peasantry as well). Their founders were so-called wonder rabbis, purportedly endowed with magical powers to save souls and cure the sick. Hasidism — that is, Jewish pietism — was a populist uprising against the dry and joyless legalism of the rabbinical establishments of the time. It emphasized joyful prayer. This was highlighted by ecstatic displays of mass enthusiasm and by cohesion within closely knit social groups. "The Holy One, blessed be He, requires the heart." The most humble of common men, even the illiterate, through love and mercy could achieve the highest level of piety. Piety required absolute subservience to the miracle-wielding *admor,* or to one of his viceroys. In the nineteenth century, there were more than thirty Hasidic "courts" in eastern Europe. They were not closed orders but mass movements. Several Hasidic courts established footholds in Jerusalem early on. Hasidism quickly provoked an intellectual countermovement, the so-called mitnaggedim (opponents). The opposition sprang up initially among Lithuanian Jews, known for their skepticism and intellectuality, and from there spread to Jerusalem, too. The mitnaggedim decried and ridiculed the mysticism of the wonder rabbis and their emphasis on prayer rather than on learning. The mitnaggedim themselves eventually developed into sects, ruled as well by charismatic rabbis, each with his retinue of loyal disciples.

Most Hasidim of eastern Europe disappeared into Auschwitz and Treblinka during World War II. Four Hasidic dynasts settled in Jerusalem after the war with their courts; their followers are heavily represented today in and around Mea Shearim. The extraordinary staying power of these fanatically loyal sects more than two centuries after their founding, and after the complete disappearance of the eastern-European feudal and mystic world that gave birth to them, is remarkable.

The names of the sects reflect distant origins that have long lost their relevance. They have not — not yet, anyway — lost their near-magic power of attraction. Belz was, and perhaps still is, a township in the marshes of eastern Poland (now a part of the Soviet Union); it was the center of a Hasidic movement said to have numbered more than two hundred thousand members before World War II. The number of Belz Hasidim today is estimated at ten thousand; half live in Jerusalem, which is also the ceremonial seat of their present dynastic head. He succeeded to his post some years ago at the age of thirteen. Four years later, he contracted a dynastic marriage with the daughter of the current head of the Wisnitzer sect, another great Hasidic court, named after a long-abandoned eastern-European locality. This not only brought about the merger of two powerful fund-raising organizations; it also assured the young man's position as undisputed head of the Belzer Hasidim. From Jerusalem, he today controls a small empire of synagogues, educational enterprises, and social institutions on three continents.

The House of Gor was founded in the village of Gora-Kalavia in southern Poland, but among the proselytizing Gorer Hasidim in

Jerusalem nowadays are many of Moroccan origin. The present
head of the Gorer dynasty is the ninety-two-year-old rabbi Simcha
Bunim Alter. He inherited his post from a brother who had transferred the seat of his court from Gora-Kalavia to Jerusalem after
World War II. When the old rabbi appears at the Gorer yeshiva in
Geulah (the word means Redemption), the run-down, former residential quarter adjacent to Mea Shearim, he attracts thousands of
ecstatic worshipers. Fervent prayer is followed by dance, drink,
song, and Hasidic music. Young and old push through the crowd
to glimpse the old man sitting motionless at a long table surrounded by leading members of his court. He leads the prayers like
drills. When he is about to speak, it would be possible to hear a
needle dropping among the hushed crowd. In the main hall, where
the walls are lined with books, there is standing room only. Tables
and benches have been removed. The worshipers press tightly together; the hot air is saturated with the odor of wool and sweat.
The great crowd, seemingly possessed, sways back and forth in the
exuberant, autosuggestive movements of prayer. The Yiddish word
for this is *shokeln* (swinging). While bodies are *shokeln,* faces take
on a transported look and shine with perspiration. The steady
motion is a movement in time as well as in space. At one moment,
the worshipers are in Jerusalem. At another, they are back in
Gora-Kalavia.

In the Sabbath-morning procession of stately, bearded figures on
their way through Mea Shearim to the Western Wall, Gorer and
Belzer Hasidim can be recognized easily by their distinctive caftans
and fur hats. The largest and most active of the Hasidic sects
is named after Lubavitch, a town in White Russia where the
eighteenth- and nineteenth-century founders of the sect held
"court" and were said to have cured many people with magic formulas, amulets, and spells. The current leader, by indirect hereditary line, is a science graduate of the Paris Sorbonne who lives in
Brooklyn, New York. He has never visited Jerusalem. His disciples
here every day await his arrival in a storm of lightning and thunder.
They have become convinced the Lubavitcher rebbe is the messiah
and his coming is delayed only by their own sins and insufficiency
in acts of pious charity. The rabbi communicates with them regularly through live sermons over the transatlantic telephone.

Endless quarrels have poisoned relations between the various eastern-European sects for generations. The animosities have followed them to Jerusalem. In this respect, there is little difference between the warring Jewish sects of Mea Shearim and the warring Christian sects inside the Holy Sepulchre. The walls of Mea Shearim are covered not only with dire warnings against the encroachments of the secular, godless world, but also with attacks on "cursed individuals" within the fold for their alleged transgressions of sacred law. The walls are covered with posters on which the various ultra-Orthodox sects accuse one another of wickedness and treason. Almost every day, new evidence of the lingering tensions between the sects is offered on the walls of Mea Shearim. Gershom Scholem, the great student of Jewish mysticism and kabbala, called Mea Shearim "a dialectical paradise," much like all other Gardens of Eden. Who represented the snake in this Eden? he wondered. "The authors of the curses and anathemas [appearing on the posters] or we, who were crawling on its walls?" (Scholem is said to have quipped that "kabbala is superstition but the history of superstition is science.")

The warring sects of Mea Shearim have been called by one scholar "the poster people." Couched in archaic Hebrew terms and phrases, their posters are hand-set and hand-printed in big, fat letters that can be read from a distance. They are the common form of social communication within the quarter. The city government long ago gave up all attempts to enforce local ordinances that prohibit this defacing of public space. The posters continue to cover and re-cover walls, doors, shutters, and fences. "Evil," "Godless," "Deadly," "Hypocrite," "So-called rabbi," "Traitors," "Slanderers," "Informers" — these are the milder epithets used. Joel Moshe Teitelbaum, the head of the Satmar Hasidic sect, once said that the decrepit walls of inner Mea Shearim "would have collapsed long ago were it not for the posters that hold together the crumbling stones."

Members of Teitelbaum's Satmar sect themselves are responsible for some of the strongest diatribes and denunciations. Equally notorious for their use of strong language are the men of Neturei Karta. Members of this sect often take to the streets as well, to burn down bus stops or to stone cars and restaurants open on the Sabbath. They also have resorted to physical measures in their attempts to stop archaeological excavations on sites in and around Jerusalem where Jewish cemeteries may have existed in ancient times. Since the environs of the city are one huge necropolis, Neturei Karta is bound to object to excavations almost everywhere. When the archaeologist responsible for excavating one famous site — the original City of David (circa 800 BC), south of the present Old City walls — died of cancer in 1987, posters went up in Mea Shearim acclaiming "with joy" the demise of an "evil, wicked, abominable apostate, the archaeologist Yigael Shilo, who is now a dead corpse, after suffering great and well-deserved pain while he was still alive. Hell and perdition will now complete his punishment."

The discord among the sects is merciless and uncompromising. The most zealous refuse to worship at the Western Wall, as this may imply recognition of the chief rabbinate of the secular state, which, since 1967, has been in charge of services there. For most other Jews, secular and observant, the Western Wall is the major site of religious and historic veneration in Jerusalem, a place of pilgrimage and worship. In the civil religion of the modern Israeli state, the Western Wall area has been accorded a unique place.

The visible part of the wall is now many times longer than before the previously described clearing away in 1968 of an inhabited quarter and of much historic debris. Seven of the original layers of huge, beautifully chiseled Herodian stones are above ground; seventeen are still buried. The stones are of such size "the mind cannot conceive how they were carried up and set in place," the Persian traveler Nasir-i-Khusrau marveled in 1047. He surmised they were the result of a miracle wrought by Solomon. Three buried layers were excavated and laid free in 1968, and the wall looks considerably higher now than before. It has an austere, forbidding presence. The space alongside it, the very air, feels tense.

It might have seemed still higher and even more forbidding if the remaining seventeen layers underground had been laid free in 1968, but the rabbinate is against further excavation. A long tunnel has nevertheless been dug along the face of the adjacent ancient supporting wall of the Temple Mount as it continues north under the houses and bazaars of the Moslem quarter. Several dark hollows and ancient underground vaults have been opened for worshipers to pray in on rainy days, in the somewhat eerie atmosphere of a catacomb. The digging of the nearly thousand-foot-long tunnel was challenged by the Moslem religious establishment as an intrusion and danger to the safety of the mosques above it on the Temple Mount, and has been a cause of bloody riots over the years.

The great plaza in front of the Western Wall can now easily hold one hundred thousand visitors and worshipers. On a normal Sabbath morning — when there are no Palestinian riots — thousands visit the wall. Many pray (individually or in groups) and some still wail. Men are asked to put on black cardboard skullcaps at the entrance. Women are given pieces of gray shawling to cover their arms and legs. Men and women are separated by a metal barrier. There are no organized prayer services to speak of; each worshiper prays in his or her own rhythm, to the music of a particular ethnic or Hasidic sect. Every group blows its own shofar.

Many touch the wall with the flat of their hand in a solemn, quietly evocative gesture; some kiss the weathered stone. Visitors stop a short distance away from the wall, to marvel at the cyclopean stones that reminded Flaubert of the Egyptian pyramids. Artfully hewn nearly two thousand years ago by the masons of Herod the Great, the huge stones are framed by a narrow border that makes them look like embossed calling cards, or perhaps invitations to a bar mitzvah. Several such ceremonies are in fact celebrated at the wall one after the other, in quick succession, twice a week. Well-to-do parents in Europe and America occasionally transport entire planeloads of relatives and friends to celebrate the bar mitzvah of a son at the Western Wall. The boy stands facing it, surrounded by male relatives and guests, and reads aloud the week's portion of the Law from a large Torah scroll.

As the sexes are segregated pursuant to Orthodox custom, women are able to approach the wall only through a special enclosure at the southern end. Couples may face it together only from a distance. Spiny capers and other wild weeds grow from the cracks between the stones of the upper layers. Lower down, the cracks between the weathered stones serve another purpose. It is here that supplicants deposit their folded pieces of paper scribbled full with prayers and pleas — in effect, turning the wall into the mailbox of God. The practice of directly communicating with the deity through written notes, which apparently originated at the Western Wall during the eighteenth century, is quite remarkable. The custom is unknown in Christianity and Islam. (Christians habitually relay messages through an intermediary; a saint is asked to intercede on the petitioner's behalf.) The written messages are taken out once a month by the caretakers and ceremoniously buried in consecrated ground. Most are said to be pleas for blessings and success in love, work, or school. According to one source, they are almost all bland and prosaic — "all requests and no thanks." (The mind wanders back to the ancient Romans, who struck or even broke the statues of the gods because of unanswered prayers.)

Occasionally, yet inevitably, you overhear heated arguments among visitors at the wall. What is there to be thankful for? Who is this God, anyway? If he is so good, why is there so much pain in the world? Most visitors, however, seem moved by the marvelous tenacity of the worshipers in adhering to ancient tradition and to hope. In the early 1970s, the American sculptor Isamu Noguchi designed a great basalt monument commemorating the six million dead of the Nazi holocaust to be built facing the Western Wall. The proposal, like many others made over the years to edify the plaza, was rejected. Another monument to the holocaust, by the Israeli sculptor Yaakov Agam, has been illegally erected on the roof of a nearby house. It emits smoke, water, and pale light from six burning gas flames, and has been the subject of protests and litigation for years. The plaza itself remains vacant, a great rectangular expanse of bright stone, sloping gently down toward the wall.

It is alive at all hours with worshipers and tourists. Psalms are read day and night. Night or day, rain or shine, there is always someone nodding toward the wall in prayer. More prayers are recited at all hours in the adjacent tunnels. The chanting echoes through the underground vaults said to be of Hasmonaean origin. Prayer shawls cover the heads of male worshipers, like hoods or shrouds. At night, the lateral searchlights directed at the wall produce a spectral effect — ghostly, bizarre, but dramatically bringing out every line and crevice in the battered stones. Late at night, black-clad worshipers line up in a single row against the lit-up wall, casting grotesque shadows on it. In the eerie, bluish light, they have the exposed look of men standing in front of a firing squad.

The Western Wall is a very far cry now from what it was earlier in this century, when it was forbidden for Jews to blow the shofar or even sit down and Moslems habitually drove cattle through the assembled worshipers. Today, there are benches and chairs; Torah scrolls, forbidden at the wall under the British mandate, are carried aloft. The wall area was commonly known as far back as the twelfth century as the "tomb of a people." Moslem and Christian pilgrims had given it this name — a tomb without inscriptions, without monuments. In the cramped, neglected alleyway where pitiful-looking old men and women wept and bemoaned "the fallen glory of their race," visitors were sometimes stirred to sympathetic feelings, but more often to nasty ones. The Reverend Richard Newton of the American Sunday School Union, a doctor of divinity, marched through the worshipers at the Western Wall late last century and concluded that their misery was well deserved as they had "neglected Jesus." The archaeologist Charles Warren deplored the habit of some Englishmen to promenade through the wall area in the afternoon pointing with their fingers, laughing and making funny remarks, "as though it was all a farce, instead of realizing that it is perhaps one of the most solemn gatherings left to the Jewish church." As late as 1912, the well-known French writer Pierre Loti noted with disgust the abject faces at the wall, which he thought were "ravished from centuries of bartering and usury." The crucifixion of Christ, Loti decided, had left a "stigma . . . imprinted on the foreheads [of the Jews] as a brand of shame with which the whole race is marked." Their noses were "longer and more pointed" than those Loti had seen anywhere before. "They have a wall here where the Jews blub," Evelyn Waugh, the English novelist, wrote home in 1935. "Very sensible idea."

There is still blubber at the wall, as there has been since the early Middle Ages when, according to a kabbalistic text, "but for the prayers of the men of Jerusalem, who pray at the Wailing Wall with weeping and supplication and are all great ascetics and saints, the world would — Heaven forfend — no longer exist." But the wall today is as much a national as a religious monument, the chosen site

for patriotic rituals and state celebrations. It has always figured in
the Israeli national anthem, "Hatikva," though only in the second,
less-well-known stanza:

> As long as eyes perceive our beloved Wall
> And tears are shed over the ruins of our Temple,
> Our Hope is not lost.

Dozens of national flags float over the wall area at all hours. In the
national religion of Israel, the wall holds the most important place,
next to the ritual shrines of Masada and Yad Vashem. There is
something reminiscent of the Japanese Shinto in these rites — an
aspect that has occasionally been criticized by religious purists. But,
as at Yad Vashem, the mythic appeal of these bare stones upon the
national imagination derives from the traditional Jewish link between catastrophe and redemption. The wall symbolizes both the
destruction and the restoration of Jewish statehood. The civil religious calendar assigns several political functions and high holidays
to the wall. It serves as a dramatic backdrop for torchlit military
spectacles. The practice recalls Durkheim's famous remark that in
religion society worships itself. Elite army units are paraded and
sworn in at the wall. (In 1987, this precipitated a bomb attack by
Palestinian terrorists on conscripts and members of their families.)
Concerts are held at the wall. Yehudi Menuhin played there on
March 26, 1979, to celebrate the signing of the peace treaty with
Egypt. There are also protest demonstrations, political assemblies,
and hunger strikes. The Western Wall has become, in effect, a
temple where people venerate not God so much as the people he is
said to have chosen, and their nation-state.

Omar, the second caliph (successor to the prophet Mohammed),
who captured Jerusalem in 638, earnestly promised the Christian
residents of the city "the surety of their persons, their goods, their
churches, their crosses — whether these are in a good or bad condition — and the cult in general." Omar's pledge was kept, more or
less, by his successors. Most Christians in Jerusalem today still follow Greek Orthodox rites, as they did at the time of the Moslem
conquest. Their clergy are vested in the same gold and purple. Each

Sunday in the basilica, they reenact rituals of the long-vanished Byzantine imperial court, in pursuit of what Saint John Damascene described as "the everlasting boundaries which our fathers have set." Austere kavasses herald the arrival of the patriarch, driving the iron points of their heavy staves against the stone flaggings with dramatically arresting effect: *kyrie eleison.* The empire that first adopted Christianity seventeen centuries ago is gone; its church and its rites survive, much as the Jewish synagogue survived the destruction of the city and of the polity that gave it birth. The Greek Orthodox church is nowhere more fascinating than in Jerusalem, where, unlike in Greece itself, it is still surrounded, like a voluptuous mother hen, by its several "heretic" or "schismatic" offspring, the so-called exotic Eastern churches, and by the church of Rome.

The name Orthodox originally embraced all faithful, as against the heterodox, who diverged. Today, Greek Orthodox is a misnomer. Most "Greek" Orthodox in Jerusalem today are Palestinians, though the upper ranks of the clergy are still jealously reserved for Greek nationals. But this, too, is changing. Mass is read in Arabic. In Jerusalem, you are constantly reminded of the fact that Christianity was originally an Eastern religion. As an Eastern religion, it survived the Dark Ages. As an Eastern religion, it thrives today in the heart of a city that is predominantly Moslem and Jewish.

The heart of Christian Jerusalem is the ancient basilica in the Old City. The Greeks know it as the Church of the Anastasis, the Resurrection. The Latins — always more baroque — call it the Church of the Holy Tomb, or Sepulchre. Like so many other churches, in Rome and elsewhere, it stands on the site of an earlier pagan temple: the "dark shrine of the unchaste demon Aphrodite," the church-father Eusebius triumphantly noted.

Ernest Renan was one of the first to remark on this curious, almost universal economy governing sacred sites. He observed that men always pray at the same sites — only the rationale for their sanctity changes from generation to generation and from one faith to another. In Bethlehem, the Church of the Nativity of Christ stands on the site of a pagan shrine, too. Saint Jerome wrote that its stones "heard the weeping of the infant Christ and the lament for Adonis." In Jerusalem itself, the mount of the former Jewish temple exemplifies even more dramatically the recycling of old holy places for new faiths. During the past four thousand years, many deities have been worshiped there — successively — on the same piece of rock. Pierced and perforated from so much use, the rock remained sacrosanct:

BC 1300–1000	Canaanite city-gods Salem or Zedek
c. 1000–168	Jehovah/Jewish monotheism
166–165	Olympian Zeus
165 BC–AD 70	Jewish monotheism
AD 135–333	Capitoline Jupiter
333–638	?
638–1099	Islam
1099–1187	Christianity
1087–	Islam

The same rock is also the legendary site where God took the dust for the creation of Adam, where Adam was buried, where Cain and Abel offered their gift to God, where Noah raised an altar after leaving the ark, and where Abraham is said to have prepared to sacrifice Isaac. Christianity incorporated all these traditions by moving them a few hundred yards west into the basilica of the Holy Sepulchre, where they are celebrated to this day.*

No single church building on earth shelters so many discordant varieties of Christianity under one roof. The truest, perhaps most moving moment in the basilica occurs shortly after the stroke of midnight. Greek matins will have begun half an hour before; at about 12:10 AM, they suddenly mingle with the Gregorian chants of the Latins and the Divornia of the Armenians to form the full dissonant chorus of the church. Shortly afterward, the language of the pharaohs is heard when the Copts say mass. The liturgy of the Syrians is in ancient Aramaic, the common language of first-century Palestine, the language of Jesus and of the Talmud (a tongue now extinct except in remote parts of Lebanon and Syria). The

* Holidays also survive the demise of religions. The Arabian hajj, or holy pilgrimage to Mecca, antedated Islam. Long before the advent of Christianity, heathens marked the birth of the sun on December 25. Saint Augustine was constrained to exhort the early Christians not to celebrate Christmas like heathens worshiping the sun, "but in the name of Him who had created it."

great rotunda reverberates strangely but not unpleasantly in the polyphony.

The Greeks control — or, as is often said, "own" — seventy percent of the Holy Sepulchre. Armenians, Latins, Copts, Syrians, and Ethiopians share the rest. Inside the basilica, order is still jealously prescribed and divided, as it has been for centuries, between the major and the minor shareholders — when and where each sect is authorized to clean, say mass, make repairs, change a light bulb, drive a nail, open or close a door. The rickety little wooden ladder seen leaning obliquely against a second-floor window in a well-known engraving of 1842 by David Roberts still leans against the same window in the west facade of the church, at the same odd angle. It is never used. It belongs to the Greeks and cannot be moved. The Greeks control the golden socket in which the true cross is said to have stood; the Latins must be content with the two openings in the rock left by the crosses of the two thieves. All this forms part of the sacrosanct "status quo" of 1757 — reconfirmed in the nineteenth century by the Treaty of Berlin, which proclaimed its "inviolability," and over and over again by a succession of rulers and conquerors: the Turks in 1855, the British in 1917, the Jordanians in 1948, the Israelis in 1967. The parties still breach it from time to time. The sweeping of Greek dust with brooms held by Franciscan hands can provoke such fury that the police must be called in to intervene. Armenians and Syrian Orthodox are not on speaking terms. Their disputes continue to delay vital repairs. Copts and Ethiopians still battle (in the courts and occasionally with fists as well) over the control of a narrow staircase and two medieval chapels. They are sometimes said to be "divided by a common faith," for both happen to be Monophysites, believers in the doctrine that Christ had but one composite nature, not two.

The foundations of the present church date from the fourth century. The original Byzantine basilica, completed in 335, rose to an immense height. "Make provision," the newly converted emperor Constantine wrote to Macarius, the bishop of Jerusalem, "that not only shall this basilica be the finest in the world but that the details also shall be such that all the most beautiful structures in every city be surpassed by it." Archaeological and literary evidence leaves little doubt that these instructions were carried out. The Byzantine basilica was probably as lavishly adorned as the chapels and tombs of a slightly later date that still stand in Ravenna.

The smaller, more modest Crusader church we see today was built at about the same time as the cathedrals of Chartres and Vézelay. Columns and vaultings of this church have recently been cleaned or reconstructed. In the process, some of the clean, medieval lines of the Crusader church have reemerged from the dark clutter that prevailed in most parts until 1975. But it still takes a lot of goodwill and imagination to conceive the original pristine beauty. The mean, imprisoned forecourt is still reached through a hole in the wall of the Arab street. The jumble of buildings and disconnected chapels, the maze of dark corridors and nondescript rooms, still make it a very ugly church, albeit historical. The Victorian-Greek "improvements" of the nineteenth century — the almost invariably bad art, the unbelievably mediocre modern frescoes — disfigure the Holy Sepulchre even more. Few discerning visitors in the past two hundred years have had much good to say about it. It jumbles together, under one roof, Christ's alleged prison, Adam's tomb, the Pillar of Flagellation, "Mount" Calvary, the Stone of Unction, Christ's sepulchre, and the Center of the Earth, as well as the site of the resurrected Christ's meeting with Mary Magdalene.

The offering of so many sacred attractions, supermarket style, conveniently under one roof has often been mocked. "When you have seen enough of the tomb of Christ you ask your dragoman whether there will be time before sunset to procure horses and take a ride to Mount Calvary," A. W. Kinglake, an English traveler, reported in 1844. The dragoman quickly reassured him. There was no problem. "Mount Calvary, signor? *Eccolo* [here it is], upstairs on the first floor."

Only a few hundred yards away from the radiantly beautiful mosques on the ancient Jewish Temple Mount, the basilica still strikes many visitors as mean and paltry, infested by sectarian squabbles and commercialism. In the words of a modern Catholic, Father Jerome Murphy-O'Connor, professor of the New Testament at the Dominican Ecole Biblique et Archéologique Française, visitors expect the basilica to "stand out in majestic isolation but anonymous buildings cling to it like barnacles. One looks for luminous light, but it is dark and cramped. One hopes for peace but the ear is assailed by a cacophony of warring chants." Its darkness appears darker than it is, its architecture worse, and its cult more degraded.

During the Mussolini years, a team of Italian architects commissioned by the Franciscan order actually proposed the razing of the basilica and the entire densely built-up area around it. They envisioned a new, gigantic Fascist-style structure, something between Brueghel's *Tower of Babel* and a modern Italian railroad station. The central rotunda with the holy tomb was to be surrounded by coiling towers and three churches (Latin, Greek, and Armenian). The project was interrupted by the war and in any event would have come to naught owing to Greek, Armenian, and Copt opposition. It was, however, approved by Gustavo Testa, the apostolic delegate in Jerusalem, who caused it to be published in 1949 in a resplendent volume entitled *Il Santo Sepolcro: Splendori, miserie, e speranze* (*The Holy Sepulchre: Splendors, Miseries, and Hopes*).

Upon discovering the "hideous kiosk" built by the Greeks over the holy tomb after the fire of 1808, the Scottish engraver David Roberts overcame his initial shock only by reassuring himself that it was trivial, since the ugly structure was, after all, covering the holy tomb. The English writer Robert Byron was less generous. "To pretend to detachment is supercilious," he wrote, "to pretend to reverence, hypocritical. The choice lies between them." Bech, John Updike's itinerant American-Jewish intellectual, chides his Christian wife as they tour the Holy Sepulchre: "You should have let the Arabs design it for you."

Edmund Wilson thought it a "macabre, claustrophobic place [that] probably contains more bad taste, certainly more kinds of bad taste, than any other church in the world. . . . What if the whole stale and rickety place, fissured by some piercing note, should come down on us and bury us?" Wilson was so dejected he walked out of the church and sat down on a bench to read *Dick Tracy* in the *International Herald-Tribune*.

At the time of Wilson's visit, the church was precariously propped up by steel scaffolding inside and out to prevent its collapse. The scaffolding has since been removed. A little more light than before reaches the dank corridors, but in the labyrinth of the closetlike interior, it is still difficult to imagine the suburban garden where, according to the New Testament, Jesus was buried among fruit trees, red poppies, and yellow daisies that flower at Easter time. Not surprisingly, a little girl is said to have once remarked: "I didn't know that our Lord was crucified indoors!"

She was expressing an uneasiness that has troubled many visitors before and since. Though Jesus was perhaps too unimportant in his time to be mentioned in any surviving contemporary source, there is little doubt nowadays, even among agnostics, about the historicity of his person and the high probability of his Passion. The same is not true, even among the pious, of the sites connected with his life and death. The authenticity of the Holy Sepulchre was first seriously questioned by pious Protestants at the beginning of the last century. Central to the dispute over the holy tomb was its dubious location within the present city walls. The ancient Jews buried their dead only outside the walls. How, then, it was asked, could this be the authentic tomb? The question was raised mostly by Protestant scholars, but it bothered Catholic savants as well. Notable among the former was Edward Robinson of the Union Theological College of New York, who conducted the first scientific excursion into the archaeology of Jerusalem. Robinson decided — perhaps too rashly, after only one short visit to the Holy Sepulchre — that it was a "pious fraud." Counterarguments were soon raised. The presence nearby of other first-century tombs, ostensibly Jewish, was cited as proof that the site must still have been outside the walls early in the first century. The church fathers, it was argued, would not have chosen a site so obviously within the walls when they could as easily have chosen one outside. The riposte to this was that the church fathers, unlike nineteenth-century savants, might have been less interested in scientifically provable, scriptural geography than in effacing the memory of the heathen shrine that had previously occupied the site of the present church. Eusebius, the sycophantic biographer of Constantine, confirmed that the holy tomb was discovered at this spot "contrary to all expectation." Why contrary? Could it be that, in ordering the basilica to be built on the site of the greatest pagan shrine in Jerusalem, Constantine, with the zeal of a new convert, was catering as much to politics as to theology?

The issue remains unresolved to this day. Its solution depends on discovering the line of the city wall at the time of the death of Jesus. For more than a century, this has been a main objective of archaeologists in Jerusalem. So far, no trace of that wall has been unearthed. Over the years, archaeologists, polemicists, urbanists, and military strategists have suggested at least seven possible lines for that wall — some "confirming" the present site of the basilica as the "true" one, others furnishing fresh doubts that it is compatible with the topographical data supplied by the Gospels.

The uneasiness about the Holy Sepulchre was so great at the end of the last century that attempts were actually made to find the true Calvary elsewhere in the city. Several alternative sites were suggested over the years, mostly by eccentric Englishmen. The most fanciful was that of a scholar named Ferguson who insisted that the present Dome of the Rock was the true Holy Sepulchre. Another possibility sprang from the feverish mind of Charles George Gordon — the English general, hero of Sebastopol and Khartoum — who announced in 1883 that he had found the true tomb as a result of a mystical experience. With unshakable certitude, he located it in a field just north of the present city wall. There were remains in that field of several first-century burial caves. The famous general was in Jerusalem on a year's furlough, the only peaceful time he had known for years, fulfilling a lifelong dream to study the geography of the Bible. He apparently had his mystical experience while poring over the 1864 "British Military Ordinance Map of Jerusalem" and quickly set out to establish his discovery as a new holy place. So widespread was the support given Gordon's discovery by distinguished Protestant clergymen — perhaps owing to their need to have a holy place all their own — that it soon gained considerable acceptance. The Anglican church officially endorsed the discovery. The endorsement was later withdrawn, but the site is venerated to this day and gives comfort to many European and American pietists. Golgotha in Aramaic means "skull," and Gordon named his shrine Skull Hill — not, as is often thought, because of the skull-shaped rock above the ancient burial cave found there, but because, he claimed, the contour line indicating 2,549 feet on his ordinance map made a "perfect death's-head, complete with eye-sockets, crushed nose and gaping mouth." It does in fact. The Garden Tomb, as the site is now called, is a pleasant, well-kept garden — actually more conducive to prayer or contemplation than is the Holy Sepulchre — though its charm is somewhat diminished by a noisy bus terminal nearby.

In the old basilica, meanwhile, tourists push through the melee all the year long, and especially at Easter time. These days, the guidebook substitutes for the devotional text of old, but the predetermined progress and ritual of medieval pilgrims from one holy site to the next remain. Few of the current travel guides do justice to the diversity of the city. In Jerusalem, even the guidebooks are divided. A dissertation could be written about the religious or the political myopia of many guidebooks, or about their deliberate selectivity. All more or less ignore Moslem monuments other than the major ones. The main Catholic guidebook, published by the Franciscan order, barely lists Greek Orthodox, Coptic, or Armenian shrines. And a recent Arabic guidebook to Jerusalem published in Amman, Jordan, lists only Moslem and Christian holy places in Jerusalem.

Pilgrims kneel at the Stone of Unction, where the body of Jesus is said to have been laid out after the deposition from the cross. On Mount Zion, they examine a Catholic and an Armenian site, some five hundred yards apart, both of which are venerated as the palace of the high priest Caiaphas where Jesus was taken after his arrest and, as described in Mark 14:66–72, Peter thrice denied him. Others gaze at the remains of the City of David and climb the ancient flight of steps to the little church of Dominus Flevit, just below the top of the Mount of Olives, where Jesus, according to Luke 19:41, "beheld the city, and wept over it."

The sightseer, bleary-eyed from the heat, wanders across Jerusalem from site to site, bravely trying to take in everything. Overwhelmed by the medley of religions, sects, and warring nationalities, and awed by a history that is by most standards too bloody and too rich, you easily weary as you push from church to synagogue to mosque, never quite sure whether to put on your hat or remove your shoes. The question of "authenticity" is of no importance at all. Whether a site has been "scientifically" certified as authentic does not seem very significant if your only object is to pray there, or to realize a sense of history or of roots, or to respect a symbol — a prism through which observers look at themselves and others.

Visitors to Jerusalem are often on a kind of interior voyage as well. They worship codes, as well as sights — what the French call *lieux de mémoire*, "memorial sites," key elements of a person's sense of identity. Many come to explore, perhaps to even live, an inner image. Jerusalem is a city you visit in your mind or heart. It does not matter that the present via Dolorosa with its stations of the cross is conclusively known to be a fairly recent tradition. (Jesus was condemned on the other side of the city. If he was led through the streets on his way to Golgotha, it was most certainly by a completely different route.) It does not matter that the building now worshiped by the Jews as David's Tomb and by the Christians as the Room of the Last Supper most probably dates from the late medieval period. These sites are defined by faith, not by science; they are sanctified by tradition — by history (Napoléon's "fable, agreed upon") and by centuries of uninterrupted devotion.

In answer to a challenge of authenticity, the Greek patriarch indignantly told a Jewish visitor a few years ago: "We don't need archaeological proof. We have an unbroken chain of faith and presence here that begins in the first century." Religion has always been rational for only the few and magic for the many. The drops formed by humidity in the cavity of Saint Helena's Chapel, deep underneath the Holy Sepulchre, have been regarded by many as tears of sorrow over the Passion. The drops of dew coagulating at dawn on the stones of the Western Wall have traditionally been described as the tears of God weeping for the suffering of the Jews. There are, nevertheless, fewer relics on display today in Jerusalem than only a few decades ago. During the eighteenth century, they still included the sponge and the reed with which Christ was purged on the cross.

Robust ecclesiastical humor nowadays finds its place, too, as when a Dominican priest who recently led a group of French ladies into the enclosure above the holy tomb was asked in a serious voice: "Mon père, is the tomb empty?" He was overheard saying: "Madame, if He is *in*, we are *out!*" In 1964, on the eve of the pope's visit to Jerusalem, the French satirical weekly *Le Canard Enchaîné* announced in a banner headline that a telegram had just arrived in the Vatican from Jerusalem: "INUTILE VENIR AVONS TROUVE CADAVRE [TRIP UNNECESSARY HAVE FOUND CORPSE]."

"In Jerusalem," writes Father Jerome Murphy-O'Connor, author of the best archaeological guide to Jerusalem, "the prudence of reason has little chance against the certitude of piety." The holy or historical sites are mostly conjectural. Some are fanciful, some unproved, and some simply arbitrary. George Bernard Shaw, visiting Jerusalem in 1930, advised the Zionists to "set up notices at every holy site saying 'do not trouble to stop here: it isn't genuine.' " The royal tombs of the family of Herod, the tomb of Mary, and that of Simon the Just are at best very doubtful. The via Dolorosa was elsewhere in the Middle Ages. Some of the present stations of the cross originated in the nineteenth century. The second station was moved two hundred feet to the west in 1914. The Tomb of Absalom is of a period at least a millennium later than Absalom himself. The great arch on the via Dolorosa where Pilate, watching Jesus being led out to the people, is said to have exclaimed "Ecce Homo" was built a century after the event, under Hadrian.

The Tomb of King David (down the stairs in the same building as the equally fanciful Room of the Last Supper) was built by the Crusaders. In the fifteenth century, bloody riots repeatedly broke out between Christians and Jews over control of this site. Eventually, both communities were expelled by order of Sultan Barsbay, who turned it into a mosque. The tomb remained an Islamic shrine until 1948, when the Moslems were evicted by the Jews. The former mosque became a Jewish synagogue and a lookout post into the Arab-controlled Old City. With the Western Wall inaccessible to Jews, it became a major Jewish pilgrimage site and *lieu de mémoire*. Visitors shared not only a veneration of the past but a construct, an idea of it. Today, the rough Moslem-looking sarcophagus inside is draped with an Israeli flag. The embroidered inscription reads in Hebrew: "David, King of Israel, Lives."

Two churches on Olivet, at some distance from one another, claim they sit on the exact spot where Jesus ascended to heaven. Pilgrims in the eighteenth century were still shown the House of the Wandering Jew, the tombs of Amos, Abner, and Caleb, as well as the twelve stones of Gilgal and Jeremiah's pit. These sites have since fallen into oblivion. Then, as now, a myth was not necessarily a fact, but the existence of a myth was a very great fact indeed. In our own time, new rituals borrow ancient symbols. Take two modern examples — one from China and the other from Mexico — both of which show how the union of legend and site can produce new holy places. In the house in Shanghai where the Chinese Communist party is said to have been founded in 1921, a visitor in 1974 was solemnly led to a room soberly furnished "with a table surrounded by twelve apostolic chairs; on the table [was] a teapot with twelve cups; on the wall, a picture of young Mao." And in the house in Mexico City where Leon Trotsky was murdered, he is venerated today as a latter-day saint. The elaborate new ritual was described not long ago by an English visitor. Like Christ or like Ché Guevara, Trotsky is in the process of being "absorbed into [a Mexican] Indian version of the past to be worshipped alongside Popocatepetl."

Among the rituals sanctified by tradition, perhaps the most stunning is the annual miracle of the Holy Fire. It takes place in the basilica every Greek Easter Sunday, according to a prepublished schedule. A few minutes after 1:00 PM, in the presence of the high clergy and thousands of ecstatic worshipers, the fire supposedly descends from heaven directly onto the tomb of Christ. It is said to be a supernatural sign marking the resurrection that took place at this spot.

Thousands will spend the previous night sleeping on the stone floors around the tomb, for latecomers on the day of the miracle cannot get beyond the main door. The church is packed tightly with people. Every spot in every gallery, in every corridor, in every chapel is taken. People stand in the windows, climb on pillars, cling to the scaffolding under the roof. A few minutes before the scheduled miracle, worshipers leap atop one another's shoulders and cry out for the fire to come down, to come down and save them. The Greek Orthodox patriarch is locked into the tomb. The door is sealed. When the fire descends — it never fails — the patriarch receives it and lights a great torch with it. He hands it out to the crowd through a narrow opening in the wall. The worshipers shout, grab, and sometimes fight one another in the attempt to reach the fire with their candles. They then rush with them out to the streets.

The rite is of great antiquity. Its origins are obscure. It echoes Greek, Zoroastrian, and Jewish myth: the flame stolen from heaven by Prometheus and the fire that "came down from heaven, and consumed the burnt offering" during Solomon's consecration of the first Jewish temple. The "miracle" is most probably the result of a simple chemical reaction between two liquids or powders mixed together behind the sealed doors of the aedicula. It was first described in 867 by the pilgrim Bernard the Wise, who reported that at Easter the Kyrie Eleison is sung in the basilica "until an angel comes down and lights the lamps." The miraculous descent of the Holy Fire every Easter at first dazzled and later enraged Western visitors, especially Roman Catholics and Protestants.

The Moslems complained early of fraud. Sultan Hakim of Egypt, who thought the magic was concocted by suspending an almost invisible silk thread soaked in sulfur from the dome above the tomb, was so infuriated that in 1010, he commanded the destruction of the basilica and of all other churches in Jerusalem. The order was partially carried out. Christian worship was banned until 1021, when Hakim, by now quite mad and a self-styled "God manifest," disappeared into the desert south of Cairo. Soon after, the basilica was rebuilt at the expense of the Byzantine emperor. The miracle was revived under Crusader rule and became a Catholic event. In 1106, when the Russian abbot Daniel witnessed it, the crowds were again so great and the press of the people around the tomb so terrible that many people were crushed, but the "Holy Light suddenly illumined the Holy Sepulchre . . . with an indescribable brightness and with a red color the likes of cinnamon." After the fall of the Crusader kingdom of Jerusalem and the resumption of Orthodox rites in the basilica, the miracle became a Greek one once again; hence it was formally anathematized by the Latins in a bull issued by Pope Gregory IX. The miracle has been celebrated since only by the Eastern churches.

Derisive comment by Christian travelers rose again after the Reformation. Henry Maundrell, an English chaplain, complained of "bedlam" and "miracle mongers" among the mob, "better becoming Bacchanals than Christians." By the nineteenth century, such reports became commonplace. According to one traveler, the Greek Easter was not only "the greatest moral argument against the identity of the spot which it professes to honor," but also "the most offensive imposture to be found in the world." Captain Charles Warren of the Royal Engineers remarked that "it is easy to comprehend ignorance and superstition welling up from beneath; but what can be said when it is propelled down from above . . . by magnates, patriarchs, bishops?" The ceremony, half political, half pagan, has often been marred by drunkenness and violence. A savage climax was reached in 1834, when at least three hundred worshipers died during the ceremony of the miracle. The event was described in great detail by an eyewitness, the English traveler Robert Curzon, in his classic *Visits to the Monasteries of the Levant*. A few minutes after the patriarch was "carried out of the sepulchre in triumph on the shoulders of the people he had deceived," all hell broke loose on Calvary and in the rotunda of the holy tomb. The Moslem guards outside the church, frightened at the rush from within, apparently thought that the Christians wanted to attack them.

> The soldiers with their bayonets killed numbers of fainting wretches and the walls were spattered with blood and brains of men who had been felled like oxen, with the butt ends of the soldiers' muskets. Everyone struggled to defend himself [and] in the melee all who fell were immediately trampled to death by the rest. So desperate and savage did the fight become that even the panic-struck and frightened pilgrims appeared at last to have been more intent upon the destruction of each other than desirous to save themselves.

Ibrahim Pasha, the Egyptian governor of the city who attended the ceremony in a "gesture of goodwill," escaped with his life only because his guards hacked a way out for him through the living mass with their swords. Curzon himself managed to get only

> as far as the place where the virgin is said to have stood during the crucifixion when I saw a number of people lying one upon another all about this part of the church, and as far as I could see toward the door. I made my way between them as well as I could till they were

so thick that there was actually a great heap of bodies on which I trod. It then suddenly struck me that they were all dead.

Curzon decided to fight his way back into the relative safety of the Catholic sacristy, tearing through and wrestling with bleeding, half-naked men who were desperately trying, like himself, to escape. He killed one man in the process. At the end of the day,

> the dead were lying in heaps even upon the Stone of Unction [and there were] twenty or thirty in distorted attitudes at the foot of Mount Calvary. . . . I saw full four hundred people dead and living, heaped promiscuously one upon the other, in some places about five feet high.

Until 1917, the rites were usually delayed until the arrival of the Turkish governor. His guards would open a way for him through the heaving crowd with clubs and whips. He would then signal the "miracle" to begin. Russian pilgrims, walking barefoot both ways, carried the fire back in little oil lamps to remote parts of the czarist empire. In the attempt to push through the melee and catch the fire, members of the various sects continued to trade blows. In 1918, during a tumultuous Holy Fire ceremony, six hundred British soldiers were employed to maintain order and some had to intervene to protect a Greek archbishop from an enraged crowd of Armenians. "Vous m'avez sauvé la vie [You have saved my life]," the archbishop murmured into the British military governor's ear as he passed, in his glittering tiara, from the tomb to the Golgotha Chamber.

Tempers have since become less frenzied. The worshipers still throng the rotunda as they reach with their candles for the fire, crying and pushing, their faces tense in the weird light, as though they were burning a heretic. But the ceremony itself is celebrated peacefully these days. Every contingency, including the miracle itself, is carefully anticipated by the organizers, and by the police. The crush is intense; the heat is excessive. Nearly a hundred Israeli police officers are posted in and outside the basilica to uphold the sacred status quo and prevent a sudden panic. A policeman is stationed inside the colonnade with a list in his hand to ensure that the spaces between columns 18 and 15 and columns 11 and 8 are reserved to Armenians. Columns 14 to 12 and 8 to 5 are exclusively Greek. The big pictures on columns 10 and 11 are, however, Coptic.

Long before the wonder is wrought, the crowd is worked up by anticipation as well as by the struggle for breathing space. The agitation is punctuated by shrieks and ululations. The staging is perfect. First, the ceremonial sealing of the tomb à la Houdini; next, a dramatic delay carefully timed to build suspense. There is not a sound in the hushed church. Then the lights go out. Then, suddenly, a deafening toll of bells rings through the dark. With perfect timing, the patriarch inside the tomb pushes the fire out through the hole, the crowd surges forward, and in a moment the entire church is ablaze, thousands of little lights spread overhead from one candle to the next. The patriarch emerges from the tomb in a flash of gold and silver, triumphantly brandishing a blazing torch in each of his hands. The crowd parts for him like the sea of weeds. The miracle is accomplished. Real or fake, there is little doubt about it being dramatic. Some of the Greek and Armenian clergy speak about it nowadays with a knowing smile. They do not see it as a deception but as the reenactment of a colorful ancient rite. The crowd most probably no longer believes in the miracle either. The ceremony is reminiscent of a professional wrestling match where everyone but the most ignorant knows that the blows are not real, but everyone nevertheless is thrilled by the spectacle. A reporter, chatting with a young Greek Orthodox clergyman a few years ago, challenged the verity of the Holy Fire ceremony. The clergyman, head of a well-known Orthodox seminary in western Greece, did not defend the miracle. He spoke Italian. "Per Bacco [By Bacchus]," he exclaimed, "it's only a tradition!"

Unlike the spooky clutter in the basilica, the Haram al-Sharif, the Moslem sacred site atop the ancient Jewish Temple Mount, is a masterpiece of airy spaciousness and design. Few architectural sites so effectively articulate space — pure, freestanding space — suffused with light: a union of the Piazza dei Miracoli in Pisa and Venice's Piazza San Marco. The two great mosques on the *haram*, the Dome of the Rock and al-Aqsa, are at once earthbound and soaring, fulfilling Walt Whitman's assignment for architecture:

> O to realize space!
> The plenteousness of all,
>   that there are no bounds,
> To emerge and be of the sky,
>   of the sun and moon and the flying clouds,
>   as one with them.

Space, mass, and time interact on the *haram*. On the very spot where the ancient Jews worshiped their unseen God, the Moslems in the seventh century revived the essentially Jewish tradition of abstract space. A great, irregularly shaped stone platform, or stage, is placed off center, a few feet above the lower, larger esplanade of the Temple Mount. Eight graceful, freestanding archways rise on the four outer edges of this stage. They enclose it, as it were, in a transparent cube of air and light.

In the center of this radiant cube formed by the freestanding archways rises the octagon of the Dome of the Rock (built in 685 to 692), a masterpiece of shape and color. The Dome is the older of the two mosques on the *haram;* it is the earliest surviving Islamic monument in the world and the Moslem religion's first major aesthetic achievement — a product of rare, harmonious, mathematically rhythmical proportions. Geometry must have been an article of faith in seventh-century Jerusalem. Unlike the ninth-century mosque of Ibn Taaluun in Cairo, which is still purest desert architecture, the Dome of the Rock is emphatically urban in its atmosphere.

Little is known of the architects. But not since the Greek temples had anyone so deftly infused space with spirit. The glazed pottery of the exterior walls is a blend of ultramarine blue, lapis lazuli, emerald green, ocher, and mauve. The mute, abstract design is most beautiful after a rain, when the water brings out the nuances. Lacelike inscriptions, quotations from the Koran, ring the upper edge of the octagon. The coiling letters, white on blue, evoke shadows of Kandinsky. Surrounding the Dome of the Rock is the vast stone esplanade held up by the massive supporting walls Herod raised in the first century to buttress the Mountain of the Lord.

Walking about the esplanade — a masterpiece in itself — with a copy of Josephus in hand, you can easily imagine the temple and the deep cloisters that surrounded it in ancient days: the royal stoa, the inner and outer courts, the high ramps and monumental staircases. Few extinct sanctuaries have been so well documented as to their exact measurements, the decor, the building materials, and even the width and color of the walls. The house of the Lord itself, where the "name" of God "would dwell in thick darkness," probably stood more or less where the Dome of the Rock now stands. Its altar perpetually smoked with sacrifice. The stockyards were filled with thousands of bleating animals — Josephus and others have vividly described everything in great detail. During the reign of Nero, no fewer than 256,500 beasts are said to have been sacrificed in less than one week. The stench and the smoke must have engulfed the entire city (much to the resentment of the Alexandrians, who, according to Josephus, complained that the Jews were turning their temple into a kitchen where they roasted sacred Egyptian animals).

If it were possible to remove the beautiful flagstones on the upper stage, the foundations of the temple might be uncovered, and perhaps some of its treasures, too. The prospect of excavating on the Temple Mount has long fired the imagination of adventurers and romantics. Since the middle of the last century, amateur and professional archaeologists have been more than eager to unearth the holy tabernacle that is presumably buried under the Dome of the Rock, much as Schliemann uncovered the mask of Agamemnon at Troy. Over the years, many requests to allow excavations were pressed, but permission was never granted. The German kaiser Wilhelm was among those turned down, as he toured the Dome of the Rock in 1898. "It is a pity there are no excavations on this meaningful site," he ruefully told the chief imam, who was showing him around. The Moslem merely raised his hands and said it was better to "direct one's eye and thought upward to heaven instead of down into the depths."

English and Italian scholars — many of them military engineers on leave of absence to explore the East — were similarly rebuffed. It is not surprising that the Moslems were not more forthcoming. Imagine the reaction of the Roman pope or the archbishop of Canterbury if a team of Moslem researchers or Turkish military engineers asked for permission to dig tunnels under the Basilica of

Saint Peter or Westminster Abbey. Clandestine excavation was
nevertheless attempted in 1912 by an English adventurer named
Montague Brownslow Parker. With a group of workers disguised
in Arab dress, Parker dug up the southeast corner of the Temple
Mount every night for a week, as well as a cave directly under the
famous rock inside the Dome. In his search for the holy tabernacle
and other treasures, Parker had been directed to these spots by an
Irish clairvoyant who claimed he was in communication with long-
dead biblical personalities. A mosque attendant came upon the
excavators in the middle of the night and sounded the alarm. In
the ensuing confusion, Parker and his men managed to get away;
they escaped with their lives only by embarking for Europe next
morning.

Until the middle of the last century, the entire *haram* was closed
to non-Moslem visitors. The last Christians to set foot on it had
been the knights of the First Crusade, when the Dome served as a
cathedral. With the return of Moslem rule, trespassers risked being
hacked to pieces by the guards or stoned to death by the mob. The
guards were Mauritanian blacks, armed with clubs and scimitars,
and with a reputation among travelers of being bloodthirsty savages. One superstition rampant among Moslem fanatics was that if
an infidel gained access to the *haram,* Allah would grant his prayers;
they assumed that an infidel's first wish would be the subversion of
the religion of Mohammed.

Chateaubriand in 1806 weighed the risks of defying the ban and,
after much to-and-fro, decided to desist; he had been warned that
he might endanger the entire Christian community of Jerusalem.
Other westerners claimed from time to time to have visited the
haram in disguise. Like visits to the forbidden city of Mecca, this
created something like a publishing vogue and a typical early-
nineteenth-century fusion of prowess, politics, piety, and soft porn.
Among the adventurers who rushed into print after a clandestine
visit to the *haram* were two women — a Signora Belzoni of Milano,
who published her exploits in *Viaggi* (Milan, 1826) and Sarah Bar-
clay Johnson, author of *Hadji in Syria* (Philadelphia, 1856). When
the presence of a European clockmaker was needed in the *haram* in
1837 for an urgent repair, he was first exorcised by an imam — not
only of his Christianity, but of his humanity as well — and declared

a beast. He was then carried in on the shoulders of Moslem porters and so completed his task without polluting the ground with his feet.

In 1833, under the more liberal Egyptian rule, an enterprising English architect named Frederick Catherwood (he later achieved renown by uncovering the Mayan ruins in Mexico) managed to enter the *haram* in European clothes and come out alive to tell his story. The Egyptian governor of the city was his friend and, according to Catherwood, "a latitudinarian as to Mahometism." Catherwood simply set up his easel one morning inside the *haram* "with an indifferent air." He sketched and surveyed the Dome and the freestanding arches around it in so cool, so matter-of-fact a manner that at first the intrusion went unnoticed. Later in the day, however, a nasty crowd gathered and a possible lynching was avoided only by the sudden appearance of the governor and his soldiers.

The ban was gradually eased in midcentury, at first only for royalty and the rich. In 1855, the Ottoman sultan personally ordered the chief imam to allow the duke of Brabant (the future king of Belgium) to visit the *haram* with his entire entourage. They became the first Christians to do so openly since the Crusades. To secure their safety, the Ottoman authorities took the added precaution of locking up the hereditary-African guardians of the *haram* for the entire day.

Like the Hagia Sophia in Constantinople, the Dome of the Rock has survived (miraculously, it is tempting to say) almost as it was built in the seventh century. Fire and earthquake have attacked in vain. Even the mass tourism of this century has not yet done it any visible harm. Its measurements still match those of the year 903, despite elaborate restorations following each of many natural disasters. Persian tiles have replaced the original marble and mosaic facade. In all other respects, it is essentially the same as the original, the first major sanctuary of Islam, built by the Umayyad caliph Abd al-Malik in 685 to 691. Disaster threatened in 1914; many of the lovely tiles had fallen from the rain- and wind-racked northwest facade, and a German architect, supplied by the kaiser, proposed that this entire side of the octagon — a miracle of color, rhythm, and geometry — "be re-covered with cast-iron tiles from the *Vaterland*." The project was approved but execution was fortunately postponed with the outbreak of World War I. The British occupied Jerusalem in 1917, and soon after located two Armenian master-ceramicists, refugees from the Turkish massacres, who agreed to undertake the renovations. They set up a kiln within the *haram* and restored the damaged facade to its former glory. (Their descendants are still active in Jerusalem, producing pale-blue and green pottery. Fast-burning electric furnaces, however, have replaced the old wood-burning kilns, resulting in somewhat inferior colors.)

Until the last century, most westerners were attracted only to the city's biblical remains. The Islamic monuments were of interest to most Christians only where they could somehow be related to events in the life of Jesus. The Crusaders regarded the Dome as the original Solomonic temple, where, they believed, the infant Jesus had been circumcised. It is not clear how they could have reconciled this identification, which appears on their maps and coins, with a simple reading of the Bible. A belated echo of this belief is found in Raphael's 1504 painting *Il Sposalizio,* in the Brera Museum of Milan, which has the marriage of Mary and Joseph taking place in front of the Moslem Dome of the Rock in Jerusalem.

The Dome is also called Mosque of Omar, after the Arab conqueror of Jerusalem; actually, that caliph had nothing to do with its construction. It was once thought that Abd al-Malik, who did build the Dome, had done so in order to divert the lucrative pilgrim trade from Mecca, which at that time was in the hands of a counter-caliph. But this view is no longer taken seriously. Most scholars today regard Abd-al-Malik's great feat as an affirmation of Arab victory bound up with missionary zeal. The Dome was built at a time when the population of the city was mostly Christian. The countryside was still, partly, Jewish. Abd-al-Malik must have hoped to dazzle the urban Christians with the Byzantine splendor of his Dome, which more than eclipsed their own churches in the city, and to impress the rural Jews by locating it on their most sacred site. A seventh-century apocalyptic Jewish hymn found in a hoard of ancient documents in a medieval Cairo synagogue suggests that Jews may well have responded to this appeal. Couched in the arcane language of mysticism, the hymn predicts that a great king will come out of Arabia and free Israel: "It will no longer be kept far from the house of prayer."

The dimensions of the Dome are almost the same as those of the fourth-century Rotunda of the Holy Tomb. The exterior is well matched by the splendid interior. The builders were strongly influenced by Byzantine and Sassanian art. It has been suggested that the masons may have been Greeks or Armenians. The decorative mosaics inside consist of vegetal motifs, cornucopias, and so-called jewels that resemble those worn by Christ and the saints in Byzantine icons. They seem to suggest the defeat of Christian Byzantium by the victorious Islamic faith. Other decorations are, in fact, missionary exhortations inscribed on the walls in beautiful kufic script on both sides of the octagonal arcades. Thousands of feet of promotional inscriptions propagate the faith, the only true faith, the only true God, Allah. Allah is great. Allah is good, Allah is merciful. Praise Allah. Love Allah. "Slumber seizes him not, neither sleep; to him belongs all that is in heaven and earth." Some of it is straightforward missionary propaganda coupled with threats to Jews and Christians to submit. There is a direct appeal to the Christians to abandon belief in the Trinity: "Jesus, son of Mary, is only an apostle of God," reads one inscription. "It beseems not God to beget a son." It is unlikely the Crusaders ever bothered to read these inscriptions or they would have defaced them.

In the center of the octagon, under the dome, is the sacred rock on which so many layers of meaning have accumulated over the ages. As in the Holy Sepulchre, lore has placed many events here, all conveniently on the same spot. Among them are the birth and burial of Adam, the installation of David's ark, and the construction of Solomon's temple — not to mention the Creation itself, when the upper world was separated by a shard from the nether pit of chaos below.

The rock may have been the summit of a hill before so many artificial terraces were raised around it. In David's day, it was probably high and exposed enough to facilitate the winnowing of Araunah's barley. Through the rock's associations with Abraham and with Jesus, Islam incorporated all these myths and added its own. From this rock, Mohammed is said to have risen to heaven on a ladder of light. Visitors are shown his footprint embedded in the rock. But the story of Mohammed's rise to heaven from this rock may have been an afterthought. None of the many seventh- and eighth-century inscriptions on the walls of the Dome refer to it.

The rock itself is probably the same "pierced" stone reported in 333 by the Pilgrim of Bordeaux — the stone the Jews visited once a year to mourn and anoint. The fractured mass of virgin rock, roughly forty feet by sixty feet in area, is carefully dusted twice a week and washed with rosewater and incense. Worshipers prostrate themselves between the arches in the ambulatory surrounding it. No services take place here; they are held at al-Aqsa, the other great mosque, on the far south side of the *haram*.

Al-Aqsa is a huge mosque, almost as big as that of Córdoba, and somewhat overornamented owing to repeated modern restorations and improvements. The latter include a graceless forest of fat marble pillars donated by Mussolini and a kitsch ceiling commissioned by one of the great kitsch kings of our time, Farouk I of Egypt. Al-Aqsa accommodates thousands of worshipers every Friday morning. Women are relegated to their own wing. (The Syrian poet Hassan Kanafani claimed the three major taboos of Moslem society are God, Government, and Sex.) Prayer services often turn into political rallies to protest real and imaginary infringements on Moslem or Palestinian rights. At the conclusion of Friday services in the mosque, demonstrators often wave Palestinian flags and demand an end to Israeli rule. From a post in the west wing that overlooks both the *haram* and the Western Wall, Israeli troops are on the alert day and night, ready to fire tear gas at unruly demonstrators inside and outside the mosque. Demonstrators and policemen often clash opposite the main gate leading into the *haram,* a gate known as *bab el salaam* (Gate of Peace). Irony in Jerusalem is always inadvertent.

Foreign visitors pause on the platform between the two mosques, awed and bewitched by the view, wondering how, if ever, the trouble will end. Ronald Storrs described Winston Churchill's visits to the platform every day and every night during a stay in Jerusalem in 1922. So appreciative was Churchill of its beauty that he begrudged every moment he had to spend away from it, and from his easel. As colonial secretary, Churchill was attending a conference in Government House where "in a few minutes" he created the new

kingdom of Jordan. It was hoped at the time that this would satisfy
Arab national aspirations east of the river, leaving the west side to
the Jews. Things turned out differently. Just outside al-Aqsa, a
newly established mastaba commemorates the 1982 massacre of
Palestinians in the Beirut refugee camps of Sabra and Shatila. The
mastaba is the site of frequent political assemblies and inflammatory
speeches calling for Islamic victory and revenge.

The text of a Friday sermon in the mosque is often reminiscent of
the arguments during the era of Saladin, according to Emanuel
Sivan, an Islamic-studies professor at Hebrew University in Jerusalem. "The same combination of claims to the title over the city
antedating the Moslem conquest, the same repudiation of the
present occupiers' allegations down to the use of the very same
hadiths."

Other political monuments on the *haram* include the venerated
tomb of Abdul Kadar el-Husseini, a Palestinian guerrilla leader
killed in action against Israel in 1948. His son, Faisal el-Husseini, is
often described as the senior representative of the Palestine Liberation Organization in Arab Jerusalem. Visitors to the *haram* are not
allowed to approach the eastern edge of the esplanade, allegedly for
security reasons. There is a good view from there into the abyss
below, the valley of Jehoshaphat. The ancients believed it to be the
site where everything began and everything will end — that is, the
site of the Last Judgment: the dead will be roused there at the End
of Days and the sun and the moon shall be darkened and the stars
shall withdraw their light. The Temple Mount was at one and the
same time the gate to heaven and the gate to hell. The medieval
Moslems superimposed upon this older Jewish tale a vision of ecu-
menical bliss. They maintained that on the Day of Judgment Abraham, Moses, Jesus, and Mohammed would be standing on the
slope like brothers at the open gates of heaven and hell. The dead
would cross the abyss on a bridge as narrow as a hair and sharper
than a knife to face the scales of justice.

The *haram* may be held sacred by all three faiths, but only the
naive would suppose that this circumstance might bring more tolerance and more understanding to Jerusalem. Christian fundamentalists continue to advocate the building of a church, or at least a
chapel, in the *haram*'s southeastern corner, known to them as the

Cradle of Jesus. Jewish extremists habitually force their way into the *haram* and try to hold a religious service, which the police are under permanent order to prevent. Without necessarily resorting to violence, many other Jews share in the unending ritual of fascination the Temple Mount evokes. The broken arch that juts out of the Western Wall (named after Edward Robinson, the American scholar who first identified it in 1838) evokes the grand staircase that once led into the temple. An ancient Hebrew inscription was found after 1967 under the arch, a citation from Isa. 66:14 — "When ye see this, your heart shall rejoice, and your bones shall flourish like an herb." It may have been carved by a Jewish pilgrim in the fourth century; or it may reflect the enthusiasm of Jewish workers engaged at the time of Julian the Apostate (AD 363), the Hellenophile and anti-Christian emperor, under whose reign the Jews were briefly enjoined to rebuild their temple. Such discoveries fascinate and at times move the modern, secular observer as well. Many Israelis still seek the emotional security implied in the discovery of roots. The monumental stairway, at the southwest corner of the former Temple Mount, has been excavated and partly restored. For Jews, this is another *lieu de mémoire* of the first order. It leads up to the now-blocked main temple entrance of the first century and prompts many a visitor to remember the psalmist's Song of Degrees:

> I was glad when they said unto me,
> Let us go into the house of the Lord.

To the believer, such finds give the sacred texts a concrete basis, a texture, a real location. Christians in the Middle Ages must have felt this upon being shown a piece of the holy cross.

It has often been said that archaeology feeds on ruins and on war. The excavations of the area below the Temple Mount took place on land belonging to the Moslem *waqf*. Archaeologists had vainly tried to dig there for over a century; in the brief period of calm — or shock — immediately after the Israeli occupation of the Old City in 1967, archaeologists were able to secure the permission of Moslem clergymen to dig up the site. (They might not have been given it a few months later.) The excavation, by a team of leading Israeli archaeologists, was financed partly by Jewish philanthropists and partly by the worldwide Church of God, a fundamentalist entity out of Pasadena, California, long run by a man named Herbert Armstrong, who claimed he was one of God's messengers on earth. The excavation lasted more than a decade, and was the most thorough, most ambitious ever attempted in Jerusalem and the only one so close to the present *haram*.

The eagerly awaited finds resulted in a curious irony. The contest in Jerusalem between Moslems and Jews, Arabs and Israelis, is not merely tribal, not only over territory, but over psychological space. The struggle is over exclusive state-power and over symbols as well. Symbols often connote power, and nowhere more so than in Jerusalem. For several generations, a school of thought had gained credence in scientific circles in Israel, according to which the Arab conquerors never really succeeded in establishing a real urban culture in Palestine, as they had in neighboring Syria and Egypt. Its proponents often argued that the Arabs had founded only one town in Palestine — Ramleh, a nondescript city on the coastal plain. In Ramleh, *not in Jerusalem,* they had established their regional capital. According to this theory, even the Dome of the Rock and al-Aqsa were essentially "Christian" structures adapted for Moslem use. And yet, the excavations at the foot of the *haram* unearthed not only the monumental Jewish staircase into the lost temple, not only great ritual baths, but also remains of a great early Arab urban center (with an important royal precinct linked to the *haram*), of the same early Islamic period as the Dome. The remains of this royal palace were at first wishfully thought by some to be "Byzantine"; the Byzantines had been great builders in fifth- and sixth-century Jerusalem. The leader of the excavation, Professor Benjamin Mazar, the grand old man of Israeli patriotic archaeology, was at home, bedridden, on the day the royal precinct was finally, and definitely, identified as Arab. A close associate, the archaeologist Meir Ben-Dov, has recorded in a memoir Mazar's initial incredulity and subsequent shock upon receiving this news.

Such are the joys and disappointments of scholars. During a long stay in Jerusalem in 1975, the novelist Saul Bellow happened upon a remote, rarely visited Greek chapel in the Old City and there experienced a curious sensation. The little flagstone court was peaceful, completely quiet. It was shaded against the sun by a large grapevine. The sun shimmered through the leafy cover. Bellow enjoyed

the calm and the verdant arbor rising from a single stem. He sensed
a sudden desire "to sit down and stay put for an aeon in the con-
summate mildness." The origin of this desire, he decided, was obvious. "It comes from the contrast between politics and peace. The
slightest return of beauty makes you aware how deep your social
wounds are, how painful it is to think of nothing but aggression
and defense . . . diplomacy, terrorism and war. Such preoccupations
shrink art to nothing."

The Armenian quarter in the Old City bristles with defensive measures. It is an enclave, a closed compound, a miniature city within a
larger one, entirely surrounded by a high, fortresslike wall. The
heavy gates are guarded and locked at night as during the Middle
Ages. During the day, visitors are stopped at the gate and asked to
state their business. Within, some eighty seminary students and
Armenian priests, headed by the patriarch, maintain a precarious
balance with fifteen hundred laymen of Armenian origin, mostly
professionals and tradespeople who rarely attend church. They
make up the only lay community in Jerusalem that lives within the
confines of a monastic order — the brotherhood of Saint James.
The compound is what remains of a large convent built in the
Middle Ages to accommodate and protect the flow of pilgrims from
Armenia. In 1918, it received the more destitute among the survivors
of Turkish massacres. A large lay community of Armenians is said,
however, to have lived in it long before.

Armenian pilgrims flocked to Jerusalem over the Roman roads
soon after their conversion to Christianity in 301, even before the
Edict of Milan in 313 and the conversion of Constantine. Jerusalem
is filled with early Armenian remains. The sixth-century Armenian-
mosaic floor of Saint Polyeuctos in Jerusalem — magnificent birds
in the branches of a vine — is the most beautiful mosaic in the
entire country. In the seventh century, on the eve of the Arab
conquest, the Armenian presence in Jerusalem and its environs consisted of no fewer than seventy monasteries and churches. The head
of the Armenian church is said to have traveled to Mecca to secure
an edict safeguarding the settlement in Jerusalem.

The Armenian compound is the only ethnic quarter in the Old City that today occupies the same site as it did in the fifth century. It takes up a sixth of the area of the Old City. Some of the refugees of 1918 and their descendants continue to live in the compound. It is a comprehensive little community with its own educational and other public institutions, a good library, a printing press (the first in Jerusalem, dating from 1833), a museum with illuminated manuscripts equaled only by those of Yerevan, residential quarters, several historical monuments, and a single shop. Narrow alleys flow into a wide public square. There are gardens with many old trees, the oldest in the Old City. The patriarch and his staff occupy a small palace where the walls are hung with portraits of long-forgotten European royalty and with a map of the long-defunct Greater Armenia (it allegedly stretched all the way from the Mediterranean to the Caspian Sea). The patriarchate's importance derives from its standing, under the famous status quo, as a principal shareholder in the holy places. It also owns extensive property in and around Jerusalem. Its bishops, gazing out of their black hoods, don the heaviest emeralds and pearl-encrusted golden crowns.

The main church inside the Armenian compound, the Cathedral of Saint James, is the finest in town. Its treasures — its miters, crowns, and gold chalices inlaid with gems, its noble vestments and lamps — have been amassed over the centuries; all were brought from Armenia and Cilicia by the pious and princely. Armenians rarely speak about their artifacts. Like the Jews, they are survivors, "people [that] dwell alone." The little quarter has always been a center of learning, much like the great Jewish yeshivas in prewar eastern Europe.

The Armenians have survived in Jerusalem for so long because as a national and a religious minority they have learned not to take sides. They are cordial with both Palestinians and Israelis. What is a mere quarter of a century of Israeli rule against the nearly seventeen hundred years of uninterrupted Armenian presence in Jerusalem?

Just outside the city walls, the fourteenth-century Armenian monastery of Saint Savior stands surrounded by an ancient cemetery. The older tombs are decorated with carvings of working tools — a mason's trowel, a tailor's scissors, stonecutters' chisels, a bishop's crown. Some are inscribed with epitaphs in Armenian quite unlike those found on modern tombs:

> Plant a rose on
> My simple grave.
> I, the sacristan Krikor
> Sang prayers
> And lit lamps
> For forty years,
> On the tomb of Christ.
>
> Here reposes
> Ghevond of Lake Van, a lover of letters.
> The scribe
> Who copied so many manuscripts
> Old and new.
>
> Sing Alleluia
> For the binder
> of books
> the monk Mekhitar.

Once a year, in April, hundreds of Jerusalem Armenians gather in the cemetery to commemorate the victims of the Armenian holocaust of 1915 to 1918, when an estimated one million Armenians were massacred by the Turks. Another half-million went into exile. Armenian spokesmen use the occasion to emphasize their belief that Armenia was a rehearsal for Auschwitz. "The Armenian holocaust was forgotten or ignored. If it had not been ignored, perhaps Auschwitz would not have happened." (Hitler, preparing for the Final Solution, is said to have reprimanded a reluctant general with the words: "Who remembers today the fate of the Armenians?") Armenians cite Israel Zangwill, the English-Jewish author, who at the time of the massacres pronounced eloquently: "I take the crown of thorns off Judah's head and put it on Armenia's brow." They will tell you that it was during a visit to Jerusalem that Franz Werfel conceived the idea of *The Forty Days of Musa Dagh,* the great bestseller of the 1930s that commemorated the Armenian catastrophe (and was also meant as a metaphor of the Nazi menace). The massacre of a million Armenians was official Turkish policy. It was carried out by a state bureaucracy similar to that used by the Nazis twenty-five years later. "Deportation" was a Turkish code word for mass execution, just as it was in Hitler's Germany. "I hate the Turks," the Armenian patriarch of Jerusalem told a newspaperman a few years ago, in a very Jerusalemite statement. "Christ enjoined us not to hate our enemy. But that was before Turks were born."

A few rooms in the art museum of the Armenian compound are dedicated to the massacres. Faded old photographs show ghastly heaps of corpses similar to pictures on the walls of Yad Vashem, the Israeli memorial on the other side of town that commemorates the destruction of European Jewry under the Nazis. Both museums are dedicated to the impossible task of tracing and registering the name of every man, woman, and child and of every erased community. The testimony of Henry Morgenthau, United States ambassador to Turkey at the time of the massacres and perhaps the only member of the diplomatic corps to protest the outrage, is prominently displayed:

> As the exiles moved they left behind them another caravan — that of dead and unburied bodies. . . . The most terrible scenes took place at the rivers, especially the Euphrates [where] the gendarmes would push the women into the water, shooting all who attempted to save themselves by swimming. . . . Tens of thousands were driven into the desert without food and water.

Among Armenians, as among Jews, an annual day of mourning is set aside to commemorate the destruction. The ghastly memory of the past nourishes a central collective trauma among Armenians, as it does among Jews. The Armenian trauma takes on an additional bitterness owing to the fact that, unlike the Germans, the Turks have never recanted, nor assumed responsibility for the disaster. As the procession of Armenian mourners winds its way back from the cemetery through the narrow streets, it passes walls covered with posters in English and Armenian protesting Turkish callousness. The sun beats down. In the mercilessly harsh light, the posters quickly fade and peel off the dusty walls. In the past, mystics used to refer to this light as the "outer garment of God."

It is not common to think of Jerusalem as an Armenian city. Not so long ago, it was a city of Greeks, of Germans, and of Russians as well. Even today, you are never far from Greece here, especially at

Easter. Large groups of Greek and Cypriot pilgrims fill the streets at Easter; parts of the Old City resemble an Aegean island. Earlier in this century, a permanent Greek colony still thrived in its own enclave. In 1909, it numbered more than two thousand souls. The Greeks of Jerusalem were a relatively well-to-do community of shopkeepers, tour guides, and artisans, clustered around their own civic institutions and church. There was constant tension between ethnic Greeks who saw the Greek Orthodox church of Jerusalem as an outpost of Hellenism — that is, the modern church of Athens — and those who wanted it to be a church of Palestinian Arabs. To this day, there is not a single Arab in the upper echelons the Greek church, even though it caters to an almost exclusively Palestinian parish. Of the lay Greeks, only a dozen or so families (and in the former Greek colony, a deserted clubhouse) remain. In the nineteenth century, Jerusalem apparently occupied so central a place in the Greek memory that there were plans to open a Greek university in Jerusalem even before a Greek national university was opened in Athens.* The chosen site for it was the ancient Monastery of the Cross, which still nestles gracefully in an olive grove below the present Israeli Knesset; the monastery derives its name from the legend that the cross of Jesus was made from a tree that once grew there. The project was abandoned only because of opposition from the Ottoman government.

Adjacent to the Greek colony was, until 1939, a large German enclave inhabited by Templers, members of a pietist Protestant sect from several rural communities in southern Germany. The Templers arrived in 1873 with the idea of founding in Jerusalem "ein kleines Reich Gottes" (a small kingdom of heaven upon earth). They were expecting the imminent Second Coming and envisaged a million likeminded European Unitarians joining them in Jerusalem and in their other settlements throughout the Holy Land. As it turned out, only a few thousand did. They were mostly peasants and artisans. Their main street in Jerusalem — the first tree-lined

* In England, at about the same time, Cardinal Newman conceived a similar plan to found a modern (Catholic) university in Jerusalem: "The spell which Oxford still exercises upon the foreign visitor," he said, "suggests to us how far more touching, how brimful of indescribable influence, would be the presence of a university within Jerusalem."

thoroughfare in the city — typified that of a south-German village and is preserved to this day: a former *Gemeindehaus* (church), a *Bierstube,* a *Lyzeum,* a few dozen one-story homes — among the first of stone, with red-tiled roofs. The sculpted portals are inscribed with pious biblical verses in Gothic script ("Pray for the peace of Jerusalem"; "Arise and shine, for thy light is come and the glory of the Lord is risen upon thee"). The area is still known as the German Colony, but the Templers and their descendants were deported by the British to Australia in 1941 (many were pro-Nazi by then).

Russia, too, had its place in Jerusalem. In the heart of the present commercial center of the New City stands a walled compound that until World War I was an outpost of Mother Russia — a city within a city. On the site of a former Turkish parade ground, it dominated Jerusalem like a fortress. The many-domed Russian cathedral was modeled after a church in the Kremlin. It was surrounded by long, barn-shaped buildings — offices, hostels, princely residences, infirmaries and canteens — inhabited, until 1914, by twenty thousand Russian pilgrims each year and the imperial bureaucracy that took care of them.

The compound was built in 1863 by the Imperial Russian Palestine Society, a pet project of the last czars, who believed that pilgrimage to Jerusalem would bind Russia's restive masses to their rule. In the jealousy-ridden 1880s, the Russian compound generated serious concerns among the other imperial powers. The British vice-consul in Jerusalem informed London, rather hysterically, that many Russian pilgrims were veteran soldiers in uniform and some had been overheard saying that Jerusalem would soon come under Russian rule.

After the revolution of 1917, Russian pilgrims stopped coming. The compound stood empty. The hospices closed. Russian nuns took up employment as maids and nannies in Jerusalem households. The compound became a British police post, courthouse, and jail. A gallows rose in the former dormitory of the peasant women; several Jewish terrorists found guilty of attacking British targets were hanged from it in 1946 and 1947. The grim site has been a national shrine since 1948. That same year, the new Israeli state recognized Moscow's jurisdiction over the premises. As a result, there were now two Russian church establishments in Jerusalem: a "red" Russian church, controlled from Moscow, in West Jerusalem under Israeli rule, and a "white" Russian church, controlled from New York by the Russian church-in-exile, in East Jerusalem under Jordanian rule.

The duplicity continued after 1967. In the former Jordanian sector of Jerusalem, the "white" Russians still exercise control over several great holdings on the Mount of Olives and in the Old City. But "whites," a dying order, are now greatly diminished in numbers, as is witnessed by the many Russian crosses on the graves surrounding their churches on Olivet. (The "red" contingent in West Jerusalem is regularly reinforced from Russia.) In the 1960s, a former grand duchess, the octogenarian Princess Bagration, was still abbess at the Russian Convent of the Ascension and could be seen, stooped and ailing, walking among the trees on the Mount of Olives. The young king Hussein of Jordan paid her an official visit in 1963. The two took tea in the convent's little salon, under the portraits of the last czar and czarina, and are said to have commiserated together on the burdens bearing down nowadays on grand dukes and on kings.

In the Israeli sector, meanwhile, "red" Russian priests, fresh from Moscow and widely regarded as KGB agents, marked their first May Day in Jerusalem by hoisting the red flag atop the Russian cathedral. It took a special protest to bring it down. In 1964, much of the compound was sold by the Soviets to the Israeli government for oranges. The Russians retained only a wing of the old czarist consulate to accommodate representatives in Jerusalem of the patriarchate of Moscow.

Today, the old Russian compound serves as a police station, a jail, various government offices, and, in one wing, the courtroom and private chambers of Israel's supreme court. The ghostlike, disembodied presence of the builders of the compound hovers over the extensive grounds. The walls are adorned with Russian emblems and Cyrillic letters. The words "For Zion's sake I will not hold my peace" curl like garlands around alpha-omega signs. The supreme court pays rent to the Soviet government. The old cathedral is still a Jerusalem landmark. Its services attract both local curiosity-seekers as well as tourists. The former noblemen's hostel, which was somehow overlooked at the time of the 1964 accord, is still registered as the heirless property of the grand duke Sergei, brother of the last czar.

An air of vanished glory marks many Christian landmarks in the New City, which, like the Russian compound, were built by the competing imperial powers during the second half of the nineteenth century. The great buildings still stand. In most cases, only the names remain. Their pompous but generally poor architecture probably reflects the nationalization of religion in the last century.* The former Italian hospital, modeled after the Palazzo Vecchio of Florence, is now the headquarters of the Israeli ministry of education. In 1979, a superstitious minister of education and culture (sic!) ordered all crosses chopped off its exterior walls; in the process, many of the majolica coats-of-arms of famous Italian cities that adorned the friezes, consoles, and arches were also defaced. The huge Kaiserin Auguste-Victoria Stiftung on the Mount of Olives is now a hospital serving destitute Palestinian refugees.

The cavernous halls of the stately Saint Pierre de Sion-Ratisbonne, built as a school in 1877 by French missionaries, are today mostly rented offices, as are the premises of nearby Terra Sancta College. Both are in the heart of the New City's best residential districts. The former Anglican cathedral of Saint George, with its frigid twentieth-century Gothic, has seen many colorful imperial rites, but is now a simple parish church, where the Lord's Prayer is said in Arabic by a Palestinian bishop. Here — during the tenure of Sir Herbert Samuel, the first British high commissioner, who was a Jew — clerics of all major denominations except Roman Catholic, including the Moslem grand mufti and one of the two Jewish chief rabbis, attended services on December 9 of every year, the anniversary of General Allenby's conquest. They all came; the service was mainly in English, but portions were read in Arabic, Hebrew, Greek, and Armenian. The services, discontinued after Samuel's departure, are remembered by those who care about such things as

---

* This is probably true everywhere. The great authority Nicholas Pevsner believed that no church designed after 1750 in Europe can be ranked among leading examples of architecture.

the last time the assorted clergy all met in one house of worship — or, for that matter, in one room.*

France, which gave Jerusalem the rulers of the Crusader state, retained a claim to be recognized as protector of all Catholic holy places and of most Western pilgrims after its fall. The claim was one of the pretexts for the Crimean War. It dates back to an alleged pact between Pépin the Short, or his son Charlemagne, and the sultan Harun al-Rashid. All that remains of French privileges today is the immunity granted certain Catholic clergymen from certain traffic regulations (they are allowed to display diplomatic license-plates on their cars, a courtesy extended by the Israeli government to the high clergy of other denominations as well).

The great block of French-Catholic institutions down the road from the Russian compound was built in the 1890s and once included a hospice, a church, a hospital, a monastery, and a convent. Of this ambitious undertaking, only a small geriatric hospital, a church-run hotel, and a gourmet restaurant remain. The hotel is probably the only one on earth today where the maître d' is a monsignor who travels on a diplomatic passport.

The Ethiopians were the single nonimperialist power to build on a grand scale in Jerusalem during the nineteenth century. They claim a special relationship with the city, reaching back to the days of Solomon. Their emperors, when they still had them, were known as "Lions of Judah." The Ethiopian emperors claimed to be descended from Solomon and the queen of Sheba. The Ethiopian monastery on the roof of the Holy Sepulchre is called House of the Sultan Solomon because, the monks claim, Solomon gave it to Sheba as a wedding gift. The walled Ethiopian compound on Ethiopia Street in the New City, begun in 1874, includes a monastery, a hospice, and a large church. The church is circular, much like the mud churches seen everywhere in the Ethiopian highlands, with a central altar under the conic roof. Here, it is made of pink

---

* After the service, the assembled clerics posed for a group photograph with the high commissioner and his staff. Sir Herbert thought it a happy coincidence that at one end of the group, as they were being photographed together, was the emblem of peace, a great olive tree. He was promptly corrected by one of his aides: "Yes, Sir, but perhaps you haven't observed that at the other end there is a peppertree."

Jerusalem stone. A few Ethiopian monks, looking like pictures of the magi, still gather here at dawn and dusk, chanting.

The annual Ethiopian ritual called Searching for the Body of Christ is said to have been borrowed from the worship of Isis in ancient Egypt. It takes place at midnight on the roof of the Holy Sepulchre. The participants (some fly in from Addis Ababa expressly for this purpose) wander about in the dark with burning candles. A colorful Ethiopian tent is pitched nearby for the visiting clergy. The flickering lights, the flares, the haunting play of shadows against the walls, the incense, the chanting, the wild, discordant drums combine to produce an extraordinary effect.

Marxist Ethiopia has not lost its interest in Jerusalem, but there are fewer Ethiopian pilgrims now than before the revolution of 1974. In the great compound on Ethiopia Street, only a handful of monks and nuns (one of them Danish) are left nowadays. Most of the picturesque houses on the grounds are rented out. The life of the Israeli city without seeps into the compound and covers up what was Christian before. Large parts are now Ethiopian by name only.

The Christian population of Jerusalem, both clergy and lay, has sharply declined during the past half-century. Most of the loss is the result of emigration to North America and South America. In East Jerusalem, the decline was at its worst during the years of Jordanian rule: the Christian population declined from 25,000 in 1948 to 10,000 in 1967. In the entire city, the Christian population, which in 1946 had been 31,000, was estimated in 1989 as fewer than 9,000. Christianity in Jerusalem may soon be a visiting rather than a living religion: the museum of its birth.

The growth of mass tourism in recent years obscures this possibility but does not make it less likely. A prominent Christian clergyman warned a few years ago that if the present rhythm of Christian emigration from Jerusalem continued, visiting Jerusalem in the future "will be like visiting Baalbek where you see the Temples of Bacchus and Jupiter . . . without any emotion except the aesthetic emotion. . . . Some religious influences will be left, some nuns . . . and highly qualified professors of theology, and archeologists . . . who will serve as natural guides for tourists." The writer is a Lebanese archbishop. The bitterness of these words was a measure of his anxiety.

Some may not consider the Christian emigration a threat; others will deplore it in the name of faith or history. A few regard the profusion of denominations and sects in Jerusalem as merely eccentric or picturesque. Others insist that, taken together, they constitute the city's unique spirit of place. That spirit itself might be put in question. Beyond the comforting, utopian generalizations that imagination, prejudice, and vanity might set free, there are human beings living in the city — Jews, Moslems, and Christians — ordinary people who, though diligent and forever on the alert, have often been crushed and plundered clean in the relentless intensity of local history. No one really knows the full human and emotional cost of living in a violent house divided against itself. The price is surely high, but no one knows the exact amount paid in terms of psychological entanglements, debilitating compensations, and illusions.

In this century, a tribal war was added to the age-old, occasionally violent clashes of sects and denominations in the city. The wars of religions continued under a new name. Religious differences were inflamed by awakening nationalisms; nationalisms were inflamed by religious differences. The result, even in the lulls between the wars, was a kind of feverish tension in the city, an air of constant emergency. There were numerous external aspects of the crisis nobody could avoid. The Arab half of the city was paralyzed for months on end by commercial strikes and demonstrations by Palestinian nationalists. In 1987, after years of acquiescence, the Palestinian population of East Jerusalem rebelled against Israeli rule. In East Jerusalem and in the Old City, heavily armed troops patrolled the streets. The streets of West Jerusalem were equally marked by the presence of armed civilians and by numerous young (and some middle-aged) men in drab army uniforms. At the entrance to supermarkets, movie houses, and theaters, aging guards checked handbags for hidden explosives. There were standing roadblocks on the main highways leading into the city as the police searched for suspect Palestinians. In West Jerusalem, there were, in addition, recurrent clashes between the police and religious fanatics.

Ultra-Orthodox yeshiva students rioted against the secular life-
style of the Jewish majority.

Historians may console us with assurances that little is new in
this restlessness. Historic Jerusalem was the restless city par excel-
lence. Crowd control, or the lack of it, has been a common theme in
the life of the city since earliest times. Civil disobedience was the
hallmark of the ancient city. Tumults were always raised in
Jerusalem for or against something. The prophets were rabble-
rousers. They arose from and appealed to the people. In the Gospels, the rioters were sometimes described as "mixed multitudes."
Josephus's name for them was "throngs." George Adam Smith saw
an early form of democracy in this perennial restlessness, "the dominant influence exercised [in Jerusalem] by the common people." He
went so far as to attribute the popular rebelliousness to the climate
and geography: "We shall never understand the history of the
City," he wrote, "without appreciating the conspiracy between its
people and the free, wild desert at their gates."

Be that as it may, Jerusalemites did stage the first recorded sit-
down strike in history. Josephus recounts how, in the first century,
multitudes of Jews from Jerusalem threw themselves on the ground
outside Pilate's house and stayed there for six days and nights. They
were protesting the introduction of Roman emblems into the city.
Pilate surrounded them with soldiers and threatened them with
death unless they would stop the disturbance and immediately go
home. But they only bared their throats, willing to be beheaded
rather than have their laws challenged. Pilate was so affected by
their resolve he ordered the images removed. The story sounds
almost modern.

The modern city of Jerusalem has almost always been intolerant
and exclusivist, harsh and hard like the consonants in the speech
patterns of the Hebrew and Arabic languages. The residence of the
Israeli president and those of the prime minister and foreign minister are under siege almost constantly by vigilantes protesting private or public wrongs. The city has never been "one" or "united,"
never a "mosaic," as its well-wishers hoped, but a collection of
alienated islands. The Palestinians of East Jerusalem, long regarded
by most Isarelis as covertly content with Israeli rule because it

afforded them higher living standards and better municipal services, in 1987 joined Palestinians on the West Bank and rose in revolt. Braving heavily armed police with a tenacity that surprised everyone, perhaps even themselves, Palestinians in East Jerusalem demonstrated almost daily. Pelting cars with stones, chanting slogans, and waving the illegal Palestinian flag, they marched defiantly through the debris, the tear gas, and the black smoke of burning tires. Little boys ran ahead firing slingshots at the troops summoned to disperse them. For the first time since the reunification of the city in 1967, curfews were imposed on some of the more turbulent Palestinian quarters. The schools in East Jerusalem remained shut for months. Thousands of East Jerusalemites tore up their Israeli identity cards. The commercial strike observed by nearly all shopkeepers paralyzed the Palestinian sections of the city for many months, turning East Jerusalem into a ghost town for many hours of the day. The "united" city seemed to be coming apart at the seams. The old (pre-1967) dividing line came into being again. West Jerusalemites, if they could possibly avoid it, no longer crossed into East Jerusalem. They could console themselves that perhaps the city was on the whole still more peaceful than Belfast; but it was not free of fear.

The fears canceled one another out. Relations between secular and Orthodox Jews in West Jerusalem also deteriorated. Long regarded by most Israelis as a quaint anachronism, the ultra-Orthodox of West Jerusalem, in the mid-1980s, broke out of their self-created ghettos. They seemed resolved to change — by force, if necessary — the life-style of the nonobservant Jewish majority. Riots by the ultra-Orthodox became an almost permanent feature in the life of the city. The religious extremists had always had strong convictions. By the mid-1980s, for the first time, their strength was also in numbers. Roughly one-third of the Jewish population of the city were now said to be Orthodox and ultra-Orthodox; 55 percent of all Jewish pupils were attending religious schools. Orthodox fanatics broke into Reform and Conservative synagogues, accusing adherents of "pornography." The Ashkenazic chief rabbi announced unequivocally that, as he understood it, there was no "religious freedom" in Israel; Orthodox Judaism was the only "legitimate" creed among Jews. His Sephardic colleague added that Reform Judaism was a plague imported from America that ought to be stamped out. The rabbis could not enforce these views, but secular and conventionally religious Jerusalem Jews grew increasingly concerned about their place in the city. The ultras were confident that the future was theirs. Almost a third of the votes cast in the city during the 1988 national election went to ultra-Orthodox religious parties allied with the ultranationalist right wing. Together, the two blocs collected 62 percent of the vote in the city.

The accumulation of so much passion and memory — much of it expressed in religious or quasireligious terms — made the city seem wondrous and at the same time quite psychotic. Tens of thousands of Jews were said to have left Jerusalem for other cities in the 1980s. One former Jerusalemite, now living in Tel Aviv, invoked a famous nineteenth-century Hasidic rabbi who reportedly warned his son not to live in frontier towns because they combine "the ill will of two countries." And yet, most of these "emigrants" were said to be secular, or conventionally religious, university graduates. Orthodox fanaticism seemed to trouble them more than Palestinian riots.

In the nineteenth century — when Paris was the heavenly city of the secular — the central- and eastern-European Jewish expression for perfect happiness was "Wie Gott in Frankreich" (like God in France). Saul Bellow wondered about this expression. Why did they not say like God in Jerusalem? Why should God be so happy in Paris? Bellow decided that God was so happy in Paris "because [there] he would not be troubled by prayers, observances, blessings and demands for the interpretation of difficult dietary questions. Surrounded by unbelievers he too could relax toward evening just as thousands of Parisians do at their favorite café."

CHAPTER EIGHT

The Future of the Past

THE rational mind has always had reservations about Jerusalem. In 1930, Sigmund Freud wrote Albert Einstein: "I can muster no sympathy whatever for the misguided piety that makes a national religion from a piece of the wall of Herod, and for its sake challenges the feelings of the local natives." Freud was attached to the Jewish world with ties he knew to be indestructible and had even contemplated, briefly, in 1922, settling in Palestine. Yet, a few years later he told his friend Arnold Zweig, the novelist, who had just returned from a visit to Jerusalem: "How strange this tragically mad land you have visited must have seemed to you. [It] has never produced anything but religions, sacred frenzies, presumptuous attempts to overcome the outer world of appearances by means of the inner world of wishful thinking. . . . And we hail from there!"

The early Zionists by and large tended to share Freud's wariness of religion. Theologically, Zionism was the great Jewish heresy of the nineteenth century. The early Zionists were sober men, more realistic than most in their fears of an imminent collapse of civilization in Europe, and eager above all to save lives. Like many national leaders of the liberal European school, they were anticlerical if not outright secular. The idea — even more so, the reality — of Jerusalem frightened or repelled them. The Zionists were, for the most part, future-oriented men and women. Jerusalem incarnated most things they had scorned and rejected: superstition, backwardness, and theocracy.

Theodor Herzl, the founder of modern Zionism, envisaged the capital of his proposed state on a new site, the western ridge of

Mount Carmel, overlooking the Mediterranean Sea. "When I remember thee in days to come, O Jerusalem, it will not be with
pleasure," he wrote after a visit in 1898. "The musty deposits of two
thousand years of inhumanity, intolerance, and uncleanliness lie in
the foul-smelling alleys. . . . The amiable dreamer of Nazareth has
only contributed to increasing the hatred." Try as he might, at the
Wailing Wall no "deeper emotion" came. "What superstition and
fanaticism on every side!"

Ahad Ha'am, the leading Zionist thinker of his time, experienced
a similar sensation in 1891 after inspecting what he called "the
terrible Wall" and the ultra-Orthodox men worshiping it. "These
stones bear witness to the ruin of our land, and these men — to the
ruin of our people; which is the greater of the two ruins? Which
should we deplore more? A ruined country . . . can be rebuilt; but
who can help a ruined people?" He would not cry for Jerusalem, he
announced, but for the Jewish people. David Ben-Gurion, the future prime minister, who arrived in Palestine as a Zionist pioneer in
1906 and during the next decade thoroughly explored the entire
country, from Galilee to the south, mostly on foot, seems to have
avoided Jerusalem almost deliberately. In his diaries and letters, so
rich in impressions of other sites, there is hardly a word about
Jerusalem. Like most pioneers of his generation, Ben-Gurion was
more interested in building a new socialist society of free men and
women than in national icons and religious relics. The Zionist
pioneers, writes Anita Shapira, a leading historian of the period,
regarded sentiments for Jerusalem as simply "reactionary." Chaim
Nachman Bialik, the great poet of the Hebrew literary revival early
in this century, avoided modern Jerusalem as a theme. He felt ill at
ease there. None before Bialik or after expressed the Jewish will to
live in words and rhymes of such beauty and poetic force. He
borrowed a well-used biblical image of Jerusalem — "joy of many
generations" (Isa. 60:15) — and applied it to Tel Aviv, the new city
on the sea, where, like Ahad Ha'am, he chose to settle. He preferred
Tel Aviv, he said, because "our hands have built it from its foundation to the roof. This after all is the purpose of our national renaissance: to cease being indebted to others, to be our own masters, in
body and spirit."

On a different, purely political level, it is noteworthy that Chaim

Weizmann, the Zionist leader who became Israel's first elected president, was known throughout his life to harbor ambivalent feelings about Jerusalem. He first visited the city in 1910 — "not without misgivings," he wrote in his memoirs in 1949. "I remained prejudiced against the city for many years and even now I still feel ill at ease in it, preferring Rehovoth [where he had built his home in 1938] to the capital." In 1937, when the first partition plans were discussed, Weizmann suggested that only parts of the modern city be included in the proposed Jewish state. As for the Old City, "I would not take the Old City [even] as a gift. There are too many complications and difficulties associated with it."

Such sentiments look preposterous today in most Israeli eyes. At the time of the establishment of Israel in 1948, they were still quite common. A few months before, in the fall of 1947, most Jewish leaders were ready to abandon all of Jerusalem if they could have an independent Jewish state elsewhere in the country. Internationalization of the city seemed a fair compromise. The 1947 United Nations resolution to partition Palestine into an Arab and a Jewish state stipulated the establishment of Jerusalem as a third, internationally administered, separate political body. The resolution was enthusiastically endorsed by the Jewish leaders. The loss of Jerusalem, in Ben-Gurion's words, was the inevitable "price we have to pay" to obtain a Jewish state elsewhere in the country. Had Israel been born in peace, had the Arabs accepted the 1947 partition resolution, the question of Jerusalem might have been resolved; as an international enclave it might have thrived as never before or since.

But the Arabs never accepted the UN partition resolution; they declared open war on it. Israel's birth came in two stages. The first was a civil war between Palestinian Arabs and Palestinian Jews, nowhere as brutal as in Jerusalem. The second was an even bloodier struggle with the regular armies of four neighboring Arab states, which invaded the Jewish-held territory on the day Israel declared its independence (May 15, 1948). The Jordanian attempt to take West Jerusalem failed after two weeks of heavy house-to-house fighting. By the following month, June, Jerusalem was a city divided, seemingly for all time.

The defense of West Jerusalem was seen by most Israelis as perhaps the most heroic feat during the war. It was popularly talked about in near-mythic terms. Nevertheless, West Jerusalem was not at this early stage accorded any special role within the new Israeli state. The new provisional government officiated in Tel Aviv. Zeev Sherf, the first cabinet secretary, later remembered that during the first nineteen months of the new state he never met anybody who thought that West Jerusalem should be Israel's capital: "The subject was never raised." Other capital sites were proposed: Kurnub in the Negev (by Ben-Gurion) and Haifa on the Mediterranean Sea (by Golda Meir). The majority seemed to favor Tel Aviv. From time to time, voices were raised abroad in favor of the aborted UN resolution on internationalization. But since both Israel and Jordan were now opposed to this and in effective control of their sectors within the divided city, such voices were not taken very seriously. The first elected Israeli parliament held a festive opening session in Jerusalem and then moved to permanent quarters in Tel Aviv. At most, Jerusalem was accorded the role of an educational or cultural center, the seat of the supreme court. The legislature and the executive established themselves in Tel Aviv.

There things stood at the end of 1949, and there they might have remained had not a new solemn resolution calling for the internationalization of Jerusalem achieved an unexpected majority in the United Nations. It was proposed by Australia, Lebanon, and the Soviet Union. A Swedish-Belgian compromise proposal calling for UN supervision over the holy places only was rejected. Shocked by the sudden prospect of having to face pressure to give up emotion-laden territory over which so much blood had been spilled during the recent war (and by the apparent callousness of an international organization that had done nothing to prevent that war or punish those who had unleashed it), the Israeli cabinet met on the next day and resolved for the first time that Jerusalem was "an inseparable part of the State of Israel and its eternal capital."

The decision at this stage to transfer the capital to West Jerusalem was reflexive rather than premeditated. The Catholic world was held responsible for the new initiative to internationalize the city. The fact that the Vatican had not protested the occupation of East Jerusalem by Jordan gave rise to suspicion that the Catholic church, reconciled to Moslem rule in Jerusalem from the Middle Ages, found it difficult, for *theological* reasons, to adjust to Jewish rule there. Had it not, since at least the third century, regarded the banishment of the Jews from Jerusalem as just penalty for the murder, or at least for the rejection, of Christ? And had not a succession of modern popes expressed concern that the holy tomb might fall under Jewish rule?* Monsignor MacMahon of the Vatican told Ben-Gurion in 1949 that had the Catholic countries of Latin America, whose vote in the United Nations had been decisive earlier that year, known of Israel's decision to move its capital to West Jerusalem, Israel would never have been established. Ben-Gurion shot back: "I don't understand you. Jerusalem was Israel's capital a thousand years before the birth of Christianity." Nevertheless, the decision to transfer the capital to West Jerusalem was carried out very slowly. A decade later, it was not yet concluded. But in the testy atmosphere of pressure, counterpressure, and heavy theological argument after a costly war, a new, defiant mood was growing in Israel, along with a strong resolve concerning Jerusalem. For Israelis, it all came to a head during the Six-Day War — and for Palestinians, as well.

Nearly a quarter of a century has since passed. The Catholic world no longer presses for internationalization, probably because the United Nations is now controlled by a communist and non-Christian Afro-Asian majority. Young Palestinians, born after the reunification of 1967, are generally more radical than their parents and even less inclined to accept the unilateral annexation of Arab Jerusalem by the Israeli state. Among Israelis, there is little readiness to meet Palestinian aspirations in Jerusalem halfway; the slightest expression of Palestinian nationalism in East Jerusalem is seen as subversive. The anger remains, the hatreds and resentments reach out of antiquity into the modern age, recasting ancient prejudice in modern words, dislodging old defenses and assembling them anew.

* The first was Pius X in 1904. He told Herzl that Jerusalem must not fall into the hands of the Jews, who denied Christ and still deny his divinity. "The Hebrews have never recognized our Lord. Therefore we cannot recognize the Hebrew people." Should they persist in their desire to return to Palestine, "we shall keep churches and priests ready to baptize all of them."

Palestinians today make every effort to remember Jerusalem — as the Jews have, for generations — in their customs, their songs, their prayers. Stylized views of the city hang on the walls of countless homes all over the Near East. Moslem religious leaders in Iran habitually call the faithful to prepare for the coming march on Jerusalem to free her sacred mosques from the hand of the infidels. There is a "Jerusalem quarter" today in every Palestinian refugee camp. In Algiers, in 1988, the Palestine Liberation Organization proclaimed the establishment of a Palestinian state "in the name of Allah, with its capital Holy Jerusalem, al-Quds a-Sharif."

The declaration was dismissed by the Israeli government as a worthless piece of paper that would soon be forgotten. There was an unexpected irony in the fact that Jews, who owed their present prominence in Jerusalem to their extraordinary memory of their own past, were now counting on the Arabs to forget theirs. Nor was the continuing Arab intransigence conducive to producing more Israeli empathy. In Jerusalem itself, the gulf between Palestinians and Israelis was deeper than at any time since 1967. Palestinians from East Jerusalem continued to work in West Jerusalem in the service industries or in construction, and a few Israelis still went to East Jerusalem — on days when there were no riots or strikes — to sightsee or shop. Otherwise the two communities lived apart.

The Hebrew University on Mount Scopus was one of the few places in town where the lethal barriers between communities and faiths were still sometimes broken down. Few modern universities have been enjoined by their founders to fulfill a nobler or more difficult task than the Hebrew University in Jerusalem. Established in 1925, its task was to resurrect Hebrew culture and at the same time, in the words of its first president, Dr. Judah Magnes, to "reconcile Arab and Jew, East and West." On the staff of the Hebrew University in recent years were a Dominican professor of philosophy and a Moslem lecturer in sociology; Arabs were studying Hebrew and Jews were studying Arabic literature. In 1988, there were about a thousand Arab students (6 percent of the total). All were Israeli Arabs, mostly from Galilee; not a single Palestinian student from East Jerusalem was attending the university.

Parts of the ugly strip of no-man's-land that divided the city before 1967 were still bare in 1989, as though in the deeper recesses of their unconscious, builders and developers recognized the continuing cleavage. Elsewhere, in and around the reunited city, Israeli and Palestinian builders were continuing the 1967 war by other means. Many building projects were politically motivated and at least partly financed from abroad. Both sides were eager to establish facts and counterfacts on the ground. The hillsides in and around Jerusalem's historic core were being covered with the resulting houses. Both sides exhausted every possible resource of law and memory. The city was overendowed with symbolisms. Each side interpreted the other's building projects, or growing birth rate, as a form of belligerence. Even archaeological excavations were controversial. In Israeli eyes, they symbolized belongingness; in Palestinian eyes, they were threatening symbols of power and aggression.

The city was held together by force. "Take away Israel's coercive power and the city splits on the ethnic fault line," Meron Benvenisti, a former deputy mayor of the reunited city, wrote in 1988. "The Arabs, one third of the population, are unable and will never be able, to acquiesce to the regime imposed upon them. Violence courts violence in a perpetual magic circle. Exotic growths — chauvinistic, fundamentalist — blossom on the rotting soil of atavistic urges," he observed. "And at its heart, a time bomb with a destructive force of apocalyptic dimensions is ticking, in the form of the Temple Mount."

This was ethnic tension, but not, as was sometimes claimed, of the kind that today bedevils other heterogeneous cities and many great metropolitan centers. The Palestinians of East Jerusalem were not pressing for equal rights and opportunities or for a bigger slice of the common cake. They wished to secede; better still, they wanted the Jews to evacuate the entire city or, at the very least, the Arab sector formerly held by Jordan. Let them go back to whence they, or their ancestors, had come. Jews and Moslems continued to present historical and literary evidence proving the "centrality" of Jerusalem in their respective religious and national consciousnesses.

The evidence was, almost as a rule, mutually exclusive. From time to time, there were also Israelis and others who raked their minds in attempts to square the vicious circle. The most far-reaching proposals envisaged Arabs and Israelis sharing sovereign rights within a united city, open to all, or, alternatively, two separate sovereignties and a jointly run Old City. Several other schemes had been mooted in the past. One stipulated continuing Israeli sovereignty over the entire city but accorded special privileges to national and religious groups. Another envisioned a capital district under Israeli rule, providing extraterritorial status to specific Christian and Moslem sites and residents. A third suggested the establishment of a sovereign Moslem enclave on the Temple Mount, like the Vatican in Rome; it might have its own extraterritorial access route from Jericho, in the form of an elevated highway or tunnel. Yet another proposal stipulated several ethnic and religious boroughs under a revolving lord mayor.

Nothing had ever come of any of these schemes. All had been stillborn — cast aside for offering too little or too much, too early or too late. To the hard-liners of both sides, the very idea of compromise was repellent. Whenever an Arab had been ready to serve on a joint municipal council, he was threatened with death and promptly withdrew. When the first "borough plan" (drafted by a commission of government and city officials) was leaked to the press in 1971, a political storm of such magnitude broke loose it convinced most Israeli politicians to stop raising such hypotheses or risk the abrupt end of their public careers. That plan, which the mayor had asked a former supreme-court justice to draft a constitution for, was shelved. Its author, Deputy Mayor Meron Benvenisti, was lambasted. The graffiti smeared on the walls of West Jerusalem read "Death to the Traitor" and "Let's cut up Benvenisti, not Jerusalem." Needless to say, his proposal was as unacceptable to the Arabs.

On both sides, religious fundamentalism has since grown considerably. The rise of fundamentalism seems to reflect a growing disillusion with politics. The new fundamentalisms will make a peaceful resolution of the conflict over Jerusalem even more difficult. Both reject any separation between the synagogue/mosque and the state. Among fundamentalist Moslems, as among fundamentalist Jews, religion *is* the state. In Islam, the prophet is sovereign; he commands armies and dispenses justice. In every Arab country today, without exception, Islam is the state religion. Orthodox Judaism, which evolved after the Jewish state ceased to exist, also postulates the synagogue militant and sovereign as a theoretical possibility for the future. Now that the Jewish state has been reestablished, with Jerusalem as its capital, it is still not certain whether it will succumb to Orthodox pressure or develop along western lines by adopting separation of synagogue and state. The disorientations generated by continuing wars militate in favor of the former alternative.

The cleavage in the city is deep, and it is made still deeper and more dangerous by the fusion, on both sides, of nationalist and religious metaphors. The futile and often obnoxious debate about who *loves* Jerusalem more is occasionally tinged with an element of male chauvinism: love or desire is seen to legitimize possession. Many Palestinians maintain the illusion that if they are only steadfast enough, the Israelis will one day vanish into thin air. Many Israelis cling to a parallel misapprehension that if economic conditions among Arabs of Jerusalem improve, they will, in the end, prefer freedom of speech and freedom of religious worship under a relatively benevolent Israeli regime over the rigid, repressive authoritarianism common today in Arab societies.

It is still sometimes said, hopefully, that the city is a "mosaic." In a mosaic, the divergent parts at least combine to make up a design; in Jerusalem, they do not. There is not even a common theme. Sensitivities and prejudices run so deep that when the ultramodern Hadassah Medical Center in West Jerusalem started performing heart transplant operations in 1987, the hospital's director general had to reassure the public that Jewish hearts would not be transplanted into Arab bodies, and vice versa. The city is sometimes compared to Brussels or Montreal. But the problems in those cities are simpler than the problems of Jerusalem. In Brussels or Montreal, the main issue lies in the realm of language and cultural domination. In Jerusalem, the main issue is religious and political. As in Belfast, national and religious loyalties are interwoven; they overshadow and complicate everything else. The Palestinian minority — roughly 28 percent of the population of the united city — repudiates the legitimacy of the existing government. As a minimum, it claims the right to secede and establish in East Jerusalem the capital of an independent Palestinian state. This is anathema to most Israelis, who persist in a related fantasy that the present situation is capable of continuing indefinitely.

On both sides, people have been governed after 1967 not by the strength of their imagination but by the poverty of it. On both sides, people continue to pray earnestly for "the peace of Jerusalem," but, as Benvenisti wrote in 1981, they might have peace *or* they might have Jerusalem — not both. The former deputy mayor has been warning for years that the conflict will not go away by itself and that its cost will go up in both human and material terms. Teddy Kollek, mayor since 1965, is a mite less flamboyant than Benvenisti but no less persistent. He repeatedly has urged the Israeli government to come up with new constitutional ideas for Jerusalem — only to be rebuffed again and again. Kollek's influence has never extended beyond the municipality into national politics. (The mayor of Jerusalem cannot move a bus stop from one corner to the next without authorization from the national ministries of the interior and of transport.)

Kollek has been complaining for years that there has not been enough consideration and respect for Arab sensibilities. He has asked the government to supply public housing not only to Israelis but to Palestinians, too. When the Jewish quarter in the Old City was being lavishly rebuilt with government funds, Kollek demanded that the adjacent Moslem quarter, one of the worst slums in town, be restored as well. The central government refused to allocate the necessary funds. Kollek was a secular Jew and a dove in a city that was becoming increasingly Orthodox and hawkish. He was not a political theorist but a man of sound instincts and humane temperament — a practical man in search of practical answers to practical questions. He never himself managed to work out the specific constitutional proposals he was asking the government to formulate. But he was always more attuned than most Israeli politicians to the complexities of Jerusalem — to the way the symbolic is intertwined with the real and endowed with a unique power of its own.

Few men have tried harder than Kollek to break the walls of hatred and suspicion that divide Jews and Moslems, Israelis and Palestinians, in Jerusalem. He realized early on that as mayor he

could not solve the big political and religious conflicts. He has tried
to help Jerusalemites in a nonpolitical way to coexist and persevere
until a political solution can be found. But in Jerusalem, everything
ultimately becomes political — that is to say, adversarial. An American columnist once asked Kollek if he did not sometimes fear that
his efforts might be futile. Kollek answered that he felt like an ant
that builds and builds: at any moment someone might poke a stick
into the heap and destroy it; but he would build it again and again,
as beautiful and as well as he knew how. And to Benvenisti, who
asked Kollek whether he thought he was being "used" to provide
good public relations for what in fact were government policies
with which he disagreed, Kollek replied that yes, he did sometimes feel he was being used — "but what else can I do? It serves
Jerusalem."

Kollek often has been attacked by right-wingers who characterize
him as "an Arab lover." On one occasion, he was physically assaulted by ultra-Orthodox fanatics and left lying on a Jerusalem
street. But for his fairness and humanity, the civil uprising that
rocked East Jerusalem in 1987 might have been worse or might have
broken out much earlier. He has always been wary of the conventional Israeli view of Jerusalem as an exclusively Jewish icon and has
warned Israelis not to forget that Jerusalem is a focus of other
aspirations as well. In a 1985 speech, he said that "in order to pre-
serve peace and justice in Jerusalem, we must go beyond the conventional formulas of national sovereignty, beyond the fears and
prejudices that drive nations into wars, and search for new forms of
freedom and of political organization." If he knew what these new
formulas of sovereignty were, he did not reveal them. His adminis-
tration proved that conflicts stemming from religious or national
differences are rarely, if ever, relieved only by fair or good government, nor by economic advantage accruing from it. In 1989, Kollek
lost his majority in the city council. He was in his seventy-eighth
year, a tired old man, embittered by what he described as the ruin of
his life's work.

Jerusalem today is once again what she has been so often in her
history: a city at war with herself. The renewed strife in her streets is

widely, almost daily, broadcast nationally and internationally on television. The situation invites easy generalizations. History making in the age of television is often encumbered by the manufacture of images. In the case of Jerusalem — her name inevitably evokes stereotypes — this is not surprising. The city is variously said to be poisoned by her past, possessed by it, haunted by demons of irrationality and superstition — the religion of feeble minds — and riveted by fear, envy, and tribalism. But there are simpler explanations. The twin roots of the renewed strife in her streets are nationalism and faith. It is difficult to say which of these two forces is the more powerful. They certainly complement and reinforce each other. Each offers the believer an identity and a plan of salvation; each also holds out a system of ultimate ends that embody the meaning of life and are absolute standards by which to judge events.

The proverbial peace of Jerusalem invoked in Psalm 122 depends, paradoxically, on a waning of religion or of nationalism, if not on the waning of both. As this book goes to print, there is little, if any, indication of the waning of either. Peace remains a remote prospect. (Notwithstanding the well-known stereotype, it seems that even in the days of the psalmist there could not have been much tranquillity in Jerusalem, or he would not have been so persistent in his injunction — endlessly repeated today on municipal billboards all over the city — "Pray for the peace of Jerusalem: they shall have quietness that love thee.")

If anything, Jerusalem is a city loved too well yet never quite wisely. Israelis are repeatedly urged to cede territory in return for peace; but the growing Islamization of the conflict on the Arab side makes it likely that even if territory is given up, the violence, especially in Jerusalem, will remain.

At the meeting point of so many cultures, creeds, images, and counterimages, of saints and of hucksters, the city continues to embody a glorious idea and at the same time a dream found vain, wanting, and destructive. The past seems to have lost little if any of its power to inspire, animate, and provoke. Where there is so much destructive memory, a little forgetfulness may be in order. Unfortunately, as these words are being written, there is little inclination for that on either side of the great national and religious divide. On the contrary, almost everywhere you turn, dark chords of memory swell the chorus of nationalism and of faith. A little forgetfulness — or compromise — seems unlikely under these circumstances.

Compromise in Jerusalem means more than merely moving a border here or there a little bit. The struggle in the city is not over a part, but over the whole. Primarily, it is over the historic core, within the ancient walls, that includes the three major holy places. One "reasonable" compromise could be the blurring of hard sovereign lines by recognizing two national rights within a united, jointly run municipal area. Even if the protagonists could mutually agree to such a plan (which remains doubtful), it must be noted that nowhere until now have two national capitals coexisted within the same city. There is reason to doubt that two nationalisms as raw as the Palestinian and the Israeli would be the first in known history to do so successfully. Another reasonable compromise might be the establishment of new capitals elsewhere by the two nationalities, within their respective sovereign territories. This seems equally unlikely in view of the strong religious component that shapes political attitudes toward Jerusalem.

The issue of Jerusalem is so emotionally charged that none of several would-be peacemakers and mediators in recent years has even dared to talk about it. Many diplomats believe that raising the sensitive issue even tentatively during attempts to initiate Middle East peace talks is sure to wreck the negotiations before they start. The subject might perhaps be tackled — very delicately — after successful accommodation has been reached on all other outstanding points, but anyone who broaches it sooner will be suspected of trying to undermine the entire process.

I was watching the sightseers one summer evening in 1967 as they streamed through the narrow gate of David's Citadel — the hills nearby were turning the color of unglazed pottery — when the idea of writing a book about this tragically mad city first occurred to me. The citadel, in the words of one of the guidebooks, "encapsulates" the city's history: saints and scoundrels, Hebrews, Hasmonaean kings, Jewish zealots, Romans, Byzantines, Arabs, Crusaders, and Turks — not to mention England and modern Israel — have all left their mark on it. No one can enter that gate without experiencing poignant emotion. The citadel's attraction overwhelms even those who try to resist it. Surely, I thought, watching the sightseers, surely this city has raised far more vexed ghosts of history than can safely be stomached locally. In the high noon of the ghosts, the human dimension is lost.

On the steps by that same gate, Yehuda Amichai, the great poet of the modern city, once sat with two loaded baskets of fruit and overheard a tourist guide saying: "You see that man with the baskets? Just right of his head there is an arch from the Roman period. Just right of his head."

"I said to myself," Amichai writes, "redemption will come only if their guide tells them: 'You see that arch from the Roman period? It's not important; but next to it, left and down a bit, there sits a man who's bought fruit and vegetables for his family.'"

Notes

Abbreviated citations in these notes refer to sources listed in the Bibliography. Unless otherwise specified, biblical passages quoted in the text are from the Authorized (King James) Version. Quoted excerpts from non-English sources listed in the Bibliography have been translated by the author ("AE").

INTRODUCTION

P. 6 "If I forget": Ps. 137:5.
   "for ever and": Jer. 7:7; 25:5.
7 "For who shall": Jer. 15:5.

CHAPTER ONE

11 "touch": Sachs, 109.
   "Stones to right": Melville, 25.
   "stones of darkness": Job 28:3.
   "for his pillows": Gen. 28:18.
   "by the sanctuary": Josh. 24:26.
   "pillar of salt": Gen. 19:26.
12 "the Rock that": Deut. 32:18.
   "The city looks": Melville, 26.
   "All these stones": Amichai, 113.
   "inside prophecies": Ibid., 117.
13 "toward Arabia": Josephus, "Wars," 4.5.3.
   "her one long": Smith, *Holy Land*, 11.
   "sight of the": Josephus, "Antiquities," 9.8.5.
15 "I had stood": Bartlett, *Walks about Jerusalem*, 13.
   "the ground around": Josephus, "Wars," 5.5.1.
16 "the grandest ever": Josephus, "Antiquities," 15.11.12.
   "in my wrath": Isa. 60:10.
17 "The heavens declare": Ps. 19:1.
   "in Switzerland": Voltaire, 96.
19 "danced before the": 2 Sam. 6:14.
   "nulla intus": Tacitus, 5.9 (p. 190).
20 "Out of the"; Jer. 1:14.
21 "How dreadful": Gen. 28:17.

23 "possessor of heaven": Gen. 14:19, 22.
   "I lift up": Gen. 14:22.
24 "Her heroes and": Lande-Nash, 7.
   "Yaqar Ammu": Pritchard, 329.
   "Jerusalem Sadness": Koestler, 236.
   "the King my" and other Abdu-Heba excerpts: Pritchard, 487–489.

CHAPTER TWO

28 "cry out": Hab. 2:11.
   "melted": Isa. 34:3.
   "an exceeding great": Ezek. 37:10.
   "rolled together as": Isa. 34:4.
   "valley of slaughter": Jer. 7:32.
   "common people": Quoted in Le Strange, 220.
29 "peace offerings": 1 Kings 8:63.
   "God Himself performed": Kotker, 5.
   "By the rivers": Ps. 137:1–2.
   "they shall beat": Isa. 2:4; Mic. 4:3.
30 "coming down from": Rev. 21:2.
   "for there shall": Rev. 21:25.
   "sadly in this": W. Shakespeare, *King Henry VI*, pt. 3, 5.5.7.
   "I give you": W. Blake, 454.
31 "as a widow": Lam. 1:1.
   "harlot": Ezek. 16:35.
   "bride": Rev. 21:2.
   "the mother of": Gal. 4:26.
32 "that the Jews": Tacitus, 2.10 (p. 193).
33 "If I forget": Ps. 137:5–6.
34 "Could I but": Trans. AE.
   "So . . . was the": Quoted in Peters, 131.
   "there shall not": Mark 13:2.

36 "if it had": Quoted in Huizinga, 98.
    "What torment to": Quoted in Peters, 364.
    "building Jerusalem daily": Quoted in Holtz, 91.
37 "on the frontier": In Heyd, 78.
    "This luckless people": Quoted in Peters, 569.
    "The only thing": Chateaubriand, 2: 212.
    "To see its": Volney, 333.
    "un charnier entouré": Flaubert, letter to Bouilhet, 20 Aug. 1850.
40 "Bring about Israel's": Quoted in Benvenisti, *Facing the Closed Wall*, 11.
    "What a divine": Quoted in Benziman, 19.
41 "in huts": Quoted in Kollek, 225.
47n "Jerusalem is built": Storrs, 310.
51 "so wondrous": Josephus, "Wars," 5.4.4.
    "to demonstrate to": Ibid., 7.1.1.
    "the other": Murphy-O'Connor, 24.
    "by the weight": Runciman, 2:466.
52 "I come as": Quoted in Haslip, 241.
    "Whoever shuffled Jerusalem": Silk, 1.
55 "strangest among the": Pliny, 5.71.
    "A thousand years": Ps. 90:4.
56 "heavenly sanctuary is": Quoted in Werblowsky, 8.
57 "Praise be to": Koran 17:11.
58 "There are no": Werblowsky, 3.
    hadiths: Quoted in Peters, 374.
59 "eating a banana": Quoted in Levine, 2:190.
    "God is in": Ps. 46:5.
60 "for the glory": Rev. 21:23.
    "My heart is": Quoted in Grindea, 75.
61 "that the sense": Levin, 93.
62 "all remember they": Amichai, 89.
    "The air over": Ibid., 135.

CHAPTER THREE

63 "great survivor of": Quoted in Grindea, 1.
    "slaughterhouse of the": A. Huxley, in *Encounter* (London monthly), Dec. 1955.
    "the hopelessness of": Ibid.
    "tragic nature of": Bedford, 2:69.
64 "Tragedy without catharsis": Koestler, 237.
    "depresses and weighs": Quoted in Grindea, 195.
    "unhappy Jerusalem has": *Palestine Pilgrims' Text Society* (hereafter referred to as *PPTS*) 9–10:262.
65 "The following nations": Ibid., 384ff.
68 "We defeated the": Quoted in Hagenmeyer, 164.

68 "Since the world": Quoted in Muller, 256.
69 "the scenes of": Cust, 8.
70 "the sacrilegious hammer": Hoade, 108.
    "provided with sticks": Finn, 2:458.
71 "Excellency": Storrs, 423.
    "with a zeal": Ibid.
72 "Oriental Stores": E. Samuel, 52.
    "contemplating with mournful": Storrs, 420.
74 "in their church": Quoted in Peters, 261.
75 "rose in the night": *PPTS* 9–10:255.
    "The Lord has": Koran 13:93.
    "O Jews!": Quoted in Curzon, 190.
76 "No gentile to": Quoted in Josephus, "Wars," 5.5.2.
    "in Jerusalem where": Quoted in Cohen, 220.
77 "as the Latins": Quoted in Silk, 139.
    "Mohammedan imposture": Finn, 2:112.
    "The Moslem clergy": Koestler, 240.
78 "Unto thy seed": Gen. 12:7.
    "By the rivers": Ps. 137:1, 8–9.
79 "no man knoweth": Deut. 34:6.
    "a horse would": Storrs, 315.
    "as a favour": Muamar al-Khatib, cited in E108, Central Zionist Archive, Jerusalem (hereafter referred to as CZA).
81 "which gate deserves": Navon, 8.
82 "as one might": W. H. Auden to AE, 5 May 1973.
83 "Their tears and": Quoted in Porath, 213.
84 "exactly like an": Quoted in Sykes, 127.
    "one side only": A. Yellin, E108, CZA.
    "Moslems will not": Ibid.
85 "Moslem property": Ibid.
85–87 Western Wall diary: Orenstein, 9 Feb. 1932–5 Nov. 1938.

CHAPTER FOUR

89 "We felt we": Benvenisti, *Conflicts and Contradictions*, 10.
90 "But people are": In Varon, 11.
    "We have returned": *Haaretz*, 8 June 1967.
91 "you have been": Gur, 317.
    "these are Moslem": Dayan, 498.
92 "the Rule of God": Kook, 102.
93 "every Jew in": Quoted in Benvenisti, *Facing the Closed Wall*, 136.
    "In two days": Kollek, 226.
94 Warhaftig interview: *Haaretz*, 18 Aug. 1967.
96 "We see with": In Warhaftig, 323.
    Getz interview: *Haaretz*, 28 Mar. 1983.
98–99 "We must condemn": YP, an eyewitness, to AE.

99 "The audience": S. Shoham in *Encounter,* June 1970, 92.
"Deviance motivated by": Ibid.

102–106 Temple Mount conspirators: See Segal, 47–54, 229–251.

107 "shall not make": Isa. 28:16.

107–109 1985 convention: Attended by AE.

110 "speak with other": Acts 2:4.

112 "Lord of hosts": 1 Sam. 1:3.
"the love of": Matt. 24:12.
"Pray for the": Ps. 122:6–7 (trans. AE).

113 "savage heroes of": Gibbon, 6:76
"in blood up": Fulcher of Chartres in Peters, 285.

114 "was to gaze": William of Tyre, 1:406.
"Let Jerusalem be": Quoted in Sivan, 82.

114n "The swords of": Quoted ibid., 86.

116 "fields of tension": In Avi-Yona, 44.
"It's sad to": Amichai, 39.
"Jerusalem": Quoted in Le Strange, 86.

CHAPTER FIVE

117 *"De profundis"*: Ps. 130:1.
"I will lift": Ps. 121:1.

118 "walk about Zion": Ps. 48:12–13.
"Beautiful for situation": Ps. 48:2.
"in the place": Deut. 16:16.
"I was glad": Ps. 122:1–2.

119 "And when the": Acts 2:1, 5, 9–11.
"There are Greeks": Quoted in Benvenisti, *Crusaders,* 40–41.

121 "united the credulity": Gibbon, 2:624.

122 "a pierced stone": Quoted in Peters, 143.

123 "extreme licentiousness": Werblowsky, 8.
"wander with the": Ibid.
"no expense where": Wright, 50.

124 "parricides, perjurers, adulterers": In Grindea, 126.
"a complete brothel": Silk, 34.

125 "from anyone traveling": Flaubert, letter from Rhodes, 6 Oct. 1850.
"faithless people who": Quoted in Peters, 144.

127 "How much longer": Ibn Ezra, quoted in Holtz, 113.
"Jhesu, for this": Chaucer, 228.

128 "a stone of": Quoted in Walker, 27.
fourteen foreskins: See Lowenthal, 408n.
"an intelligent man": Quoted in E. N. Adler, 234.

129 "The Swabians who" and other Fabri excerpts: PPTS 7–8:398–427; 9–10: 257–259.

131 "Allah is well beyond": Quoted in Peters, 319.

131 "It is said": Quoted in Sharon, 40.
"I have never": Voltaire, 223.
"write back only": Quoted in Raba, 3.

131–134 "I went out" and other Chateaubriand excerpts: Chateaubriand, 2: 702, 1112–1113, 1125–1127, 1733n.

132 "stinking egotism": Quoted in Said, 171.

134–137 Disraeli in Jerusalem: See Buckle and Monypenny, 2:96; R. Blake, *Grand Tour,* 7; idem, *Disraeli,* 67; letter to Lytton, 27 Dec. 1830; Tuchman, 219.

134n "the most corpulent": Quoted in R. Blake, *Grand Tour,* 67.

137–138 Lamartine in Jerusalem: See Lamartine, Oct. 1832; Thubron, *Mirror to Damascus,* 157.

138–139 "Until I have" and other Gogol excerpts: Quoted in Troyat, 333, 372, 373.

139–140 Flaubert in Jerusalem: See Flaubert, 1:290; idem, letter to Bouilhet, 2 Aug. 1850; Starkie, 198.

140n "pioneers of the": Ohne and Wahrman, 68.

141 "You are hurting": Quoted in Warren, 89.

142 "There was an": Quoted in Nooks, 111.
"that vile place": Ibid, 112.
"could no more": Twain, *Innocents Abroad* 2:295.
"pauper village": Ibid., 359.

143 "some good morals": Twain, *Letters from the Earth,* 14.
"the abode of": Twain, *Notebooks,* 93.

144 "a force much": Graham, 88.
"28 servants": Howard, 6.

145 "25 tents of": Ibid.
"to convey to": Ibid.
"by the same": Quoted in Gilbert, 178.

146 "It is a": Goodrich-Freer, 35.
"a fire shall": Jer. 48:45.
"if thy right": Matt. 5:29.

148 "They are disappointed": *Jerusalem Post,* 18 Mar. 1987.

CHAPTER SIX

149 "from the number": Gibbon, 6:72.
"that this was": Josephus, "Wars," 5.7.3–4.

150 "despoiled Ashdod": In Pritchard, 283.
"The city and": Ibid.
"slew the people": Judg. 9:45.
"broke down the": 2 Kings 25:10.
"as a man": 2 Kings 21:13.

151 "no man dwelleth": Jer. 44:2.
"as dung upon": Jer. 9:22.
"as an enemy": Lam. 2:5.

151 "How lone she": Lam. 1:1 (trans. Raphael, 90; this translation captures the extraordinary rhythm, the full elegiac beat and sound of doom).
152 "The Lord was": Lam. 2:5, 7–9; 5:18.
155 *"immense bonheur"*: Renan, *Discours et conférences,* 20.
     "the Sabbath of": Quoted in Hertzberg, 119.
156 "I, who am": Quoted in Muller, 303–304.
159 "Why should the": 2 Chron. 32:4.
160 "large and great": Neh. 7:4.
     "what my God": Neh. 2:12–13.
     "factual record in": Kenyon, 181.
     "I went on": Neh. 2:14.
     "Come": Neh. 2:17.
161 "O miserable people!": Josephus, "Wars," 5.9.3–4.
162 "Their multitude was": Ibid., 5.2.1.
     "your heaven as": Lev. 26:19.
     "What aileth thee": Isa. 22:1.
163 "made the whole": Josephus, "Wars," 6.9.5.
     "a reminder of": Kenyon, 254.
163 "Woe is me": Quoted in Avigad, 130.
164 "How lone she": Lam. 1:1.
166 "It was this": Runciman, 1:287.
167n "The conquest of": Gibbon, 2:76.
     "Strongly suggest": Quoted in Knightly and Simpson, 73.
168 "It has never": Quoted in Mack, 157.
     "Walls are nothing": Sophocles, *Oedipus Rex,* line 56.
169 "the city of": Neh. 2:5.
     "No silver and": N. Avigad in *Israel Exploration Journal* 3(1953): 137.
     "Men from all": Grindea, 123.
170 "you will find": Quoted in Wright, 392.
     "husband and wife": Silk, 3.
171 "Redemption here loses": Friedlander, 1:1.
172 "We have seen": Ibid.

CHAPTER SEVEN

176 "in order to": Quoted in Wilhelm, 81.
178 "The mediators": Amichai, 30.
180 "The Israeli-born": J. Frankel in *Dissent* (New York), Spring 1984, 192.
181 "Jerusalem, ungoverned": Quoted in Silk, 60.
     "maketh himself a": Jer. 29:26, 27.
     "Well, isn't it": Quoted in Hazleton, 86.
182 "only city on": Amichai, 51.
     "I do not give": C. Kallman, "Dome of the Rock," *New York Review of Books,* 12 Dec. 1974.

182 "being sacred to": Tchernichowsky, 506.
183 "I do not know": Bartlett, *Jerusalem Revisited,* 71.
184 "Thus saith the Lord": Zech. 8:4–5.
185 "the directness and": Huizinga, 9.
186 "proud or cruel": Ibid.
189 "skin tone a": Roth, 88.
     "the disembodied ghost": Weizmann, *Statement,* 11.
     "Because of Hitler": Oz, 11.
     "they overwhelm us": Ibid.
193 "a dialectical paradise": Scholem, *From Berlin to Jerusalem,* 205.
193 "would have collapsed": *Kol Hair* (Jerusalem weekly), 8 Jan. 1988.
194 "the mind cannot": N. Khusrau in *PPTS* 4:42.
196 "all requests and": Hazleton, 181.
197 "the fallen glory": Robinson, 1:350.
     "neglected Jesus": Quoted in Gilbert, 139.
     "as though it": Warren, 212.
     "ravished from centuries": Loti, 117.
     "They have a wall": Waugh, letter to Asquith, 23 Dec. 1935.
     "but for the prayers": Scholem, *Sabbatai Zevi,* 73.
198 "the surety of": Quoted in Peters, 185.
199 "the everlasting boundaries": John of Damascus, *Icons* 2:12.
     "dark shrine of": Quoted in Peters, 132.
     "heard the weeping": Quoted in Frazer, 359.
200n "but in the name": Ibid., 259.
201 "Make provision": Quoted in Peters, 133.
202 "When you have": Kinglake, 233.
     "stand out in": Murphy-O'Connor, 42.
203 "hideous kiosk": Roberts, 1 (plate 14).
     "To pretend to": Byron, 7.
     "You should have": Updike, 79.
     "macabre, claustrophobic place": E. Wilson, 475.
204 "pious fraud": Robinson, 329.
     "contrary to all": Eusebius, *Life of Constantine,* as quoted in *PPTS* 1:3.
206 "perfect death's-head": Vester, 97.
207 "We don't need": To AE.
208 "In Jerusalem": Murphy-O'Connor, 33.
     "set up notices": Quoted in E. Samuel, 112.
209 "with a table": Leys, 138.
     "absorbed into": P. Marnham in *Granta* 10 (London, 1986): 187.
210 "came down from": 2 Chron. 7:1.
     "until an angel": Quoted in Wright, 27.
     "Holy Light suddenly": *PPTS* 4:78.

211 "bedlam": Wright, 462.
"the greatest moral": C. W. Wilson, 202.
"it is easy": Warren, 426.
211–212 "carried out of" and other Curzon excerpts: Curzon, 196–204.
212 "Vous m'avez sauvé": Storrs, 318.
213 "Per Bacco": To AE.
214 "O to realize": "A Song of Joys," in Whitman, 153.
215 "would dwell in": 1 Kings 8:12.
"It is a pity": Quoted in *Die Reise des kaiserlichen Paars im heiligen Land* (Berlin, 1899), 283.
217 "a latitudinarian": Bartlett, *Walks About Jerusalem,* 149.
218 "be re-covered with": Storrs, 325.
219 "It will no longer": Quoted in Peters, 192.
220 "pierced" stone: Ibid., 143.
"in a few minutes": Storrs, 449.
222 "I was glad": Ps. 122:1.
224 "to sit down": Bellow, 122.
225 "people [that] dwell": Num. 23:9.
227 "I hate the Turks": *Kotheret Roshit* (Jerusalem weekly), 24 Apr. 1985.
"As the exiles": Morgenthau, 317.
228 "ein kleines Reich": Elan, 18.
228n "The spell which": Quoted in Bentwich, 8.
232n "Yes, Sir, but": H. Samuel, 166.
233 "will be like": Quoted in Cragg, 110.
235 "the dominant influence": Smith, *Historical Geography of the Holy Land,* 435.
"We shall never": Ibid., 451.

237 "because . . . he would": S. Bellow in *Granta* 10 (1986): 173.

CHAPTER EIGHT

238 "I can muster": Quoted in Gay, 598n.
"How strange this": Letter of 8 May 1942, in Freud and Zweig, 40.
239 "When I remember": Herzl, 2:145 (31 Oct. 1898).
"the terrible Wall": Ahad Ha°am, 29.
"reactionary": A. Shapira, *The Life of Berl Katznelson* (in Hebrew, Tel Aviv, 1980), 112.
"our hands have": Quoted in Ben-Baruch, 118.
240 "not without misgivings": Weizmann, *Trial and Error,* 169.
"I would not": Note of 8 July 1937, Weizmann Archive, Rehovot.
"price we have": Quoted in Shaltiel, 386.
241 "The subject was": Ibid., 400.
242 "I don't understand": In Shaltiel, 395.
242n "The Hebrews have": Herzl, 4:1603 (26 Jan. 1903).
243 "reconcile Arab and": Quoted in Bentwich, 16.
244 "Take away Israel's": Benvenisti, *New York Times Magazine,* 16 Oct. 1988.
248 "in order to": Speech delivered at Paulskirche, Frankfurt am Main, 10 Oct. 1985, in Kollek, *Friedenspreis,* 39.
249 "Pray for the": Ps. 122:6 (trans. AE).
250 "encapsulates": Murphy-O'Connor, 23.
251 "You see that": Amichai, 177.

Bibliography

Adler, C. *Memorandum on the Western Wall*. Prepared for the Special Commission of the League of Nations. Philadelphia, 1930.

Adler, E. N. *Jewish Travellers from Nine Centuries*. New York, 1966.

Ahad Ha'am. *The Collected Works of Ahad Ha'am* (in Hebrew). Tel Aviv, 1954.

Amichai, Y. *Poems of Jerusalem*. Bilingual ed. (in Hebrew and English). Jerusalem, 1987.

Avigad, N. *The Upper City of Jerusalem* (in Hebrew). Jerusalem 1980.

Avi-Yona, M., ed. *The Book of Jerusalem* (in Hebrew). Jerusalem, 1956.

Bartlett, W. H. *Jerusalem Revisited*. London, 1852.

———. *Walks About Jerusalem*. London, 1843.

Bedford, S. *Aldous Huxley: A Biography*. London, 1973.

Bellow, S. *To Jerusalem and Back*. New York. 1977.

Ben-Baruch, S. *Jerusalem in Our Modern Poetry* (in Hebrew). Jerusalem, 1955.

Ben-Dov, M. *The Dig at the Temple Mount* (in Hebrew). Jerusalem, 1982.

Bentwich, N. *The Hebrew University of Jerusalem*. London, 1961.

Benvenisti, M. *Conflicts and Contradictions*. New York, 1986.

———. *The Crusaders in the Holy Land*. Jerusalem, 1970.

———. *Facing the Closed Wall: Divided and United Jerusalem* (in Hebrew). Jerusalem, 1973.

———. *The Peace of Jerusalem* (in Hebrew). Jerusalem, 1981.

Benziman, U. *Jerusalem: City with No Wall* (in Hebrew). Jerusalem, 1973.

Biale, D. *Scholem: Kabbala and Counterhistory*. Cambridge, 1979.

Blake, R. *Disraeli*. London, 1967.

———. *Disraeli on the Grand Tour*. London, 1982.

Blake, W. *The Portable Blake*. Selected by A. Kazin. New York, 1946.

Bovis, H. E. *The Jerusalem Question, 1917–1968*. Stanford, 1971.

Buckle, G. E., and W. F. Monypenny. *The Life of Benjamin Disraeli*. London, 1929.

Burgoyne, M.H. *Mamluk Jerusalem: An Architectural Study*. Jerusalem, 1987.

Byron, R. *The Road to Oxiana*. London, 1981.

Carmel, A. *Palestina Chronik*. Ulm, 1978.

Ceruli, E. *Etiopi in Palestina: Storia della comunità Etiopica di Gerusalemme*. Rome, 1943.

Chateaubriand, F. R. *Journal de Jérusalem: Notes inédites*. Edited by G. Moulinier and A. Outrey. Paris, 1950.

————. *Oeuvres romanesques et voyages*. Edited by M. Regard. Paris, 1969.

Chaucer, G. *The Complete Works of Geoffrey Chaucer*. London, 1974.

Clarke, E. *Travels in various countries of Europe, Asia and Africa*. Pt. 2. London, 1810.

Cohen, A. *Sixteenth-Century Jerusalem according to Turkish Documents*. Jerusalem, 1976.

Condor, C. R. *The City of Jerusalem*. London, 1909.

Cragg, K. *This Year in Jerusalem*. London, 1982.

Curzon, R. *Visits to the Monasteries of the Levant*. London, 1849.

Cust, L. G. A. *The Status Quo in the Holy Places*. Reprint. Jerusalem, 1980.

Dayan, M. *The Story of My Life* (in Hebrew). Jerusalem, 1976.

Drori, J. "Jerusalem under the Mamluks." In *Jerusalem in the Middle Ages* (in Hebrew), edited by B. Kedar. Jerusalem, 1979.

Elan, S. *Deutsche in Jerusalem von der Mitte des 20. Jahrhundert bis zum Ersten Weltkrieg*. Wertheim am Main, 1984.

Eliade, M. *Cosmos and History: The Myth of the Eternal Return*. Translated by W. R. Trsak. New York, 1959.

Finn, J. *Stirring Times*. London, 1878.

Flaubert, G. *Notes de voyage*. Vol. 19 of *Les oeuvres complètes de Gustave Flaubert*, edited by L. Conard. Paris, 1910.

Flusser, D. *Jesus*. Hamburg, 1984.

Frazer, J. G. *The Golden Bough*. New York, 1949.

Freud, S., and A. Zweig. *The Letters of Sigmund Freud and Arnold Zweig*, edited by E. L. Freud. New York, 1970.

Friedlander, S. *History and Memory*. Tel Aviv, 1989.

Gabrieli, F. *Arab Historians of the Crusades*. Berkeley, 1969.

Gay, P. *Freud: A Life for Our Time*. London, 1988.

Gibbon, E. *The History of the Decline and Fall of the Roman Empire*. Notes by D. Milman et al. 6 vols. New York, n.d. [1845?].

Gilbert, M. *Jerusalem: The Rebirth of a City*. Jerusalem, 1985.

Goodrich-Freer, A. *Inner Jerusalem*. London, 1904.

Graham, S. *With the Russian Pilgrims in Jerusalem*. London, 1913.

Grindea, M., ed. *The Image of Jerusalem: A Literary Chronicle of 3,000 Years*. London, 1980.

Gur, M. *The Temple Mount Is in Our Hands* (in Hebrew). Jerusalem, 1973.

Hagenmeyer, H., ed. *Kreuzzugsbriefe, 1088–1100*. Innsbruck, 1901.

Haslip, J. *The Sultan*. New York, 1972.

Hazleton, L. *Jerusalem, Jerusalem*. New York, 1986.

Hertzberg, A. *The Zionist Idea*. New York, 1959.

Herzl, T. *The Complete Diaries of Theodor Herzl*. Edited by R. Patai. Translated by H. Zohn. New York, 1960.

Heyd, U., ed. *Ottoman Documents on Palestine, 1552–1615*. Oxford, 1960.

Hoade, E. *Guide to the Holy Land*. Jerusalem, 1971.

Holtz, A., ed. *The Holy City: Jews on Jerusalem*. New York, 1971.

Howard, A. *Howard's Guide to Jerusalem and Vicinity*. Jaffa, 1888.

Huizinga, J. *The Waning of the Middle Ages*. New York, 1954.

Hyamson, A. M. *The British Consulate in Jerusalem*. London, 1939.

John of Damascus. *Icons*. Translated by F. H. Chase. Washington, 1970.

Jones, E. *The Life of Sigmund Freud*. Vol. 3. New York, 1960.

Josephus Flavius. "Antiquities of the Jews" and "Wars of the Jews." In *The Life and Works of Josephus Flavius*. Translated by W. Whiston. Philadelphia, n.d.

Kaplan, J. *Mr. Clemens and Mark Twain*. New York, 1966.

Kenyon, K. *Digging Up Jerusalem*. London, 1974.

Kinglake, A. W. *Eothen*. London, 1844.

Knightly, P., and C. Simpson. *The Secret Lives of Lawrence*. New York, 1971.

Koestler, A. *Arrow in the Blue*. London, 1969.

Kollek, T. *For Jerusalem*. New York, 1978.

———. *Friedenspreis des Deutschen Buchhandels* (acceptance speech). Frankfurt am Main, 1985.

Kook, Z. Y. *Royal Theory* (in Hebrew). Jerusalem, n.d.

Kotker, N. *The Earthly Jerusalem*. New York, 1969.

Kotting, B. *Peregrinatio Religiosa: Wallfahrten in der Antike und das Pilgerwesen in der alten Kirche*. Regensburg, 1950.

Lamartine, A. de. *Voyage en orient: Souvenirs, impressions, pensées et paysages pendant un voyage en orient, 1832–1833*. Paris, 1835.

Lande-Nash, I. *3,000 Jahre Jerusalem*. Tübingen, 1964.

Le Strange, G. *Palestine Under the Moslems*. London, 1890.

Levin, S. *Kindheit im Exil*. Berlin, 1935.

Levine, L. I., ed. *The Jerusalem Cathedra: Studies in the History, Geography, and Ethnography of the Land of Israel*. Jerusalem, 1982.

Leys, S. *Ombres Chinoises*. Paris, 1974.

Loti, P. *Jerusalem*. London, n.d.

Lowenthal, D. *The Past Is a Foreign Country*. Cambridge, 1985.

Mack, J. E. *A Prince of Our Disorder: The Life of T. E. Lawrence*. London, 1976.

Melville, H. *Journal of a Visit to Europe and the Levant*. Princeton, 1955.

The Midrash on Lamentations. Vol. 5 of *The Midrash* (Soncino edition). Edited by H. Freedman and M. Simon. Translated by A. Cohen. London, 1931.

Morgenthau, H. *Ambassador Morgenthau's Story*. New York, 1919.

Mujir al-Din. *Histoire de Jerusalem et d'Hebron*. Translated by H. Savere. Paris, 1876.

Muller, H. *The Loom of History*. New York, 1958.

Mumford, L. *The City in History*. New York, 1961.

Munib el-Mady and M. Suleiman. *The History of Jordan in the Twentieth Century* (in Arabic). Amman, 1959.

Murphy-O'Connor, J. *The Holy Land: An Archaeological Guide*. Oxford, 1986.

Navon. Y. *The Six Days and the Seven Gates*. Jerusalem, 1978.

Nooks, Y. *Edward Lear: Life of a Wanderer*. London, 1968.

Onne, E., and D. Wahrman. *Jerusalem: Profile of a Changing City*. Jerusalem, 1986.

Orenstein, I. V. *Diary of the Western Wall* (in Hebrew). Jerusalem, 1951.

Oz, A. *Here and There in the Land of Israel* (in Hebrew). Tel Aviv, 1982.

Palestine Pilgrims' Text Society (PPTS). Edited by C. Wilson. Translated by S. Aubrey et al. Reprinted from the edition of 1887–1897. 13 vols. New York, 1971.

Peters, F. E. *Jerusalem: The Holy City in the Eyes of Chroniclers, Visitors, Pilgrims, and Prophets from the Days of Abraham to Modern Times*. Princeton, 1985.

Pliny the Elder. *Historia Naturalis*. Translated by H. T. Riley. London, 1857.

Porath, Y. *Growth of the Arab Palestinian National Movement, 1918–1929* (in Hebrew). Jerusalem, 1971.

Prawer, J. *The Latin Kingdom of Jerusalem*. London, 1972.

Pritchard, J., ed. *Ancient Near Eastern Texts Relative to the Old Testament*. Princeton, 1955.

Raba, J. *Russian Travel Accounts of Palestine* (in Hebrew). Jerusalem, 1981.

Raphael, C. *The Walls of Jerusalem: An Excursion into Jewish History*. New York, 1968.

Renan, E. *Discours et conférences*. Vol. 4 of *Histoire des origines du Christianisme*. Paris, 1928.

———. *Letters from the Holy Land*. Translated by L. O'Rourke. New York, 1904.

Robert, M. *From Oedipus to Moses: Freud's Jewish Identity*. New York, 1976.

Roberts, D. *The Holy Land* (engravings). London, 1855.

Robinson, E. *Biblical Researches in Palestine, Mt. Sinai and Arabia Petraea*. Boston, 1841.

Roth, P. *The Counterlife*. New York, 1986.

Runciman, S. *A History of the Crusades*. London, 1971.

Sachs, A. *Light-Handed* (in Hebrew). Tel Aviv, 1988.

Said, E. W. *Orientalism*. New York, 1978.

Samuel, E. *A Lifetime in Jerusalem*. Jerusalem, 1970.

Samuel, H. *Memoirs*. London, 1945.

Saulcy, F. de. *Les derniers jours de Jerusalem*. Paris, 1866.

Schleifer, A. *The Fall of Jerusalem*. New York, 1972.

Scholem, G. *From Berlin to Jerusalem* (in Hebrew). Tel Aviv, 1982.

———. *Sabbatai Zevi: The Mystical Messiah*. Princeton, 1973.

Seetzen, U. J. *Reisen durch Syrien u. Palaestina*. Berlin, 1854.

Segal, H. *Dear Brothers* (in Hebrew). Jerusalem, 1987.

Shalev, M. *Poems (Kol Anot*, in Hebrew). Jerusalem, 1959.

Shaltiel, E., ed. *Studies in the History of Modern Jerusalem* (in Hebrew). Jerusalem, 1981.

Sharon, M., ed. *Issues in the History of the Land of Israel under Islamic Rule* (in Hebrew). Jerusalem, 1976.

Silberman, N. A. *Digging for God and Country*. New York, 1982.

Silk, D. *Retrievements*. Jerusalem, 1977.

Sivan, E. *Interpretations of Islam: Past and Present*. Princeton, 1985.

Smith, G. A. *The Historical Geography of the Holy Land*. London, 1904.

———. *Jerusalem: History and Historical Geography*. London, 1907.

Starkie, E. *Flaubert*. London, 1967.

Storrs, R. *Orientations*. London, 1945.

Sykes, C. *Crossroads to Israel*. London, 1965.

Tacitus. *The Histories*. London, 1896.

Tcherikover, V. *Hellenistic Civilization and the Jews*. Translated by S. Applebaum. New York, 1970.

Tchernichowsky, S. *Poems* (in Hebrew). Tel Aviv, 1943.

Thomas, H. *History of the World*. New York, 1979.

Thubron, C. *Jerusalem*. London, 1986.

———. *Mirror to Damascus*. London, 1986.

Troyat, H. *Divided Soul: The Life of Gogol*. Translated by N. Amphoux. Garden City, N.Y., 1973.

Tuchman, B. *Bible and Sword*. New York, 1968.

Twain, M. *The Innocents Abroad*. New York, 1911.

——. *Letters from the Earth*. Edited by B. De Voto. New York, 1962.

——. *The Mark Twain Notebooks*. Edited by A. B. Paine. New York, 1930.

Updike, J. *Bech is Back*. New York, 1982.

Varon, L., ed. *Living in Jerusalem: An Anthology* (in Hebrew). Jerusalem, 1987.

Vester, B. S. *Our Jerusalem: An American Family in the Holy City*. Garden City, N.Y., 1950.

Volney, C. de. *Voyage en Syrie et en Egypt, 1783–4*. Paris. 1959.

Voltaire. *The Portable Voltaire*. Edited by B. R. Redman. London, 1979.

Walker, F. *Irreverent Pilgrims: Melville, Browne, and Twain in the Holy Land*. Seattle, 1974.

Warhaftig, I., ed. *Tekhumin: A Halakic Compendium* (in Hebrew). Jerusalem, 1982.

Warren, C. *Underground Jerusalem*. London, 1876.

Waugh, E. *The Letters of Evelyn Waugh*. Edited by M. Emory. London, 1980.

Weizmann, C. *Trial and Error*. London, 1949.

——. *Statement Made before the Palestine Royal Commission* [25 Nov. 1936]. London, 1939.

Werblowsky, R. J. Z. *The Meaning of Jerusalem to Jews, Christians, and Moslems*. Jerusalem, 1978.

Whitman, W. *Leaves of Grass and Selected Prose*. Edited by S. Bradley. New York, 1949.

Whittemore, E. *Jerusalem Poker*. New York, 1986.

Wilhelm, K. *Roads to Zion: Four Centuries of Travelers*. New York, 1946.

William of Tyre. *History of Deeds Done beyond the Sea*. New York, 1943.

Wilson, C. W. *Picturesque Palestine, Sinai and Egypt*. London, 1880.

Wilson, E. *Red, Black, and Olive*. New York, 1956.

Wright, T., ed. *Early Travels in Palestine (the narratives of Arculf, Willibald, Sigurd, Benjamin de Tudela . . .)*. London, 1848.

Index

Jewish, 93–94, 100–109, 110, 146, 185, 222, 237, 248 (*see also* messianism)
memory and, 58
Moslem, 3, 146, 166, 216
See also fundamentalism; sects and sectarianism; violence/terrorism
fantasy, 11–12, 31, 155
of heavenly Jerusalem (*see* Jerusalem: heavenly)
of messianism, 97, 102, 103, 146, 147
Farouk I (king of Egypt), 220
Feast(s):
of Liberty, 118 (*see also* Exodus, the)
of Tabernacles (or Booths), 118–119
of Weeks (Shabuoth; Pentecost), 40, 118, 119
Ferguson (English eccentric), 205
fetishism. *See* religion: and relics
Fidelio (Beethoven), 13
Finn, James, 77, 82
fire worship. *See* paganism: fire worship
Fish Gate. *See* Jaffa Gate
Flaubert, Gustave, in Jerusalem, 37, 124, 139–140, 153, 195
Florus, Gessius, 33
Forty Days of Musa Dagh, The (Werfel), 226
France, 21, 49, 69, 70, 113, 133
in Crusades, 132, 232
and French as "chosen people," 134
Jerusalem buildings constructed by, 45, 46, 231, 232
Jewish expression referring to, 237
pilgrimages/visitors from, 36, 131–134, 137–138
Franciscan Order, 70, 133, 134, 168, 176, 203
Custodia di Terra Sancta of, 77
guidebook published by, 206
and sectarianism, 71, 76, 201
Francis Joseph I (emperor of Austria), 145
Francis of Assisi, Saint, 71, 124
Frankel, Jonathan, 180
Frederick I (Barbarossa, Holy Roman emperor), 35
Frederick II (king of Jerusalem), 113
French Academy of Sciences, 140n
French Revolution, 167
Freud, Sigmund, on Western Wall, 238
Friedlander, Saul, 171
Fulcher of Chartres (French chronicler), 114
fundamentalism
Bible as viewed by, 109, 110
Christian, 61, 106, 110, 221, 222–223
Jewish, 78, 92, 93, 95, 102, 105, 106, 110, 174 (*see also* Orthodox Jews: and ultra-Orthodox)
Jewish and Moslem, similarity and growth of, 78, 108, 245–246
nationalism and, 61, 78, 90, 92
and Six-Day War, 90

terrorist, 102, 105, 110
See also holy wars; messianism

"Galilee of the Gentiles," 89
Garden Tomb, 307. *See also* Calvary; tomb(s)
gate(s) of Jerusalem
closed at sunset, 38, 141
Mandelbaum, 39
of Mercy (*see* Golden Gate)
of Peace, 220
"speak," 81
of the Valley, 160
See also Damascus Gate; Jaffa Gate; Lions' Gate
Gehenna (Hell), naming of, 28. *See also* Valley of Hinnom
Genesis, Book of, 23, 185
genizah, discovery of, 126
George V (king of England), 145
German colony in Jerusalem, 226
Germany, 36, 69, 100, 227
Jerusalem buildings constructed by, 45, 46, 231
Templers (Protestant sect) from, 228–229
Gerusalemme Liberata (Tasso), 35
Gesta Francorum et aliorum Hyrosolymitanarum, 35
Gethsemane, 45, 53
Getz, Meir Yehuda, 96–97
Geulah (district), 188, 192
Ghirlandajo, Domenico, 129
Gibbon, Edward, 20, 27, 113, 121, 149, 167n
Gibeon (city), 53
Gilgal, twelve stones of, 209
Ginzberg, Asher. *See* Ahad Ha'am
Gnostic doctrine, 99, 127
Godfrey of Bouillon, 35, 70, 133
Gogol, Nikolai, in Jerusalem, 138–139, 182
Golan Heights, 104
Golden Gate (Gate of Mercy), 73–74, 83
Golgotha. *See* Calvary
Goodman, Alan Harry, 100–101, 104
Gora-Kalavia (Poland) and Gorer Hasidim, 191–192. *See also* Hasidic sects
Gordon, General Charles George, 147, 205
Goren, Major General Shlomo, 93–94, 96
Gospels. *See* Bible, the
Gothic art and architecture, 30, 231. *See also* arts, the
Graham, Stephen, on Russian pilgrims, 144
graves. *See* tomb(s)
Great Britain. *See* Britain
Greece, 17, 18, 19, 21, 29, 227
consulate of, 49
cultural influence of, 22, 44, 45, 50, 180, 219
and Hellenism, xii, 13, 50, 56, 67, 222, 228
pilgrimages from, 228